Rec Center

HEATH

HEATH

A FAMILY'S TALE

JANET FIFE-YEOMANS

FALL RIVER PRESS

CONTENTS

SIR FRANK LEDGER / LADY GLADYS

COLIN FRANCIS LEDGER
/ ESMA KATHLEEN

JUNE SYME
/ JOHN SYME

BETSY COX
/ PETER COX

KIM LEDGER
/ SALLY BELL
/ EMMA BROWN
/ INES IANOLLO

SALLY BELL
/ ROGER BELL

WAYNE LEDGER
/ VIRGINIA

MIKE LEDGER
/ DIANNE

HAYDN LEDGER
/ APRIL

HEATH / MICHELLE ———■——— MATILDA ROSE
KATE
OLIVIA

ASHLEY

BRUCE
PEGGY
NATALIE
STURT
ESMA

ADAM
VERITY
TIM

JESSICA
MITCHELL
SAMMY
LUKE

01
NO MORE BRIGHT LIGHTS

A FREEZING NEW YORK WINTER'S EVENING, THE AIR TURNING EVERY BREATH INTO A CLOUD OF FOG. ALL AROUND, PEOPLE ARE HEADING HOME FROM WORK THIS TUESDAY NIGHT, OR SEEKING REFUGE FROM THE COLD IN THE NEIGHBOURHOOD'S HIP LITTLE COFFEE SHOPS AND ARTY RESTAURANTS. FROM HERE ON THE EDGE OF LITTLE ITALY AND SOHO, IT'S AN EASY STROLL TO THE BRIGHT LIGHTS OF BROADWAY, BUT TONIGHT ALL THE LIGHTS ARE FOCUSED ON THIS FIVE-STOREY WHITE AND GREY APARTMENT BUILDING AT 421 BROOME STREET. THE ARC LIGHTS, SATELLITE DISHES AND FLASHBULBS OF THE MEDIA ARE SENDING THE NEWS LIVE AROUND THE WORLD. THE COLD CREEPS UP FROM THE PAVEMENT THROUGH EVEN THE WARMEST BOOTS, CHILLING BODIES TO THE BONE—BUT NO-ONE IS MOVING.

Not the hundreds of American and foreign reporters, nor the fans standing quietly behind them, some clutching bunches of hastily bought flowers. No-one is leaving until the show is over.

Inside the trendy cast-iron building that used to be home to industrial workshops, each of the floors has been carved out into loft-style apartments. There's one to every sprawling floor apart from the street level, which houses a designer furniture store. On the fourth floor, $24,000 a month buys 4,400 square metres of space, with floor-to-ceiling windows letting the lights of the media flood in. There are soaring tin ceilings, three bedrooms, two and a half bathrooms and private balconies.

Loft apartments by their very design are meant to be spacious and sparse, but this one on the fourth floor takes it to an extreme. It's bare and empty, with hardly any furniture on its polished wooden floors. It looks unlived in, apart from a collection of skateboards lying around.

Since the day its current tenant moved in, four months earlier, apartment 5A had never been as crowded as it was this evening. There were uniformed NYPD officers, detectives, paramedics and medical examiners—the coterie of strangers that attend a suspicious death. The man they were zipping up into the black body bag and lifting onto the stainless steel gurney was Heath Ledger. They all knew who he was, though he had not met any of them when he was alive.

Teresa Carino Solomon had been recommended to Heath by the superintendent of the Broome Street building. A petite Filipino-American, the fifty-six-year-old had been doing light cleaning and laundry for Heath since he rented the place in September 2007. Every Tuesday she took the subway from her apartment building in the Astoria section of Queens, New York, where she had been living for twelve years, and let herself into 5A with her key. Not that she had much to do once inside.

'His place was always clean. That's why I told him, "What else am I going to do here?"' Solomon later recalled.

The mother of five is by all accounts a decent and hard-working housekeeper who counts a number of wealthy New York families among her cleaning clients. She arrived in the United States in 1985 after working for three years in Athens at the home of the Saudi Arabian ambassador to Greece, and took US citizenship after being sponsored by the family for whom she worked as a nanny, looking after their little boy.

On Tuesday 22 January, Heath had stuck a note on his fridge before he went to bed to remind Solomon that his masseuse, Diana Lee Wolozin, was due for a 3 p.m. appointment. Solomon saw that his bedroom door was closed.

As she went about her chores, she had to go through the bedroom to get to the en suite bathroom, where she changed a light bulb. It was about 1 p.m., and she heard Heath snoring and saw him lying face down on the bed, with a sheet pulled to his shoulders.

'I didn't think anything was wrong. I thought he was sleeping,' she later said.

At 2.45 p.m., Wolozin arrived with the fur collar of her parka pulled up against the cold and a blue cap pushed down on her sandy hair. She was fifteen minutes early for her appointment, and filled in the time chatting with Solomon.

When Heath still did not emerge from his bedroom, Wolozin knocked on the door. Nothing. So she called him on his mobile at 3.10 p.m. His phone clicked through to his voicemail with an upbeat, 'Hi, I'm not here. Leave a message. I'll get back to you.' She opened the door and went into the bedroom, where she saw him lying face down at the foot of the bed, naked. She thought he was still sleeping so she opened the closet where the massage table was kept and set it up in the bedroom.

When the noise didn't wake him up, Wolozin leaned down and shook him.

Heath Ledger was unconscious and his body was cold.

But she didn't dial 911. The first person she called for help wasn't the ambulance service or the police. It wasn't Heath's father Kim Ledger or his estranged partner Michelle Williams, the mother of his beloved daughter Matilda Rose.

Wolozin used the speed dial on Heath's mobile phone, but she bypassed the numbers for his dad, his mum and Michelle. Bizarrely, Wolozin scrolled down to the number of actress Mary-Kate Olsen and pressed the call button.

'Heath is unconscious, he's cold to the touch!' she cried over the phone.

The former child star, who was in LA at the time, didn't advise her to call for medical help.

'I'm sending my private security there,' she said.

Moments later Wolozin called Olsen back.

'I think he may be dead. I'm calling 911,' she said.

Olsen told her, 'I already have people coming over.'

It was 3.26 p.m. when Wolozin dialled 911, fifteen frantic minutes after she realised Heath was in trouble. With help finally on the way, the emergency operator gave her instructions and Wolozin tried in vain to resuscitate him.

The paramedics were there by 3.33 p.m., at almost exactly the same moment as a private security guard summoned by Olsen. The medics lifted his body to the floor and tried CPR. They used a defibrillator to try to shock Heath's heart into beating again. Nothing was going to work. He was pronounced dead at 3.36 p.m.

By that point, two other private security guards summoned by Olsen had arrived, along with the first of the police officers. News travelled fast, and within the hour the media started to gather on the pavement outside.

⊹

Back home, in Heath's home town of Perth, it was early in the morning when the news started to filter out.

'Actor Heath Ledger has been found dead in his Manhattan apartment, possibly of a drug overdose,' a newsreader announced as Tim Ledger dropped his car off for a service at his local garage.

'Lieutenant John Grimpal from the New York Police Department says drugs were found at the scene, but investigators are yet to determine how he died.

'Police do not suspect foul play.

'The body of the young Perth star has been removed from his apartment.'

Tim, one of Heath's young cousins, walked outside the garage, his face white as a sheet, where his mum, Di Ledger, Heath's aunt and godmother, was waiting for him. She had just heard the news on her own car radio.

'Why didn't he just ring us up, Mum, if he was having problems? He could have come to stay with us on the farm and had a swim and a beer and hung out,' cried Tim in his innocence.

✚

Heath died an unbelievably lonely death, with no-one with him who loved him, and far away from home. What inner demons was he battling?

✚

02
PEA-GREEN TIGHTS AND SEQUINS

HEATH LEDGER PICKED UP THE AFRICAN TRIBAL MASK HE HAD BEEN WORKING ON AND CARRIED IT BETWEEN THE DESKS ACROSS THE ART ROOM. THE METRE-WIDE WOODEN DESKS WERE SET UP IN A U SHAPE SO THE STUDENTS ALL HAD A CLEAR VIEW OF SUBJECTS THEY HAD TO DRAW OR PAINT, WHICH WERE PLACED IN THE MIDDLE OF THE ROOM. BARRY GARDNER WAS SITTING AT A DESK ON THE OUTER EDGE OF THE U. HEATH PUT THE MASK DOWN IN FRONT OF BARRY, PULLED OUT A CHAIR AND SAT OPPOSITE HIM. HE PUT HIS ELBOWS ON THE DESK, HIS HEAD ON HIS CLENCHED HANDS. 'WHAT SHOULD I DO?' HE ASKED HIS TEACHER. GARDNER, WHO TAUGHT ENGLISH, SOCIAL STUDIES AND ART AND WAS HEAD OF GUILDFORD GRAMMAR'S ART DEPARTMENT UNTIL 2002, WAS A WISE AND APPROACHABLE TEACHER AS WELL AS A FAMILY FRIEND.

He had become a mentor to Heath, who often sought him out to discuss problems. The rest of the small class was working away quietly on their masks, but Heath's mind was soaring far beyond the art room.

It was a day Gardner probably had seen coming—if not quite so soon.

Guildford Grammar was a Ledger family tradition. Heath's father Kim and his uncles Wayne, Mike and Haydn had all gone there, their parents sacrificing a lot to make sure the boys got a good education. Heath and some of his cousins carried on the tradition, maintaining the family link with the school. It was the sort of school where you left your Christian name at the gate and were known as Ledger by the teachers as well as your mates.

Guildford Grammar makes some of those old, established English public schools, upon which it was modelled in 1896, look shabby. Its red-brick buildings would look austere if they were not softened by the white, wooden verandahs, and with 100 acres straddling the Swan River, it is not only picturesque but maintains a rural feel. Guildford Grammar is not just a part of Guildford—it *is* Guildford, dominating the historic suburb 15 kilometres from the centre of Perth.

Inside the school grounds, it looks as though time has stood still. Nothing is out of place, with green lawns as smooth as silk upon which not even the stately sugar gums that shade the buildings dare to drop a leaf. In Heath's father's day, the manicured grass was out of bounds to the schoolboys.

Heath's uncle Haydn held the record for the number of canings in one day—sixteen. He decided that a day at the zoo would be more interesting than the classroom, and when he got back, every teacher whose class he had missed caned him twice. Eight teachers, two strokes each.

Tradition also dictated that all the Ledgers, including Heath, were members of the same house, Woodbridge. Heath's closest friendships also began at Woodbridge House, with friends who stuck by him after their schooldays, including twins Ben and Tom Rogers and N'fadeynde Forster-Jones. His best friend from when he was a toddler, Trevor Di Carlo, was also a member of the Woodbridge gang.

It was named after Woodbridge House, where Charles Harper lived, and in the billiard room of which he first set up a school that formed the beginnings of Guildford Grammar. Eight houses with seventy boys to a house makes up the pastoral structure of the school, and its job is to develop a boy's character—as much as any school can.

There was nothing subtle about life at Guildford Grammar. At every moment of the day you knew exactly where you had to be—and woe betide you if you were not there. The day started at 8.25 a.m. at each of the houses. The Woodbridge boys met for rollcall before housemaster Graham Hartley, in their dark-blue blazers, grey trousers, crisp white shirts and school ties. Woodbridge House is a single-storey red-brick building down towards the river at the back of the school. Rollcall was in a large bare room with a polished-concrete floor in the middle of the house. Bags were dumped in lockers, and the only times the boys would be back here during the day was to change for sports or, if it rained, for a game of pool at lunchtime. The pool table is in a room of its own, surrounded by battered but comfortable couches, with a wooden honour board on the wall. However, the rain had to be a torrential downpour before the boys were allowed to spend lunchtime inside, as school rules encouraged them to stay outdoors as much as possible. It was considered much healthier, as was bringing lunch from home, although Woodbridge House was the closest of all the houses to the tuckshop and to the wooden-panelled dining room with its white tablecloths, flowers on every table and heraldic banners around the walls.

Twice a week between 8.30 and 9 a.m., the day boys filled the school chapel, the Chapel of St Mary and George. They were all taught its history. One of the first headmasters, Percy Henn, believed that a school without its own place of worship was like *Hamlet* without the Prince of Denmark. An appeal to his homeland of England led to a surprising and generous benefactor. Clive Oliverson, a bachelor, was prepared to spend several thousand pounds on a chapel for this obscure school in faraway Australia.

The chapel is one of the finest examples of Gothic architecture in Australia, but its dark wooden pews running from the front to the rear always seemed too sombre to the boys. The pews are lit by electric candles in brass holders, spaced along the rows, with hand-embroidered cushions on every seat, one for every boy to kneel on during worship. The cushions are made and maintained by the boys' mothers, and are a bright spot in a magnificent but rather gloomy chapel. Looking at it today, it conjures up images of Hogwarts Castle in the Harry Potter novels.

The chapel played a large role in the Ledger family's history. Heath's father Kim was the first of the four brothers to marry, and the chapel was the setting for his wedding to Sally.

Guildford Grammar was strong on military training, and when Heath's father was there it was compulsory to belong to the army cadets, with its marching and rifle training. Kim really got into the tradition and was a commanding officer in the cadets by the time he left school. Standards were very high, and Kim was accepted for officer training at the military college at Portsea in Victoria. He left after a year and came back to Perth to marry Sally Ramshaw. Kim's family adored Sally—she was quiet, kind and loving, and would never complain about anything. She fit in really well, which was pretty tough when there were four brothers who knew each other so well they could usually tell what the others were thinking.

Kim got to know Sally because she had been the girlfriend of his best friend from Guildford Grammar, Roger Bell. Roger's father had established the original Bell Brothers earthmoving and trucking business, which was taken over by Perth millionaire entrepreneur Robert Holmes à Court, and formed the basis for his flagship Bell Group of companies before entrepreneur Alan Bond took it over and left it penniless. Roger's mum is one of Sir Frank Ledger's sisters, making Kim and Roger related. All this shows that while Perth pretends to be a city, it is really a small town where everyone knows everyone else's business.

Sally's family descended from one of the oldest Scottish clans, the Campbells, who treacherously slaughtered the Macdonald family in the Glencoe massacre of 1692. This sounds much more romantic than saying that her dad was a Perth insurance agent. Sally's mum, Jackie Ramshaw, is a big lady in size as well as personality, and wonderfully outgoing and flamboyant. She could fill every moment with drama and make everyone around laugh with her. She was popular with the whole family, and her theatricality made a huge impression on and greatly influenced the young Heath.

At their wedding, Wayne was best man and Mike and Haydn, who were still at school, were groomsmen. Just as they had when they were growing up, the four brothers still did everything together. As one after the other got married, they all played a role in the weddings and took turns being best man or groomsman. Later, they were named as godparents to each other's children, who all grew up together.

Mike and his wife Di were two of the first people at the St John of God Hospital in Subiaco, an inner city Perth suburb, on 4 April 1979, when Heath was born. He was Sally and Kim's second child, following his sister Kate, who had been christened Catherine. Mike and Di were Heath's godparents, and wanted to buy him something he could add to over the years, so they got him a stamp collection. For quite a few years Di went to the post office and bought the latest stamps for him for his birthday.

While much was made of it in later years, none of them had any idea that Sally, who was a French teacher, had named Kate and Heath after the passionate but frustrated lovers Catherine Earnshaw and Heathcliff from Emily Bronte's brilliant but ominous and turbulent novel, *Wuthering Heights*.

For Heath Andrew Ledger's christening, the brothers were all back together at the school chapel at Guildford Grammar.

Twelve years later, the chapel was the setting for 12-year-old Heath's first title roll in a school play—wearing pea-green tights as Peter Pan.

'It took a lot of guts,' he later said of the skin-tight costume. 'For a 12-year-old kid, that can be damaging among your peers.'

Heath's first school was Mary's Mount Primary School, a co-educational Catholic school at Gooseberry Hill, near where Kim and Sally lived in the hills behind Perth. From its tidy grounds, there is still the best view across the suburbs to the city centre. It was actually here that Heath took his first steps onto the stage, as a sheep in the school's nativity play. The following year he graduated to the role of the donkey.

He moved on to Guildford Grammar's prep school, where he made his mark playing chess. The school prides itself on its magazine, called *Swan Magazine*, which is almost as old as the school itself, and Heath featured in its pages often during his school career. In a 1988 edition is a photograph of nine-year-old Heath sitting at a chess board, looking grown-up in a short-sleeved white shirt and tie but characteristically unable to suppress a giggle as the picture is taken, while he pretends to work out his next move. His teachers were Mr and Mrs Spick, and Heath was part of the flourishing Junior Chess Club, which at that time had a record forty members.

Heath got his love of chess from his dad, and just a year later he fulfilled another of his dad's ambitions when, at the age of ten, he was West Australian go-kart champion for his age group.

The go-karting grew out of a little side business his grandpa Colin Ledger had, importing rotary engine pumps for farms. They were popular with the farmers because they were simple, with few moving parts. Kim learned all about them helping his dad out at work. When Mazda started to put rotary engines in its production-line cars in the early 1970s, Kim saw the business potential there, and set up Rotomotion. The company, situated in a small green-painted workshop in a residential area of Guildford opposite the railway line, became the first in Australia specialising in rotary engines.

The benefits of the rotary engine are that it is quiet, fuel-efficient and has only three moving parts, with no valves or pistons. They also go like stink, and Kim could see there was a market not only in servicing the engines in the Mazdas, but in using the motors in high-performance cars. When he started turbocharging rotary motors, it was real pioneering stuff. Brother Haydn, who is a first-class machinist, worked with Kim for a while, helping build high-performance engines—all those years of racing hotrods around in the dirt behind the family house in Gooseberry Hill paid off for the brothers. They were now doing it for real. In 1977, Kim got into speedway racing, and Haydn followed a couple of years later when he married and moved north to Geraldton.

It was a noisy, dirty, testosterone-charged world, with the roar of the cars and the smell of burning tyres, made more exciting because it was held at night under lights—every Friday was speedway night in Perth. Sally would take Kate and Heath down to Claremont Speedway to join the spectators and watch their dad race. Cars are a religion in Perth, which is still a city of revheads with a bigger membership of car clubs than anywhere else in the country, and Claremont was one of the world's oldest speedway tracks. It opened in 1927 and sadly closed in 2000.

Kim was good at racing—he had great cars and he liked to win. He came third in the 1981–82 and 1982–83 seasons, then second in 1984–85, before finally snaring the top spot as WA Speedcar State Champion in 1985–86. He loved it when Heath was down in the pits with him working on the cars, and he would have loved it if Heath had followed him into speedway racing. He had always told his son that you could never be good at anything unless you enjoyed it 150 per cent.

Kim encouraged him to start off with go-karts and an old speedway associate of Kim's, Kevin Hilgert, accompanied Heath around the go-kart races. Kevin had come third to Kim's second in the state speedway championships in 1984–85, and he and Kim were very close. They were constantly tuning and tweaking Heath's machine so that he got the best out of it—it was a matter of pride for them as well as for Heath. Heath loved the adrenalin fix of flying around the track so close to the ground, and it was his razor-sharp reflexes that took him to the top at the age of ten.

But Heath never had the killer instinct needed to keep going in the sport and while he liked to please his dad and was enthusiastic, his dreams lay elsewhere.

Drama was compulsory at Guildford Grammar, meant to build self-confidence and the ability to speak in public. The school has a huge and very professional drama department with a significant budget, and a purpose-built drama theatre that would be the envy of many professional companies. The David Law Davies Theatre was built with the help of a substantial endowment from an old boy's family in 1978. This was after Heath's father and uncles had left school, so none of them graced its stage—not that they were particularly interested in drama at the time. Acting up in class, yes. Acting in drama class, no.

The school theatre has an impressive foyer, with stairs sweeping up to a balcony and the entrance to the Kyle Auditorium, which can seat audiences of several hundred and was the scene of Heath's first performances after *Peter Pan*.

Like every dad, Kim was proud of Heath's first starring role, but he had realised by then that his son had better-than-average talent. He was so excited that he rang Mike and Di to tell them what a good performance young Heath had given as the boy who never grew up. Kate, who was four years older and had already decided that she wanted to be an actress, sat with her parents in the audience and—despite the pea-green tights—thought her little brother was 'really good'.

The Guildford Grammar acting year revolves around major productions, which are staged either in the theatre or in the more dramatic setting of the chapel. After *Peter Pan*, Heath appeared in every major school drama in his time at Guildford. His drama teacher, Gillian Kerr-Sheppard, saw his potential. She recognised his fantastic focus and the rare ability to listen intently to what the director wants, to understand and interpret it, and then to personalise it with his own skills.

'Heath's a perfect actor,' she later said.

Unfortunately for Heath, his drama teacher's son, Alex Kerr-Sheppard, was in the same year at school, and was often cast in the lead roles over him. Alex was no slouch himself in the acting sphere, and joined local drama groups. But Heath was always going to outshine him.

Barry Gardner saw other parts of Heath's personality in his acting. He said that Heath had a belief in himself, and the talent and ability to get into the skin of whoever he was portraying; that he could become that person. Gardner also saw that Heath had a maturity beyond his years.

'He had this incredible awareness and sensitivity for someone so young,' Gardner said.

There was also an inner sadness about Heath that may well have had a lot to do with his parents' divorce. He was seven when Kim and Sally split up.

The family had moved to Millson Avenue, Maida Vale, a tidy single-storey house tucked away in the corner of a quiet cul-de-sac, surrounded by gum trees. Kim always had an eye for the ladies and eventually it came between him and Sally. When they split up, it was Kim who moved out.

Kim and Sally were very conscious of making sure Heath and Kate never felt pulled between the two of them, and the rest of the Ledgers made sure they all remained part of the larger family.

Sally remained in the Maida Vale house and eventually her old boyfriend Roger Bell moved in after the couple rekindled their teenage romance. Heath's bedroom was papered with modern art posters and he spent a lot of time in there watching videos of old movies, his escape from what was happening with his mum and dad. He adored old musicals, especially *The Wizard of Oz* and anything starring Gene Kelly. The first Kelly movie he saw was *The Pirate* and it wasn't just Kelly's talent that blew him away, but his energy and his grace and power as a dancer. He was also a fan of Fred Astaire, impressed with the way Astaire and Kelly could reach an audience, make people believe in what they were doing on the screen. He admired Jack Nicholson and Daniel Day-Lewis for the same reasons.

His eclectic taste extended to music, and he grew up listening to Led Zeppelin, Janis Joplin, Eminem, Beck, the Doors and Radiohead as well as U2 and INXS.

There was—and still is—truly nowhere better in the world to be a child than Australia, and in particular Western Australia. Rockingham is a holiday resort about 50 kilometres south of Perth, and for years it was one of those places the developers had thankfully forgotten, a small town of fibro holiday shacks along the calm, protected beaches of Cockburn Sound. It hadn't progressed much since its days as a port for the timber industry. Just off Rockingham is Garden Island, connected to the mainland by a causeway. It was here that Heath's grandpa Colin Ledger's Z Force was trained during World War II.

Rockingham was one of the places Heath spent his summer holidays after his mum and dad separated. Sally bought a house at Rockingham, but she was not a great fan of the beach. Mike and Di rented a house down there for the holidays, and Heath spent a lot of time with them. Adam, four years younger than Heath, thought his older cousin was the 'duck's nuts', and Heath took him under his wing. They would head off fishing for dinner, and Heath invariably caught something worth cooking. The Ledgers joked that he charmed the fish out of the water.

The house was right on the sand, without even a road between it and the beach. It really was idyllic, with postcard colours and long, hot days. The days were spent on the beach, or out on the water on a boat owned by friends of Mike and Di, or on one of the pedal boats that were licensed to carry two people but often fit four or five kids and one of the uncles.

Evenings were spent on the verandah of the house watching the sun sink into red over the ocean. A couple of low-slung wooden chairs were pulled out of the lounge for the grown-ups, and an esky would double as a wine cellar, beer fridge and occasional table.

One evening Heath got Di by herself and confided in her how he had been trying to make sure that his parents didn't worry about him. Di asked him how it was going at home and Heath said that when his mum asked him if he was okay with the arrangements, he had to say yes, otherwise she would cry; when his dad asked him, he also had to say yes, otherwise his dad got angry.

Heath used to analyse things a lot, often too much. All kids find it difficult when their parents split up, and Heath was no different, but he was very aware of how his mum and dad felt and thought more about them than himself. When he was famous and was interviewed many years later, he was quoted as saying that he was okay with his parents being divorced, because it made him realise that they were human. That was Heath hiding his true feelings behind his privacy, something he did even as a kid. It was a character trait of his that was probably heightened by the divorce, because no matter how much parents try to shield their kids from it, a divorce makes them grow up overnight.

Heath had stars stuck on his bedroom ceiling, which he would lie and look at before going to sleep. There was a whole world out there, and he had already decided that acting was going to be his ticket to it.

Heath was passionate about acting, and the drama theatre at school became like a third home, counting his mum's house at Maida Vale and the granny flat beneath his great-grandfather Sir Frank Ledger's house on the Swan River where Kim had moved after the separation—it was the granny flat with the best views in Perth. Sir Frank had been alone since his wife Gladys had died, and the rest of the family were pleased that Kim was there to keep the old man company. Heath and Kate filled the house with laughter when they visited their dad.

Kate was also interested in acting and had signed with a local agency, which further inspired Heath.

It was a boom time in Perth for the arts. The state had its own acting school, the Western Australian Academy of Performing Arts, which was producing actors of the calibre of Marcus Graham and William McInnes. It certainly focused the attention of agents and producers on Perth's talent.

Another boost came with the formation of the state's first drama production company, Barron Films. Major production houses felt it was not viable to travel to Western Australia to make movies when they could get the same backdrops back east without the cost of moving an army of production staff the equivalent distance of London to Moscow. Paul Barron, who was director of the Perth Institute of Film and Television, saw the potential in the material that was being submitted to the institute and came up with an innovative way of raising finance—money being the biggest hurdle for anyone wanting to produce a film. He listed a prospectus on the Perth Stock Exchange, which meant investors could buy and trade shares in the prospectus as if it were a mine or manufacturing company.

Heath's first time on the big screen had come a few months before he climbed on the stage as Peter Pan, when he was cast in Barron Films' *Clowning Around*. It was a four-hour TV series aimed at children aged seven to twelve, a family tale about a star-struck kid played by Clayton Williamson who wants to be a circus clown. It had a strong cast of Australian actors including Ernie Dingo,

Noni Hazelhurst, Rebecca Smart and Jill Perryman. Heath played an orphan clown who comes on in the last ten minutes and delivers the film's closing lines.

His cousins got a great buzz from seeing Heath on the screen, but they remember him best in a Chicken Treat ad he did around that time!

Two years later, he got a small role in an Australian children's television series, 'Ship to Shore', about a group of children living on Circe Island off the coast of Perth. Heath's character was simply called 'the cyclist', but he was excited beyond the size of the role because the series was sold to New Zealand, the UK, Ireland, Germany, Iceland, Israel, Portugal and Latin America.

The productions at Guildford Grammar were no less professional, with the school able to afford professional set designers and make-up artists, and contracting other experienced theatre workers as needed. However, it still usually came down to the mums to make the costumes, as when Heath played Dandy Dan in the gangster spoof *Bugsy Malone* in 1993. The smooth, charismatic Dandy Dan, named for his fashion sense, is by far the best role, and Heath played it to the hilt, with spats on his shoes, pork pie hat and Tommy gun.

As he grew up, so did his roles. And as Barry Gardner noted, Heath lived every part he took on.

In 1995, the school's major production was *Royal Hunt of the Sun*, the 1964 play by Peter Shaffer. It was chosen by Gillian Kerr-Sheppard, and the boys thought it was the hardest play they had ever done, because it dealt with complex feelings. The play portrays the destruction of the Inca empire by conquistador Francisco Pizarro, and what the drama class saw at first was the potential for on-stage massacres and bloodshed, highly decorative sets—and a bit of emotion on the side. Their previous plays had all been fast-moving and full of thrilling action, but their director, Father Roy Gilbert, who was also the school chaplain, knew that would have been too easy. He wanted to challenge the boys, and his plan was to perform this play with no basic costumes, no swords and no girls.

Everyone's immediate thought was, 'Boring!'

But as one of the students wrote in the school magazine, the meaning soon came to them. In an indication of how seriously they all took their acting, one of Heath's classmates, Julian Tompkin, credited the play with maturing their acting and making them more open-minded.

'This wasn't just a play we were putting on to show our acting skills. This was an event which really took place, the Incas were slaughtered and the theme was timeless. It was amazing how this story actually touched the whole class,' he wrote.

What also amazed the boys were the expressions on the faces of the audience when they left after the play. Heath headed the cast in its main role as the narrator Old Martin, a jaded man in his mid-fifties. Wearing an old check jacket and glasses, carrying a walking stick and sporting a furrowed brow, he made the part his own. The school still talks about what everyone calls his incredible performance.

His stunning rendition snared him the Open Drama Monologue prize as well as the Ramsey-MacLean Trophy for the most outstanding Art of Speech item at the North Perth Festival that year. The 15-year-old Heath kept the room silent for a full fifteen minutes. It wasn't quite the Oscars, but nonetheless twenty-nine schools competed fiercely for the honours. Heath had more than the others—he had a presence that no amount of teaching can instil. Kim later said that it left everyone in the audience with goosebumps.

Heath had already confided in Barry Gardner that he felt acting was his future, and that it gave him the self-assurance to be himself. But he was still at school and had to toe the line and continue with the rest of his school work. He had got his love of chess from his dad, and his closeness to Kim also influenced his choice of school sport. Boys could only choose one winter sport and one summer sport, simply because the games were all played on a Saturday, so there was no time to play more than one game competitively. Like Kim, Heath played cricket in summer and hockey in winter. Every Monday, Wednesday and Friday after the academic day finished, at 3.25 p.m. precisely, sport was compulsory until 5 p.m.

Years later, he upset his old school by saying that he had only chosen sports to get out of joining the cadets, where they had to learn to fight, and fired automatic weapons. That was probably Heath using a bit of artistic licence and portraying himself as more of a rebel than he actually was. Cadets and sports was never an either/or thing, and the boys fired rifles, not automatic weapons. But, hey, it sounded more dramatic the way Heath told it.

Barry Gardner says Heath was not the rebel in the corner chewing gum—he was just a delightful young man.

He could easily have become a professional hockey player, and by 1992 had won the school's hockey trophy, the David Minchin Cup, donated by an old boy. In 1993 he won the AJ Clark Cup for his hockey, and in 1995 was playing for the combined Public Schools Association state team. He also played for the prestigious Curtin Trinity Tigers, where his coach was three-time Olympian Julian Pearce, who had played on bronze- and silver-medal-winning Olympic sides in Tokyo and Mexico City. Kim Ledger had his sights on Heath making an Olympic hockey team himself! Heath's hockey coach at Guildford, Lloyd Tompkin, and Gillian Kerr-Sheppard found themselves having spirited arguments about whether hockey or drama would triumph.

While *he* knew what he wanted to do, it was 1996—a year that passed for Heath like a whirlwind—that finally persuaded everyone else. While his schoolmates were burning the midnight oil swotting for their exams, Heath was learning his lines for what was his biggest break so far, as the gay cyclist Steve 'Snowy' Bowles in another Barron Films series, 'Sweat'. In what would turn out to be a prophetic role, it was the first time a homosexual teenager had been portrayed on Australian television. Heath could have chosen an easier role as the swimmer, but at sixteen he had already worked out that to be noticed you had to stretch yourself as an actor, and he was hugely adventurous. When he told his dad he wanted to play the gay cyclist, Kim said: 'Oh, God … well, okay.'

Despite the writer and creator of the series, John Rapsey, having worked with Heath before on 'Ship to Shore', it took Heath eight auditions to secure the role. All good, character-building stuff, because in the Ledger tradition nothing should be handed to you on a plate. 'Sweat' was about the trials and tribulations of nine young students at a West Australian sports academy. The publicity blurb said Heath's character was a promising cyclist from the country with 'a fierce competitive spirit'. It didn't talk much about how Snowy grappled with the problem of coming out as gay. His best mate was Danny, another cyclist, and Snowy dragged along behind him, getting 'involved in all his hiccups' as Heath put it. One of the stars of 'Sweat' was a New Zealand actor, Martin Henderson, who was five years older than Heath and had already made it big in his homeland. The two became good friends, and Martin went on to be an acting mentor for his young mate.

The $4.95 million thirteen-week drama was shot at locations around Perth in sessions that ran as late as 3 a.m. It also generated a lot of excitement at Guildford Grammar, where the school's 50-metre Olympic swimming pool was used as a backdrop.

Heath's cousin, Adam, then in Year 8, revelled in the attention and liked to proudly tell anyone who would listen, 'That's my cousin.'

The pool is surrounded by a fence and the production crew had a freezer full of Streets ice-creams—on the wrong side of the fence. Adam and his mates would hang around while Heath smuggled ice-creams through the bars to them.

But Adam was not as happy when the series screened on ABC TV and Heath's character kissed another guy. 'Don't do it!' he shouted at the TV screen. The next day at school he was mortified when people kept coming up to him and saying, 'Give us a kiss!'

John Rapsey recognised that Heath possessed unusual talent.

'What was noticeable about him was he was concentrated, very quiet, and you could see that he was really observant of other people,' he said.

Heath wasn't as pleased with his work on 'Sweat', especially after a scathing newspaper review called the series clichéd.

'I was crap,' Heath said. 'I remember just burying my face in my hands thinking, "This is the end, it hasn't even begun".'

Unlike his older cousin, Adam Ledger had no inclination to sing or dance, and especially not in public. Not long after Heath had finished filming 'Sweat', Adam went home from school one day and told his mum that Heath had said Adam had no choice but to perform in the school's Rock Eisteddfod show.

'Heath says I have to,' said Adam, saying Heath had told him that it was compulsory.

Di Ledger rang her nephew to sort it out. Heath 'fessed up.

'No, it's not compulsory, but I told Adam that and you have to get him into it because he will love it,' Heath replied.

He was pulling the same stunt on other boys at Guildford Grammar, many of them farmers' sons from the bush who, like Adam, thought dancing was sissy. But when Heath turned on the charm, resistance was futile. In 1996 he had been appointed the school's co-captain of drama, along with his friend Aaron Beach. It was a position that brought with it the honour of wearing the distinctive white edging on the school blazer.

In his new position, Heath had decided Guildford should enter the Rock Eisteddfod Challenge for schools, and a bunch of sixty boys who had never danced in their lives was not going to stop him. His theme was male fashion and how young men struggle to impress the girls by dressing in the right way.

Weeks of work were put into it, and Heath was helped a lot by his friend N'fadeynde Forster-Jones, who later shortened his name to simply N'Fa and became a hot rapper star. Heath choreographed all the routines, which covered the eras of top hat and tails (his Fred Astaire influence), hippies and disco, as well as Michael Jackson's 'Thriller' period and, appropriately because of N'Fa's influence, rap. It showed his incredible drive and the competitive spirit he had for everything he did.

He did not take part, deciding to work behind the scenes. Once again, the mums made the costumes, and they must have bought up every sequin in Western Australia.

Heath was rigorous with rehearsals and drove the boys hard, but it was worth it. The finals were held at Perth's Burswood Casino, and when Guildford were announced as the winners—the first all-boy team to win the state title—the roof almost lifted off the dome with all the screaming from the girls' schools. It was a huge win, and netted them the $20,000 prize.

A couple of hours afterwards, the euphoric schoolboys, who all felt like superstars thanks to Heath, were back in the Kyle Auditorium with their parents and headmaster Dr Matthews, watching their triumph on video. There was much cheering, fists were pumped in the air and Heath leapt up at the front of the crowd and shouted, 'We kicked their arses!'

Then he realised what he had done.

'Oops, sorry, Doc Mat,' he said to the headmaster. 'We kicked their bottoms.'

His last appearance on a Guildford Grammar stage was much more sedate, when he took on the role of Laertes in *Hamlet*—the key role of the Prince of Denmark going to the drama teacher's son, Alex Kerr-Sheppard. Gillian Kerr-Sheppard chose *Hamlet* because as well as being an actor's dream play, its combination of drama, humour, passion and tragedy allowed the students to test out and find the true depths of their talents. As part of this, they had to learn vast quantities of complex Shakespearean lines and then say them as if they had just thought of them. Heath's performance as the broken-hearted Laertes was said to be a masterpiece.

It was during the preparations for the Rock Eisteddfod that Heath sat down opposite Barry Gardner and had that chat in art class. He knew that he wanted to be more than just one in a long line of high school students who toyed with drama but went on to do something 'sensible', like become a lawyer or a doctor. He was very strong-willed, and that path in life was not for him. He told Barry that he wanted to travel to Sydney, because all he wanted to do was to be an actor.

'He asked what should I do, and I remember saying to him, follow your dream. I told him life is too short, and you only get these opportunities once in a lifetime,' Barry recalls.

'Heath said, well, what about staying until the end of the year? And I told him that if his passion was to be an actor, do it. I told him if he waited until the end of the year, he would be competing with everyone else going for work, and that he should grab it now because it may never come again.

'And he did.'

Later, Barry would look back on that moment and think it was possible that there was something else bothering Heath— something he was trying to escape from.

03
WHERE'S THE MONEY?

WHILE HEATH WAS IN HIS FINAL YEAR AT SCHOOL, FOCUSED ON HIS ACTING, HE WAS OBLIVIOUS TO THE REAL LIFE DRAMA BEING PLAYED OUT ALL AROUND HIM. HIS FAMILY WAS QUIETLY TEARING ITSELF APART. AND THE ISSUE IN QUESTION WAS SIR FRANK'S MONEY. SIR FRANK LEDGER WAS THE PATRIARCH OF THE LEDGER CLAN AND TO FULLY GRASP HEATH'S LIFE AND CHOICES, AN UNDERSTANDING OF SIR FRANK—HIS ROOTS, HIS CHARACTER, HIS WEALTH AND HIS ROLE AS PART OF THE FABRIC OF THE WILD WEST STATE—IS CRUCIAL.

HEATH IS STRAINING AGAINST HIS DAD'S ARMS, BURSTING WITH EXCITEMENT, DESPERATE TO JUMP INTO THE CENTRE OF THE LOUNGE ROOM AND ORGANISE ALL THE KIDS. THE LEDGERS BREED LIKE RABBITS. HEATH'S GREAT-GRANDFATHER WAS ONE OF NINE, HE HAD TEN GRANDCHILDREN AND BETWEEN FOUR OF THESE—BROTHERS KIM, WAYNE, MIKE AND HAYDN—THERE WERE EVENTUALLY FIFTEEN CHILDREN.

Heath was one of the oldest of the tribe, and loved to take centre stage.

It's Christmas morning before the family's traditional opening of the presents at lunchtime and there are so many of them, they are almost bursting the seams of Heath's grandfather Colin's Gooseberry Hill house, as big and sprawling as it is. Heath is about four, Mike is behind the camera and the photograph shows everyone wearing their Sunday best, squashed on the lounge and comfy chairs around the coffee table, which already has a few empty beer stubbies on it. Heath wears a pair of blue jeans and a striped T-shirt. Kim is trying to restrain him and maintain decorum before the festivities begin.

This was the Christmas that Heath followed Colin when he sneaked off downstairs just before lunch to the workshop under the house. Heath caught his grandfather in his baggy underpants as he climbed into the red trousers of his Santa Claus suit. Colin told Heath to shut up and not tell the other kids, but Heath raced upstairs and blurted out the secret.

'I know who Father Christmas is. He's Papa!'

Heath's great-grandfather—christened Joseph Francis Ledger, but always known as Frank—is also in the photograph, or rather his expansive belly is, as he stands at the right-hand side of the picture, stomach pushed out, his hands high on his hips as he watches everyone. Frank had bought his son Colin a shrub and left the price tag on. Colin watered it for a year, crossed the price out, doubled it and gave it back to Frank for his birthday the year after.

You can see Frank is talking and laughing. He's probably saying how great it is to have everyone together at Christmas. He loved the whole family thing. He also loved being in charge.

﬙

Frank Ledger didn't talk much about how tough life must have been when he was growing up in Perth, for two reasons. The first was that he wasn't into the 'poor me' thing. He just got on with life and work, didn't ever feel sorry for himself and expected everyone else to do the same. The second was probably that even though he was the patriarch of the family, they would have teased him about his 'sob story' in that anti-authoritarian, irreverent way that only Australians can. You never got away with much in a big family like that.

It's hard to imagine what life was like in England's industrial heartland when the first member of the Ledger family to come to Australia, Joseph Edson Ledger, left Leeds in Yorkshire in 1879 at the age of twenty-eight. The sailing ship *Robert Morrison* was as hardy as its passengers, regularly ploughing the seas between European ports and Australia in the 1800s, at times carrying over 150 people. When the immigrant ship docked at Fremantle on 6 July 1880, there were only twenty-two on its decks, including Joe, his wife Jane and their daughter Clara.

However harsh life was in Yorkshire, it probably seemed like luxury compared to living on one of those ships. The journey took between three and four months depending on the weather, with the ship rolling and pitching constantly. Most passengers were horribly seasick and spent a lot of time below decks. It was not a trip for the fainthearted.

When they landed in Australia, the family first had to walk the 20 kilometres from Fremantle into Perth, to what remains the world's most isolated city. They had little money, no guarantee of work and nowhere to live.

Joe was a fitter and turner, and set up a small business in the laneway between Hay Street and Murray Street in what remains the centre of Perth. Once established, he sent word home for his brother Edson to join him, and on 30 June 1882, Heath's great-great-grandfather was among the sixty-five passengers who stepped ashore from the *Fitzroy*.

The Ledger family always admired Edson for making that long trip alone at the age of fourteen, just a boy. Edson was an apprentice tinsmith and once he had finished his apprenticeship, the two brothers opened the Stirling Foundry in Pier Street. In their bowler hats and sporting thick moustaches, they cut dashing figures—demonstrating the good looking genes which augured well for the rest of the Ledgers.

The brothers' luck held when ten years later the state was besieged by gold fever. Gold had been discovered in 1885 way up north at Halls Creek in the Kimberleys, but it all went crazy in 1892 when gold was found much nearer Perth, just 550 kilometres east of the city at Coolgardie. A year later it was discovered 40 kilometres further out at Kalgoorlie. But not for nothing were the local landowners in Western Australia known as sandgropers. Water on the goldfields rapidly became scarcer and more precious than gold. Enter the Ledger brothers.

Even today the Goldfields Pipeline would be an engineering marvel. It carries water 557 kilometres through a steel pipeline from Perth to Kalgoorlie. The Ledger Brothers, as their business was then known, cast many of the 60,000 special, massive pipes. By 1896, they were employing forty to fifty people. However, to the locals in Perth the brothers were better known for the old-style red cast iron pillar boxes with J & E Ledger's name moulded into them.

Edson was as busy building a family as he was building a business. In 1896, he married Annie Frances Sumner and they had nine children, eight of whom survived. Frank—Joseph Francis—was born in October 1899, the third eldest. Despite the success of the business, the children were certainly not born with silver spoons in their mouths. Like so many of the large families of the era, they were strictly brought up, loved with discipline, a 'fine family' of 'repute and integrity', as later described at Frank's funeral by one of his closest friends, Sir Charles Court.

Frank exhibited a trait shared by many Ledgers down the line: he liked learning, but he didn't like school very much. By the age of fifteen, he had begun his apprenticeship with his father's firm. He chose general engineering, which encompassed fitting and turning, blacksmithing and foundry, and worked 48-hour weeks for seven shillings and sixpence, doing a bit of everything. He might have been the boss's son, but he was shown no favours— that would have been a sign of weakness for the Ledgers, who have all been expected to make their own way. Not only did he not really like school, Frank developed serious reservations about those with academic qualifications, which he would harbour for the rest of his life. He believed everyone should do what he did: start at the bottom and work their way up.

Frank finished his apprenticeship not at the family business, but at a firm that built motor bodies, to get more experience. He was then earning the princely sum of three pounds and five shillings a week. Enough to get married on.

Frank had met Gladys Lyons a couple of years earlier. Her dad was Councillor Lyons on the Perth City Council and one half of another well-known local business, Lyons and Hart. Frank and Gladys had a traditional marriage in 1923 at the grand Trinity Church in the heart of the city. They lived in a rented house for a couple of years while they saved, then built a house on land near the Swan River with a loan from the War Services Homes.

Frank had moved back to the family firm just as the depression hit. Things were so bad they had to lay men off to enable the business to survive, and Frank went back on the machines himself. But he knew it was not sensible to put all his eggs in one basket. He developed a sales arm of the firm and diversified into print machinery, brick making and pottery work.

His brother Ted joined the family firm as the accountant, and the Ledgers started to win contracts in the eastern states' markets. Customers who Ledger Engineering won around that time in the 1930s in Melbourne, Adelaide, Sydney and Queensland were still with the firm fifty years later.

Frank and Gladys had a very traditional relationship, as befit the time. They were intellectual equals, but she was the backbone of the family and a tower of strength at home while he went out into the world and did business. Gladys was frustrated all her life by having to take a back seat, but Frank, a risk-taker in business but not in relationships, still believed women should be seen and not heard. Gladys held Frank in great respect—sometimes in too much respect, his family thought. They felt it was a shame that she was held back. She wanted to get out there and kick arse, but was too proper to say so. All the same, it was a match made in heaven, and they adored each other.

Colin, Heath's grandfather, was born in 1925. Tradition dictated that he was named after his dad, so he was Colin Francis Ledger. He had two sisters—June, who was older, and Betsy, who was younger—and growing up sandwiched between two girls taught him a lot about women. The sisters were far more boisterous than Colin and, although he never said so, the family felt he was overshadowed by them, as well as by his father. It led to Colin growing up a rather sensitive man.

While Frank could be strict, Gladys was a softie with all her family, gentle and sweet, and loved by everyone. Though from a well-to-do family, she was very down to earth.

Frank's kids didn't have a posh upbringing. The house was not grand but comfortable, and although it was in one of the better streets of East Perth, it was a lower middle class existence. The kids played on the banks of the river and out in the street in the shadow of East Perth Power Station.

In 1940, Frank's father, Edson, died at the grand age of eighty-nine and Frank officially became head of the Ledger family, a position he relished. He was always community minded, and had started to take on leadership roles in Western Australia, becoming part of the fabric of the state.

'He was a leader in his day,' Sir Charles Court, Frank's close friend, said at Frank's funeral. 'He carried more than his share of the burden as committeeman and office bearer in many organisations. He was quick to remind others of their responsibilities.'

But he was still a businessman first! When he was asked whether J and E Ledger, as one of the leading foundries in the country, could make aerial bombs, he didn't flinch when he said that of course they could. In reality, he knew less than nothing about aerial bombs, and even less about making them, but that wasn't going to stop him. He figured they would need high-tensile cast iron and that was something he knew more about than almost anyone in the country, so the company moved into the munitions business.

Frank put so much into what he did that he used to say that every time he completed a job, his 'brains went out of the gate with it'—another quality passed on to the Ledger clan. But there were those who could see that Frank's total dedication to the business had an effect on his family life.

Frank's son Colin was one of the few people who never pandered to him. When World War II broke out, Colin joined up and became part of the legendary Z Force (as it was popularly known). The Z Force flew out of the Philippines at night, without radar, on instruments alone through the mountains, to drop off spies and bring back intelligence on the enemy. With the idealism of a nineteen-year-old, coupled with the bravery and confidence that came from flying into the face of death every night and coming out alive, Flight Sergeant Colin Ledger wrote to his father during the war, reminding him that there were more important things than work.

'I told Mum this letter was coming and she said telling you was like water on a duck's back. Well, you've asked for it and you're going to get the works.

'What about easing up this night work, Pop? It's all very nice to say that you are on this and that committee and board etc but [will] those same people that appreciate you now be so thoughtful when you have worked yourself to a premature breakdown or even death. After all, Pop, your life is your own and you can live it as you please but the main thing in life is the search for happiness and if you can think of any other reason we are on this earth, I would like you to name it. I'm sure Mum doesn't like being by herself nearly every night of the week. Remember the office is the office, and home is the home and why you spend as much time there is beyond me …

'You have got to admit, Pop, that someone had to talk to you like this and as everyone seems to have shirked it, the baby is left for me. Anyhow I think too much of our combination to try to forget it. Please don't feel cut up about the way I have written. I only hope you take it in the spirit it was meant, and not as a symbol of disobedience or ingratitude, after all the only way to drive a point with you is to have it out man to man as we always have.

'My advice to you is to sit back and start to enjoy the fruits of your labour as you aren't getting any younger, you know, Pop, forty-six this year …

'Anyhow Dad I will drop this for a while, hoping you will answer it in a kindly manner ...

Love to all at home

Your loving son'

The letter was so special to the family that after Frank died, Kim had copies made, had them framed and gave one to each of his brothers to hang on their wall. But if Frank heeded the message in his son's letter at all, he did not let it change his life.

He was a doer, and he wasn't afraid to bend the rules to get things done. In the 1960s when Western Australia began to flex its muscle, with the development of the rich resources in the state's north-west, men like Frank, Charles Court and the mining entrepreneur Lang Hancock were the tendons. They were a formidable group, and some wonder what the state would be like today without them.

The wealth of the state's mineral resources would far outstrip the gold rush, but it was real pioneering stuff to tap into it. J and E Ledger already had a toehold in the region, providing some of the heavy machinery for the fledgling mining ventures.

With his mate Charles Court as the Minister for Industrial Development, Frank chartered a DC-3 and filled it with twenty-three businessmen, got them to pay their own fares and took them up north to whip up enthusiasm for the region. Kununurra—meaning 'big water' in the language of the local Aboriginal people—is in the Kimberleys. It's still a long way from anywhere, but back then it was even more of an outpost, a purpose-built town for an ambitious government dream.

Frank had the plane land there, and took these businessmen out to Bandicoot Bar, to look out at the Ord River. It was winter and the dry season, and the river was mainly a trail of isolated pools. In the hot, wet summer months it would have been in tropical flood. He wanted them to see the government's bold vision for the north-west—a dam harnessing the floodwaters of the river for the rest of the year and the rest of the region.

J and E Ledger built and transported the massive cranes and other heavy machinery needed to make the project a reality. The Ord River Scheme created Lake Argyle, an inland sea nine times the size of Sydney Harbour, a hydroelectric station and irrigation for 14,000 hectares. Bandicoot Bar became a good fishing and picnic spot just below the dam wall, though its strong currents and saltwater crocodiles made it too dangerous for swimming.

Frank travelled all over the world to sell Australia, including to New York and Ceylon (now Sri Lanka) and south-east Asia. In 1963, he was knighted for his services to industry and to Western Australia. He and Gladys flew to Canberra to meet the Queen at the Governor-General's residence in Yarralumla. Secretly they would have liked the drama and ceremony of going to Buckingham Palace, but the Queen and the Duke of Edinburgh were on a royal visit to Australia to mark the fiftieth anniversary of the naming of Canberra as the capital.

It was around this time that Frank and Gladys started to enjoy the fruits of their labour. They now lived in Peppermint Grove, one of Perth's most beautiful suburbs, on the Swan River, in a beautiful old house with gardens complete with a fountain. The family loved it not for its aesthetic qualities, but because the lawns were nice and flat to kick a footy ball around on. It was on the elbow of the Swan River and still has the best uninterrupted views right along the waterway. When the tribe descended on the house, Gladys always had something home-baked for them. At Christmas, she still hid an old threepence in the Christmas pudding. She was a great person to sit down and talk to, and her grandkids could talk to her about anything.

Colin was working as general manager at J and E Ledger when in 1969 Frank decided to sell the family company to the UK-based Mitchell Cotts Group. Mitchell Cotts was a conglomerate of companies expanding across Australia, snapping up building, transport and engineering firms. They thought Ledgers was an ideal fit for them, and Frank thought it was time to move on. They promised to keep the J & E Ledger name going, which they did. Frank, however, had no intention of retiring and stayed on as a director, with Colin remaining as general manager.

Frank was a philanthropist, and he set up the Sir Frank Ledger Charitable Trust, which has been operating since at least 1982 and continues to this day. The trust, which is run through the University of Western Australia, provides scholarships that allow students who would otherwise not be able to afford it to take part in the Advanced Management Program.

Frank's legacy was in giving his children, grandchildren and great-grandchildren the confidence in themselves to go out and make their mark on the city they called home. Or on the world.

In his study at Peppermint Grove, he had a favourite rolltop desk where he did most of his work, often with young Heath sitting on his lap. Heath was the first boy among Sir Frank's grandchildren, and they got on like a house on fire. Frank enjoyed Heath's energy and enthusiasm, and Heath was always taking the piss out of him. Like Heath, Sir Frank could be a joker.

Sir Frank was very indulgent of the boy—Heath was such a ham, and he could wrap the old man around his little finger.

But not as much as his dad, Kim, could. As the family later found out.

╫

It was Ric Syme who first suspected something dodgy might be going on with Sir Frank's money.

Retirement suited Sir Frank and Gladys Ledger. The couple had been living very comfortably, mortgage-free and with a considerable income from $865,000 cash in various deposits. They could relax on their verandah with no worries, taking in their multi-million-dollar views over Freshwater Bay on the Swan River.

Sir Frank had his toys—a stylish Halvorsen wooden cruiser and a stretch limo limited edition Mercedes-Benz 600—and he maintained his membership of most of Perth's major sporting organisations. He liked a drink, and had a formidable appetite for alcohol. One legendary tale told about his flight home to Perth from Brisbane with a well-known Perth race caller. The race caller decided to try and outdrink him. Sir Frank walked upright off the plane while the race caller had to be half-carried.

But money can't buy health, and sadly, not long after they moved to Peppermint Grove, Gladys began to suffer from dementia. She died in July 1981, aged seventy-eight. Sir Frank was lost when she went, and had trouble finding things to fill his days. It was also around this time that the family realised from his bizarre behaviour that Sir Frank was also suffering from dementia. It advanced quickly until by 1986, at the age of eighty-seven, the man who had been such a business powerhouse was unable to handle his own financial affairs. Ross Ledger, an experienced chartered accountant, was managing Sir Frank's money matters with input from Frank's children, Colin Ledger, June Syme and Betsy Cox. Ross Ledger was a cousin of Colin, June and Betsy's and had worked for Sir Charles Court's accounting firm—another example of Perth's small-town syndrome.

Sir Frank had the care and support of the whole family. He still loved having his grandchildren, including Heath, around, even if he didn't always remember who they all were.

Under the terms of his long-standing will, Sir Frank had appointed his son and daughters as joint executors of his estate, and bequeathed $10,000 to each of his ten grandchildren.

It was in mid-1986, after Kim and Sally split up, that Kim, aged thirty-six, moved into the downstairs flat beneath Sir Frank's house at The Esplanade. Heath and Kate lived with their mum, but regularly spent nights sleeping over at the flat. It was an arrangement that increased to two to three weeks at a time once Kim moved into his own home six months later.

Mitchell Cotts, the international conglomerate which had bought J & E Ledger Pty Ltd from Sir Frank almost twenty years earlier, was struggling, and trying to offload its businesses. In 1987, Kim bought it out, including the old Ledger company, and renamed it Ledger Engineering Pty Ltd. It caused a huge buzz in the family that Kim was bringing the firm back into the fold, albeit no longer as a family firm.

Kim took over the Mitchell Cotts foundry at Welshpool, where he built large mining equipment. He had a payroll of about a hundred and an annual turnover of around $10 million. Mike Ledger, who could turn his hand to most things to make a buck, including shearing sheep and breaking horses, was employed as manager of the foundry division. Haydn was working up the west coast at Geraldton, where he had a successful mechanical business and service station and refuelled the planes at the small but busy airport, and Wayne ran a nursery just outside Adelaide.

Colin Ledger had an old saying: 'What you put out in life is what you get back.' He was proud of what his four sons were achieving in their lives. There are only five years between the Ledger boys, with Kim the oldest, then Wayne, Mike and Haydn, and the family was still very close.

Colin and their mum, Esma, had sold the farm where the boys had grown up racing hotrods around the paddock and swimming in the creek and moved to the whitewashed brick house on Sundew Road, Gooseberry Hill. Sundew Road was the scene of most of the family gatherings, including the Christmas where Heath sprung his Papa, Colin, dressing as Santa Claus.

Colin had a green thumb and out of the front garden he created a land of homemade creeks with little bridges and islands so impressive that it won him Kalamunda Shire's Garden of the Year one year. That garden was a wonderland for Heath and his cousins, who created all sorts of adventures among its hidden paths, always happily led by Heath, king of the kids. He invented a ghost in the garden and embellished the story for years, keeping his young cousins mesmerised and terrified by turns. Kate was the oldest of the cousins, then came Heath, and then Jess, Haydn's oldest daughter, who became very close to Heath.

As the oldest son, Kim held regular meetings with Sir Frank's children—Colin, Betsy and June—to keep them up to date with what was happening. The family would gather around the table in the boardroom of the Welshpool plant, or meet at Sir Frank's house.

However it wasn't Sir Frank's children who first became suspicious about where Kim was getting his money, but his grandchildren, specifically Ric Syme, June's son. Ric and his cousin Kim were close in age and in looks, both sporting the baldness that creeps up on most of the Ledger men in their twenties.

Ric was puzzled as to how Kim was raising the money when the company he was buying only had one main asset, so there did not appear to be much to borrow against. Kim's other business, Rotomotion, was successful, but not making anywhere near enough money to fund the takeover of Ledgers.

Ric, one of Perth's leading professional photographers, turned into the family detective. According to court documents, when he did a title search of 2 The Esplanade, his suspicions were confirmed. The house, which just a year earlier had been unencumbered, was mortgaged to the hilt and Sir Frank up to his eyeballs in debt. Ric broke the shocking news to his mother, June.

Sir Frank's house was a fitting backdrop for the family showdown. They had gathered together over tea and biscuits for the next meeting. It was 1988.

According to Ric Syme, his mother, June, asked Kim to tell them all how Sir Frank's house had been remortgaged to raise the money for Ledger Engineering.

'It isn't,' Kim replied.

Ric said June had been holding the mortgage documents in her right hand and slammed them down on the table in the middle of them all.

'Well, what's this?' she asked.

Everyone sat there horrified, waiting for Kim to reply and hoping he had a good answer. A court would later hear that Colin was visibly upset and emotional—his son had already assured him that the money for the business had come from Kim's own assets and had nothing to do with Sir Frank.

Kim tried to calm them all down, assuring them that the move was only technical, the NatWest Australia Bank would never foreclose on the mortgage and he would get a 'comfort letter' from the bank putting all that in writing. But the seeds had just been sown of the row that none of them wanted—the row that would rip the heart out of the Ledger family.

Six years later, in August 1994, lawyer David Price rose to address the judge of the West Australian Supreme Court.

'It is common ground that my client has no money,' he told Justice Graeme Scott.

His client, Kim Ledger, was broke. Over the previous eight years, he had lost everything, the court was told. Ledger Engineering had gone into receivership in 1992. Kim was also locked in a $15 million legal fight with the NatWest Australia Bank, and he was in court on this particular day because his own family wanted back the money they alleged he had taken from them.

Sir Frank, the glue that had held the family together, had died in 1993, and his family was at loggerheads.

Colin Ledger had died two years before that. Haydn was in Geraldton and Wayne was in Adelaide when Mike called in August 1991 to say their father had collapsed in the driveway of his house, of a stroke. The family gathered in Perth, and Colin held on for another two weeks at the Hollywood Repatriation Hospital. His body became weaker, but his mind remained sharp, and he kept the bawdy Ledger family humour alive until the end. Haydn recalls visiting one night and realising, after placing his hand on his dad's forehead, that Colin was hot and sweaty. Haydn asked if his dad wanted the window open and his dad said he was okay, but that he got sweaty 'when the nurse sat on my face'. The nurses thankfully were not offended by his offbeat humour.

Colin's funeral service at Karakatta Cemetery was packed with mourners including the old family friends Sir Charles Court, former senator Sir Bruce Mackinlay, and former MP and champion of Aboriginal rights, Fred Chaney. His four sons were pallbearers, and Kim delivered the eulogy.

After the service, Heath got a lift home with his uncles and they called into Hungry Jack's for a feed. As they stopped at the window of the drive-through, Heath leaned out of the back of the car and asked the women serving them how many burgers they had sold last year.

'Because this year you'll be selling only half as many, because we've just buried my Papa and he ate the rest!' Heath shouted, using humour to make light of the occasion. They drove off giggling somewhat manically, like schoolboys.

Colin had been surviving on fast food because his wife, Esma—who had been diagnosed with Alzheimer's at fifty-seven— had been taken into a nursing home.

Esma's four sons felt she was the last person who deserved to have anything bad like this happen to her. She had grown up in a poor, strict Catholic farming family at Kellerberrin in the West Australian wheat-belt, and met Colin while training as a nurse at Royal Perth Hospital. A born carer, she was always doing favours for the neighbours and found time for a regular meals-on-wheels round. The boys had grown up with laughter and joking around the kitchen table, which continued when they took their own children around to Sundew Road. Esma had never had a bad word to say about anyone, and the brothers always said it was from her that Heath got his caring, compassionate nature.

Esma's illness and the trouble over Sir Frank's money took their toll on Colin, and Mike and Haydn think the stress may have caused their father's stroke.

Sir Frank's funeral, again at Karakatta Cemetery, was even bigger than his son's, with everyone who was anyone at the big end of town turning up to pay their respects, including his friends and business associates from a lifetime at the epicentre of Perth business. Sitting at the front were his daughters June Syme and Betsy Cox, and his ten grandchildren, including Kim, who had walked in wearing a ten-gallon hat and looking very much like the star of his favourite TV series, J.R. Ewing from 'Dallas'. Sir Charles Court delivered a dignified eulogy to a man who he said was a pioneer, one of the great personalities who coloured the heady days when Western Australia was built into the state it had become.

'We say farewell to a true friend who served his country, his industry and his community beyond the call of duty. We are the richer for his life and work,' Sir Charles said.

But what struck Mike and Haydn was Sir Charles describing Sir Frank as one of the real 'flesh and blood proprietors who had put their own money as well as their own careers and their family fortunes at risk'. It stuck in their craw that he had died a pauper, with nothing left of the Ledger family fortune—at least not in his name.

In August 1986, just weeks after Kim moved into Sir Frank's granny flat, Sir Frank had signed a codicil to his will dismissing his son and two daughters as joint executors. In their place was Kim Ledger.

Sir Frank had also given Kim power of attorney and appointed him as administrator of his financial affairs, the West Australian Supreme Court was told in 1994.

After Sir Frank's death, Colin's sisters spent months trying to find out from Kim what was going on with their father's estate. Eventually frustration gave way to anger, and they regrettably felt they had no option but to take Kim to court. Ric Syme rang his cousins to let them know what was happening. One by one the cousins gave their aunts their support, some more willingly than others, and some of them also put their hands in their pockets to fund what would grow into a $100,000 legal bill.

The only one not contacted, of course, was Kim. From this moment, he was out on his own.

The family's solicitor, Stephen Scott, told the Supreme Court that probate for Sir Frank's estate had been granted on 26 October 1993, but that Kim had done nothing to administer the estate. There had been no reading of the will, nor had Kim spoken to the beneficiaries—June and Betsy—about the disposition of the assets.

The sisters applied for him to be removed as executor, arguing that Kim had a conflict of interest in administering the estate.

In her affidavit, June Syme said her father had been incapable of handling his own affairs since the early 1980s. Since the mid-1980s, he had been unable to understand the purpose of transactions into which he entered.

Sir Frank's doctor, Dr W. Allan Hutchinson, made a statement that from the time he began caring for Sir Frank in 1988 'there had never been any time [he] could have made a competent business decision'.

Yet he died with his estate around $2.5 million in the red.

'From 1986 through until he died, effectively his estate was eroded by a number of transactions that were entered into with the enthusiasm of [Kim Ledger],' said the solicitor, Stephen Scott.

It emerged that Kim had remortgaged The Esplanade property several times to guarantee the liabilities of his two companies, Ledger Engineering and Fella Pty Ltd. Fella Pty Ltd was the trustee of the Ledger Property Trust, and as each of Sir Frank's cash term deposits had matured, Kim used his power of attorney to lend $500,000 unsecured and interest-free to the trust, the court heard.

This drew Sally, Kate and Heath unwittingly into the financial maze, because they were the beneficiaries of the trust. A co-director of Fella Pty Ltd was Kim's long-time friend and business associate, Robert Collins.

In addition, there were not one but three deeds of option to buy The Esplanade property signed by Sir Frank in favour of Kim. They were set at a bargain basement price that never increased despite the rise in house prices. Mortgage documents lodged with the state government utility Landgate show that on 4 February 1987, Sir Frank first raised $1.85 million using his house as collateral. The last deed of option was signed by Sir Frank in April 1992.

'The deceased had been a very careful businessman and he would not have placed his assets in such a precarious position had he understood the impact of these commercial decisions,' said the sisters June Syme and Betsy Cox in their court submission. '[Kim] has placed his own interests before that of the trust and used the trust assets in order to advance his own business interests.'

They said that if Kim had been correctly managing the estate, he would have sued his own companies—and himself—to get the money back.

But the millions had gone and there was nothing to retrieve, his lawyer Mr Price told the court.

He said Kim agreed to be removed as executor, but only because he had no money to pursue the estate's best interests.

'The deceased did appoint this man as his executor, his entrusted servant, as it were,' Mr Price said. 'His motives for capitulating are honourable and correct.'

The court officially removed Kim as executor and replaced him with June Syme and Betsy Cox. Kim's costs for the court case were awarded against the estate.

Sir Frank's Peppermint Grove home, which had always been immaculate, had fallen into disrepair because there was no income to maintain it. Worth around $10 million in today's prices, it was sold by the NatWest Australia Bank in a mortgagee sale for $1.2 million, of which half was eventually given to the estate.

Families are like marriages—no-one outside really knows what goes on inside. The Ledgers wanted to keep it that way. The court case had garnered no media attention, and none of them talked about what was going on with anyone outside the family. This became more important to them as Heath's star rose and they wanted to protect him.

Heath was sharing his time between Sally and Roger Bell and his dad, who was with a new, young partner Emma Brown. They lived on a farm at rural Janebrook, east of Midland, where Mike agisted some of his horses.

In 1996, Emma was twenty-five and closer to Heath's age than to Kim's, with the result that Heath found her easy to talk to. Heath would get his best mates together and camp up the back of the property where there were 180 degree views of Perth. They would party up there, watching the sun set, surrounded by horses and kangaroos.

Kim protected Heath from details of the family row. That year, when Heath was seventeen, he bumped into Mike on the steps of Guildford Grammar's David Law Davies Theatre during rehearsals for the Rock Eisteddfod. He wanted to know why Mike and his dad weren't getting on. Mike told him that Kim had not been honest with his brothers, and that they felt they deserved an apology. He told Heath to ask his dad and discuss it with him.

Meanwhile the sisters' marathon legal battle against Kim to recover Sir Frank's money continued. Records show that while he had control of his grandfather's wealth, Kim had bought a stake in Barron Films as a shareholder, and had become a director between 1990 and 1995. Barron Films was the company that gave Heath his big break in television. There was no doubt that Heath deserved the roles—and he did audition no less than eight times for his part in 'Sweat'.

With Ledger Engineering in receivership, Kim had been forced to look for work. Capitalising on his love of cars, especially fast ones, he found a job right up his street as after sales manager at Western Australia's major Porsche dealership, Chellingworth Porsche.

At the time, Kim was still racing, but had moved on from speedway to road racing, driving Mazdas and Mitsubishis. According to Western Australia District Court documents, he came up with an ambitious plan to upgrade to a Porsche. His idea was for Chellingworth to buy a $75,000 Porsche 944 Turbo racing car. He said it would give the dealership a project, build staff morale and give the mechanics something to work on when they weren't busy with customers' cars.

His boss, Greg Arnold, didn't agree, and did not want the company involved. He made his feelings clear to both Kim and the man selling the Porsche, Clive Hartz.

However, District Court documents show Kim went ahead with the deal. Mr Hartz produced a written agreement with Kim dated February 1997, a month before Kim quit Chellingworth. When Kim did not pay up, Mr Hartz, and his company Cleveland Nominees Pty Ltd, took him to the District Court. Kim told the court he had only signed the agreement under pressure and saw it as more of a 'comfort letter' than a formal contract. His lawyers submitted that Kim had been bankrupt and had no money to pay for the car.

Judge Mary Ann Yeats did not believe him.

'Those submissions are not supported by the evidence,' she said in her judgment in 2000. 'I note that his family's company receivership was as long ago as 1992. There was also evidence confirmed by the defendant under cross-examination that he did have a sizeable sum of around $100,000 set aside in his wife's name to assist with a Supreme Court action he was involved in in relation to the family company.'

Judge Yeats said Kim was an astute businessman and she did not accept his evidence that he believed the contract was only a comfort letter. She said the evidence supported Mr Hartz's case that Kim had on 'numerous occasions in telephone conversations with Mr Hartz admitted that the $75,000 was due and owing and asked for extensions to pay'.

She found against Kim and ordered him to pay the money with interest, a total of $88,500.

However the case dragged on through a successful appeal by Kim until finally the state's highest court, the Full Court of the Supreme Court, ruled Mr Hartz's lawyer should have been claiming for damages and not the cost of the car. Mr Hartz kept his car, but it was back to square one. He decided to cut his losses and drop the case.

In 1998, with his businesses finally out of receivership, Kim signed a legally binding deed with his aunts, June Syme and Betsy Cox, to pay them $1 million once he had settled the $15 million case with the NatWest Australia Bank. Two years later, while the bank and Kim settled the action out of court on a nil-all draw basis, June and Betsy were still waiting for their money.

In April 2000, the aunts issued a writ against Kim and records show that Kim challenged the writ and made a counteroffer—of $50,000. His new law firm told the sisters that Kim still had no money and was facing bankruptcy if they pressed their claim. He listed his total assets as $43,700, including $2,000 in clothing and personal effects, a car, a bike and two personalised numberplates of VMX-1200 and WA 6655. His liabilities were $29,500, including $4,600 in credit card debts and two loans. (Records with the Insolvency and Trustee Service Australia show Kim was never bankrupt.)

None of this did anything to heal the rift in the family. Brothers and sisters can treat each other much worse than they would treat their friends. By the same token, they will forgive and forget even the cruellest barbs because, after all, blood is thicker than water.

For the Ledgers, there was no healing balm that could salve the wounds. By 2000, Kim and his brothers Haydn and Mike were communicating only by letter and email. It was a heartbreaking series of direct missives that became increasing bitter and crushingly sad.

Haydn to Kim: 'If you really want to know what I want, I want a brother back. I want an uncle for my kids, one they remember as funny, loving and kind. For that, you can stick all the money in the world up my fat hairy arse!'

Kim replied to Hadyn that he had always been true to his family, until all the trouble began. He was disappointed that his brothers had listened to their aunts' side of the story instead of his. He emphasised that he had not deliberately lost his grandfather's assets.

Ric Syme to Haydn: 'Nothing seems to stay the same anymore … except dysfunctional families usually stay dysfunctional.'

Haydn to Kim: 'Imagine what Dad or Mum would feel if they knew the wheels had dropped off this family and more importantly the reasons why. I guess though that Dad's death and Mum's illness have been a blessing in disguise.

'In closing (if you have got this far) I'd just like to say that I have tried with you but as I said earlier, it resulted in egg on my face. Whether you like to admit it or not, only you can initiate the moves to turn this thing around. The ball's in your court. Your family is here to support you, but you've got to have both the desire and the guts to take a risk.'

Mike to Kim: 'The reason you think of me as being "that irrational Michael as only he can be" is because there are several things in yours and my life that you will never properly front.'

Meanwhile, Clive Hartz had dragged Heath into his row with Kim, slapping a caveat on a property in the Perth suburb of Cloverdale owned by Heath's company Act 6 Pty Ltd, in a final bid to try to claw back the money for his Porsche.

The caveat was eventually lifted, but the whole episode was lampooned in the local daily newspaper, the *West Australian*. It dubbed Kim 'The Litigant', as a play on his son's starring role in *The Patriot,* which had just hit the screens at the time. It was excruciatingly embarrassing for all concerned.

In April 2001, an anonymous letter arrived in the letterboxes of 200 Perth households, including that of the Premier Richard Court, his father, Sir Charles Court, and many of Kim's clients. A copy was received by Kim's brothers and every one of his cousins. The letter also landed on the desks of news and features editors at the *West Australian* and the city's weekend newspaper, the *Sunday Times*.

It was a carefully written, detailed, twelve-page account of Kim's alleged dealings with Sir Frank's money, which it went on to link to Kim's management of Heath's financial affairs. 'If Kim has control of Heath Ledger's financial affairs,' it stated, 'which seems likely ... one must feel at least a little concerned for his talented son's financial welfare.'

It was obvious the letter had been written by an insider with intimate knowledge of the case, an insider who was not a fan of Kim's. However no-one 'fessed up to it, not then and not since. But Kim had his suspicions, none of them proved.

A few days later, Haydn received a call from a former cop turned private detective who said he had been hired by Kim. He wanted Haydn to visit his office and have his fingerprints taken. Haydn refused the invitation. Ric Syme found his rubbish bin had been ransacked one night, and presumed it was by someone looking for something bearing his fingerprints. Mike had a strange customer, a huge Maori who said he wanted to buy wheels for a massive earthmover. However, Mike quickly realised that everything his customer knew about wheels could be written on the back of a postage stamp. The man kept pressing Mike for his business card, and Mike surmised he only wanted it so he could check fingerprints. He gave the customer short shrift.

For the two aunts, June Syme and Betsy Cox, all those years in litigation were enough and the women, in their seventies, gave up.

The last time the brothers were all together as a family was at their mother's funeral in May 2004, after she died in the nursing home. Esma Ledger was the last thread that tied them all together, and the funeral marked not only the death of their mother, but the death of the family.

But that 2001 anonymous letter, with its prediction about the management of Heath's affairs, would return to haunt Kim.

04
LET HIM
FLY

THE FRONT OF THE BIRTHDAY CARD READ 'HAPPY BIRTHDAY, MUM', BUT THE MESSAGE INSIDE WAS NOT QUITE AS WHOLESOME. IT SAID, 'LET'S PARTY IN THE EAST, LOVE HEATH.' THE 'MUM' CARD WAS A JOKE BIRTHDAY CARD FOR TREVOR DI CARLO, HEATH'S BEST MATE AND SOMEONE WHO SHARED HIS SENSE OF THE RIDICULOUS. THE TWO TEENAGERS WERE LOOKING FORWARD TO BREAKING AWAY FROM PERTH AND EXPERIENCING LIFE OUTSIDE THE WORLD'S MOST ISOLATED CITY. THEY WERE HEADED FOR SYDNEY, AND WHILE IT WOULD HAVE BEEN CHEAPER TO FLY, A SEAT ON A PLANE LACKED THE THRILL OF A RIDE IN A CAR HEADING ACROSS THE NULLARBOR. KIM BOUGHT HEATH A MAZDA, AND THE TWO FAMILIES HELPED THE BOYS PACK IT FOR THE DRIVE EAST.

They hadn't long had their driving licences, although Heath had his experience on the go-kart track, and the families waved them off telling them to take it easy and go slow. Three days and close to 4,000 kilometres later they telephoned home—from Sydney.

'I'm sure my parents were really concerned, but they were wise enough not to show it to me too much. They knew they were not going to stop me. They knew I was going to go. They're amazing. They really just fucking let me fly!' Heath told *Vanity Fair* four years later.

Kim would never have held his son back, however much he missed him.

'I've always been a person who believes that people who break kids' spirits should be jailed. It should be a capital offence. We all have our individual spirits,' Kim later said. 'He does seem to have a destiny that he's in charge of.'

It is trite but true to say that Heath and Trevor had the time of their lives on the journey. The windows down, the music of INXS, U2 and Janis Joplin blasting from the tape deck, surfboards tied to the roof, and Heath smoking openly—he had been doing it secretly since he was fifteen. The two boys were real soul mates, who had grown up closer than brothers—as his uncles would attest. When Heath was heading for his eighth birthday and Trevor was staying with his family in Kalgoorlie, Kim asked his son what he wanted as a present. Heath said he just wanted his best buddy, so Kim flew Trevor over to Perth. They had a bond that would endure.

They also had a place to stay in Sydney. Heath had kept in touch with Martin Henderson, the actor who played Tom Nash, one of his fellow alumni from the school for the athletically gifted in 'Sweat'. Henderson had encouraged Heath to move to the big smoke and give Sydney a go. The road to an acting career is paved with wannabes, but Henderson thought Heath had what it took, as well as being great fun to have around. So when the two young sandgropers knocked on his door in Bondi, Martin gave them a bed and a beer.

There was nowhere better to be at the age of seventeen than Bondi, party central with beach, babes and bonking—Heath had already lost his virginity back in Perth. Bondi's cafes were full of yuppies, rogues, millionaires and out-of-work actors. At night there was the Bondi Hotel with its foreign backpacking crowd, the world-famous Bondi Icebergs, still grungy and cool before its trendy makeover, the edgy Liberty Lunch nightclub, and BB's, a bar that attracted a weird and interesting crowd. Heath liked to dine out on the tale that he had left Perth with just 69 cents in his bank account, which was true—but his dad made sure he didn't starve. While Heath wanted to stand on his own two feet, there were limits to being independent.

Despite the later belief that Heath grew up a surfie—while his dad and uncles were champion swimmers, none of them could stand up on a surfboard—he was brought up miles from the ocean in Perth's eastern suburbs. He got his love for the surf from holidays down at Dunsborough, a laid-back spot in the south-west of the state where he regularly stayed with his grandparents on his mum's side, John and Jackie Ramshaw, who had a beach house there. Dunsborough is on a sheltered bay, but just down the road, around Margaret River, are some of the world's best-known surfing spots, with swells that roll in uninterrupted across thousands of kilometres of the Indian Ocean. The water is pristine, the beaches never have more than a handful of people on them and there is always a wave somewhere.

When the swell was up back in Perth, Heath liked to get a lift to Cottesloe, one of his favourite city beaches. He had the natural rhythm, balance and athleticism of a surfer, and when he wasn't on the water he was always on a skateboard.

So at Bondi, with the beach on his doorstep, Heath was up at 6 a.m. to catch a sunrise wave. If the waves weren't cranking, he would drive to check out Dee Why and Narrabeen on the city's northern beaches. It was a lifestyle he slipped into easily.

He briefly thought about auditioning for the National Institute of Dramatic Art but, like Sir Frank Ledger, Heath wasn't big on lessons, deriding acting school as a place where people ran around dressed in black pyjamas on an empty stage. He was pleased to escape the clutches of method-driven acting.

'I feared four years in acting academy would spit me out like a Toyota model with a set of rules, when I felt acting was about defying rules,' he later said. While lucky that his talent was instinctive and spontaneous, the result was that he was able to develop his own style.

As it turned out, his art teacher's advice to get out there and 'grab it' was spot on. Within months he had won a role in *Blackrock*, which began shooting in August 1996. The movie was based on the chilling rape and murder of fourteen-year-old Newcastle schoolgirl Leigh Leigh (she was christened Leigh and her mother later remarried a man with the surname Leigh) during a sixteenth birthday party at the old North Stockton surf clubhouse on 3 November 1989.

There was evidence that as many as ten teenagers, aged between fifteen and nineteen, took part in attacking her. But eighteen-year-old Matthew Webster soon pleaded guilty. He said he had tried to have sex with Leigh Leigh, but when it all went wrong, he strangled her until she was unconscious, then bashed her head time and time again with a lump of concrete. Many people, including Leigh Leigh's mother, believe the truth has still not been told and that Webster, who went to jail, did not act alone.

It was a sickening episode that brought shame on Stockton, one which the town has spent years trying to forget. It was a brave move by the late Nick Enright (who also wrote the original version of *The Boy From Oz* and the drama *Lorenzo's Oil*) to take a taboo subject and turn it into a play, and then a screenplay. Enright's movie is set in a fictional working-class suburb called Blackrock, and revolves around a 'welcome home' party thrown by Jared for his mate, Ricko, a local surf legend. Fifteen-year-old Tracy is found raped and murdered on the beach. Jared had witnessed a gang, including Heath's character Toby Ackland, raping Tracy. It was a small role for Heath, but one that tested him nonetheless, and a great way to get his face known.

Blackrock was screened at the prestigious American Sundance Film Festival, chaired by Robert Redford, and nominated in 1997 for five Australian Film Industry (AFI) awards.

Heath quickly moved on from *Blackrock* to an equally small role—and equally small pay cheque—in a movie called *Paws,* in which Scottish comedian Billy Connolly puts his distinctive voice to the movie's namesake, a Jack Russell terrier, who holds the secret to a $1 million fortune. It was an altogether much gentler movie than *Blackrock*—a cute little family film that took advantage of the current popularity of Nathan Cavaleri, who had picked up a guitar at age six, and went on to play with Dire Straits' Mark Knopfler at the age of nine. Heath played a student playing Oberon, king of the fairies, in a stage production of *A Midsummer Night's Dream* as part of a sequence in the film.

He also scored a fleeting role in the series 'Bush Patrol', which was based on the life of a national park ranger, her family and lots of Australian fauna.

One of the first people Heath met in Sydney was an aspiring young model from Melbourne, Christina Cauchi. They had a lot in common because, like him, she was at the start of her career and trying to make a name for herself. Both were about the same age and living away from their families. Christina was 178 centimetres tall (that's 5 feet 10 inches in the old style), slim and very attractive and, more importantly for Heath, she had a great sense of humour. They got on well, and while their romance didn't really get off the ground at that time, they kept in touch as friends.

Heath was having a ball.

'My lifestyle was: wake up, eat a bit and walk down to the beach and go for a surf, then just go out looking for jobs. I loved the whole process of it,' he later said.

His job hunting took him on the rounds of casting agents, a task he tackled with the politeness of a well-brought-up young man and the confidence of a seventeen-year-old who had yet to face rejection. The late actor Hayes Gordon used to say that an actor had to have the heart of a dove and the hide of a rhinoceros. Heath was blessed with the first and had not had time to grow the latter.

In early 1997, with *Blackrock* and *Paws* in the can but not yet released, Heath was doing some meeting and greeting when he propitiously wandered into the Glebe headquarters of casting agents Maura Fay and Associates. Sisters Maura and Ann Fay had been enlisted by former teen idol Shaun Cassidy to find him the lead for his planned new TV series, 'Roar'. Cassidy and co-producer Ron Koslow planned to film in Australia, but they were looking worldwide for the actor who could carry off the job of portraying their reluctant hero, the orphaned Celtic prince, Conor, who in the year 400 AD harnesses the magical power of the land to unite the Celtic clans against the Romans. The agents were looking for a twenty-five-year-old, but it was all over when the raw-boned, 185 centimetre (6 feet 1 inch), spunky Heath Ledger walked in. The Fays were knocked out by his energy and his sparkle.

'He was one of the most charming young men ... confident, engaging and charismatic,' Ann Fay later said.

Heath had flown back to Perth to see his baby half-sister, Olivia, the daughter of Kim and his girlfriend Emma Brown, when he was called back to Sydney to do an audition tape for the part of Prince Conor.

Fox TV was investing more than $20 million in 'Roar', and Shaun Cassidy, the half-brother of 1970s heart-throb David Cassidy, knew he had to have the actor with the right stuff to make it work—someone the boys wanted to be and the girls wanted to have sex with. Heath's Perth agent, Vivian Poulton of Frog Management, got him a copy of the script, and Heath realised he wanted the part 'desperately'. The medieval adventure built on the success of Mel Gibson's *Braveheart*, which had been released the previous year, and the fantasy series 'Xena: Warrior Princess'.

He was called back for another audition, this time to Warner Bros studios on the Gold Coast in Queensland, where the series was to be filmed. Then he got word that he had to go to Los Angeles to audition in person for co-producers Cassidy and Koslow. Cassidy would later say that he had bought Heath his first plane ticket to America.

But Heath was working on the television series 'Home and Away', earning decent money playing bad boy surfer Scott Irwin, the boyfriend of Sally Fletcher, played by Summer Bay veteran Kate Ritchie. Scott, as one wag put it, 'pops Sally's cherry in the back of a panel van'. The series had already proved the training ground for a string of local talent, including Dannii Minogue, Julian McMahon and Naomi Watts. Despite a less-than-flattering hairstyle that stuck out at right angles from his head, Heath was offered a long-term contract on the show, an offer he rejected after talking it over with his dad.

The only time he could make it to LA was on a weekend. He flew out on the Friday night after shooting all day.

'It was a fourteen-hour flight and I didn't sleep a wink,' Heath said in a media interview to promote 'Roar'. 'It was the hardest audition I've ever done and I really wasn't sure how I'd gone.' He thought he'd blown it.

It was also his introduction to the real Hollywood power elite—the suits. He came from Australia, a suit desert unless you work in the banks or the law courts. In LA, Heath said the room was 'full of suits', the money men from Fox and Universal television.

'After every shot they swarmed together like a pack of ants on a sweet biscuit, whispering. It was definitely not my best performance, but something must have gone right,' he recalled, always a good storyteller.

Shaun Cassidy knew what he had just seen, and knew then that Heath was going to be a star. 'He was exactly the type we wanted for the role of Conor.'

Ron Koslow was willing to take the calculated risk of casting an unknown: 'It probably sounds a risk but when you meet him, he has such presence. He has a tremendous amount of experience for someone his age, including stage work and Shakespeare.'

Heath flew straight back to Sydney and was back on set on Monday morning, describing the trip as being like 'time travel'.

Two tense weeks later he got the news that he had the part. He was the youngest actor who had been interviewed, and beat a hot field, including experienced actors from the US, Canada, Ireland and England.

It was less than a year since he quit school to follow his passion—and justified a few Heinekens and a nice red (his favourite was Margaret River's Vasse Felix cabernet sauvignon) back at Bondi with Trevor and Martin, to celebrate.

Up to this point, Heath had been cruising. This was his entry to the film factory where time was money, and now it all got serious—still fun, but hard work. He got into the character by studying books on Druidism, and worked six months with only two days off, describing it as a tough apprenticeship.

'It was shocking, but it totally paid off. It shows you've got to go through that pain, doesn't it?' he said, during his media rounds to publicise the series.

'It started off being *Braveheart*-the-television-series, very passionate. The first two episodes I did with a full-on Irish accent, but then the Americans couldn't understand it and said "Modify it", which sucked, critic-wise.'

All actors lie when asked if they can ride a horse, fly a helicopter, scuba dive, if it means getting the role (and then rush out and do a crash course), but Heath didn't have to stretch the truth too much when he heard he had to ride bareback with a sword, in fine swashbuckling fashion. He had ridden before, albeit briefly, at his godfather Uncle Mike's farm at Gidgegannup in the Perth hills, and had been around horses at the Jane Brook property where his dad and Emma lived.

'Roar', which screened on Fox in the 9 p.m. slot, attracted both an audience of young women (handsome, blond, muscular, knockabout, half-naked male lead dressed in leather and chains) and a cult audience, much like some of Cassidy's other projects, including the standout series 'American Gothic'. However, looking at it now it is obvious that Heath's acting ability was still in the process of being honed. *TV Guide* later said gracefully that it was 'a shining example of a young star starting to take shape'.

After mixed reviews, it failed to reach a big enough audience and the suits at Fox pulled the plug after just eight of the thirteen episodes (although all are available on DVD). Cassidy and Koslow felt that Fox had missed the boat with Heath by failing to build him into a star.

But Heath himself was smitten, and not just with acting. Someone who admitted to wearing his heart on his sleeve, he had fallen in love with his leading lady—the first of many. She was the petite, sultry Lisa Zane, who played the evil Queen Diana. Adversaries on screen, they became lovers off-screen, despite Heath being eighteen years her junior. Zane—already well-known, and with many roles under her belt including Dr Maggie Burroughs in *Freddy's Dead: The Final Nightmare*—is the sister of Billy Zane, best known in Australia for his spooky role opposite Nicole Kidman in *Dead Calm*.

It was no surprise to his mates when Heath went back to Bondi, packed up his suitcase and followed his heart and Lisa to LA, leaving with Trevor the Mazda they had driven over from Perth not a year earlier.

'I'm a real softie and I fall in love easily, but I have loads of friends and friendship is more important than romance right now,' he told Perth's *Sunday Times*.

His parents were concerned that Heath be safe and financially secure. In April 1997, Kim set up a company that would manage Heath's affairs, Act 6 Pty Ltd, with himself as the founding director, secretary and sole shareholder. A month later, Heath joined Act 6 Pty Ltd as a director. It was the only company Heath was involved with in his own name, but the first in an intricate and increasingly secretive series of companies and trusts that would manage his properties and his wealth, squirrelling it away from prying eyes.

Kim asked one of Heath's uncles to keep an eye on his son in LA. Neil Bell, the brother of Sally's new husband Roger Bell, was firmly entrenched in California where he had lived for several years. Bell, a bisexual world champion arm wrestler and bare-knuckle fighter, was tough mentally as well as physically. As Heath would later tell it, when Bell's father, a multi-millionaire, found out about Neil's sexual preferences at the age of twenty, he suggested he go to hospital and have his 'illness' fixed. Bell years later became one of the inspirations for Heath's role in *Brokeback Mountain*.

However, even though he had the support of his uncle Neil and would be living with Lisa Zane, Heath was still only eighteen and arrived in LA feeling like the proverbial deer in the headlights. 'I was following my instincts and my heart and that's all I do. I keep moving through whatever my instincts tell me to do. It's all an adventure. I love travelling. It was easy because I was moving over with the people I did "Roar" with—they're from LA, so I moved in with one of them. It was hard to do, but in a way I was cradled into it,' he later said.

Doing the rounds of the agents in Sydney was like feeding the chooks compared to enduring the cut-throat casting scene in LA, where pretty young things wanting to get into movies are two a penny. Heath could only be himself, open, personable and confident. Four months of wearing out his shoe leather finally brought Heath to the glass, feng shui-ed Beverly Hills building of Creative Artists Agency, where veteran talent agent Steve Alexander recognised him as someone who was going somewhere.

Alexander, one of the world's top agents, said later, 'He had all the characteristics of a man, and yet he was a boy. But you could just feel that there was something important going on right away. Everyone who met him had that impression of him.'

Back in Australia, Heath's performance in 'Roar' had caught the eye of laid-back young director Gregor Jordan. Jordan's five-minute film *Swinger*, a dark comedy set in an inner city loft, had just been awarded the Jury Prize at the 1995 Cannes Film Festival and won Sydney's prestigious Tropicana Short Film Festival. Jordan had written his first feature film, based on the villains, wise guys and spruikers he watched every day from his office window on the corner of Bayswater and Darlinghurst Roads in Kings Cross. 'There's always some crazy shit going on,' he said.

That crazy shit turned into one of the funniest films ever made in Australia, the black comedy gangster flick *Two Hands*. On the strength of seeing Heath in 'Roar', Jordan set up a taped audition in LA in which an American agent played opposite Heath.

'Ten seconds into watching the tape, I knew. He's that rare combination of a real screen presence and charm,' Jordan later said. He knew he wanted Heath without meeting him and flew to LA to persuade him to come home to take the part.

Heath and his suitcase were on their way back to Bondi.

Day one of his new job was spent at Annandale Town Hall in Sydney's inner west, where all the actors pulled together by Jordan met for a two-day read through. Having written a razor-sharp script, Jordan wanted the film to deliver on the level of a Hollywood movie 'without wimping out on the Aussie-ness'. A sort of *Goodfellas* in shorts and thongs, as he put it.

You couldn't get more Aussie than the cast he chose—or their cars. The goodies drive Holdens and the baddies cruise around in a big, grunting, chocolate-brown Monaro.

There was Bryan Brown in too-tight stubbies in his best role in years as neighbourhood mobster and drug kingpin Pando; Tom Long as one of his sidekicks; Rose Byrne as the sweet art student Kate; and Heath as Jimmy, who works in Kings Cross as a street promoter for a strip club. Byrne, who ended up bedding Brad Pitt in *Troy* several years later, beautifully underplays the role of Jimmy's love interest. Steve Vidler, the director of *Blackrock*, plays Jimmy's dead brother, who acts as his guardian angel.

Trying to make a bit more money, the naïve would-be crook Jimmy agrees to deliver $10,000 of dirty money for Pando, but loses it on Bondi Beach after burying it in the sand while he goes for a swim. With Pando's gang on his tail, Jimmy decides to rob a bank to pay back the money.

Heath had always looked up to Bryan Brown as an actor, and working with him was not a disappointment.

'It was so cool. He's extremely professional, he teaches you a hell of a lot, not by sitting me down and saying "You've got to do this", but just when you work with actors of that calibre and experience, it feeds out of them. It's really exciting to work with people like that,' he said.

Brown said the thugs in the movie were deadly but not earnest, because Gregor had written Australian criminals, not American crims who took themselves far too seriously.

With the money gone, Jimmy meets up with a couple of tattooed and experienced crims—one of whom has to get a babysitter for his kids before he can do the job. But the heist is botched when Wozza, played by Steve Le Marquand, hilariously trips and falls off the bank counter with the cash.

Le Marquand and Heath became friends during the shoot.

'He was one of the most unassuming, nicest guys I have ever met for his age. I have never heard anyone say a bad word about Heath, ever.'

He said Heath treated everyone the same on the set, from the director to his co-stars, make-up artists and catering staff. 'He was a bit of a chameleon in a nice way, and could fit in anywhere. He treated everyone as an equal.'

Heath was also pleased to be able to dye his hair, play someone other than a pretty blond boy—and rob a bank. He said he had always wanted to rob a bank. He played Jimmy by looking at the character's world through the eyes of a child.

'I tried to play him as a little boy stuck in this crazy world where everything's new and innocent,' he said later. 'I thought the script was really interesting because it was about current day Australian gangsters, and I don't think that's ever been done before. Jimmy was one of the best characters I'd read because he goes through so much, both love and pain.'

On set, Heath was a total professional, building his reputation as a diligent and thoughtful actor. In the middle of the organised chaos that is a film shoot, he would sit quietly at one side, smoking and reading his lines. He listened to the director, but threw out his own ideas.

Gregor Jordan later said of him, 'He's a complete actor: he's never late, never chucks a tantrum, can hit his marks, comes up with ideas, and he has great technical skills. He understands where the camera is, where the best angle is, which some really good actors never learn.'

With his mate Martin Henderson in New Zealand filming *Big Sky*, Heath was living by himself. *Two Hands* was supposed to be set over two days in summer, but April 1998 was one of Sydney's notoriously wet autumns and the shoot was, in Jordan's words, 'a fucking nightmare'.

With long days on the set, there was no time for partying at night, and Heath had already established a pattern for relaxing.

'One of the first things he asked when he came to Sydney to do *Two Hands* was, where can I score some grass?' one reliable source reveals. 'He was a big pot smoker and used it to relax. But not serious drugs, just pot.'

Heath had started smoking dope while still at school—not that any of the teachers knew—and even sneaked a few puffs behind the change rooms while filming the series 'Sweat'.

If it took Gregor Jordan ten seconds to decide Heath was right for the role in *Two Hands*, it took all of three minutes and forty seconds for director Gil Junger to seal his next role, his first movie filmed in America. Only this time, he was the second choice for the job.

With *Two Hands* winding up, Heath was summoned back to LA for an urgent audition. Two years earlier, Baz Luhrmann had taken Shakespeare to a mass younger audience with his radical approach to *Romeo and Juliet*. *Romeo + Juliet* sacrificed some of the Bard's language, but capitalised on his timeless take on how people tick, at the same time making overnight stars of Leonardo DiCaprio and Clare Danes. *10 Things I Hate About You* was a similar modern-day adaptation of *The Taming of the Shrew*.

Rehearsals had already started, but the producers were not happy with the choice of actor for Patrick Verona, Shakespeare's Petruchio. Enter Heath's agent Steve Alexander, and Heath was on a plane back to California.

'My first reaction to Heath Ledger was, this guy is great-looking,' Junger told journalists when the movie opened. 'When I talked to him, I realised how bright he was. Then he read for me, and it took about three minutes and forty seconds. I knew that he was the right actor for the role.'

There was also an instant spark with his co-star Julia Stiles, who played Katarina, known as Kat, the shrew of the two sisters.

Patrick is a rebellious outsider, so it helped that Heath didn't turn up until three days into shooting.

'I wasn't there for two weeks of rehearsals, and I didn't know any of the cast,' he said later.

'Everyone was checking me over and I was doing the same to them, and that's the same as what my character goes through in the movie, so I used those feelings to play him.'

Junger also encouraged him to stick with his Aussie accent, because it played beautifully into him being from out of town, and he kept his hair dark, as it had been during *Two Hands*.

Heath's relationship with Lisa Zane had ended, and his best friend Trevor Di Carlo joined him during the eight-week shoot of *10 Things* in Seattle. He was maturing quickly and learning that self-analysis is vital to bringing characters to life.

'You've got to know yourself so you can use yourself. It's like a tool, like a saxophone. You've got to know every button and when to press them. You have to analyse every decision. You have to know yourself inside and out,' he told Perth's *The West Magazine*.

To get into the 'zone' for *10 Things*, he re-read the Shakespeare text and watched the many screen versions of the play, the best of which was Franco Zeffirelli's 1967 film starring Richard Burton and Elizabeth Taylor. Heath's ambitious suggestion that he make Patrick a bit like a drunken young Burton wasn't taken up by Disney, but showed he was already trying to do something edgy—with a teen flick! Instead, he added the cheekiness of a Jack Nicholson grin.

The *10 Things* storyline revolves around the 'good' sister Bianca, who is not allowed to go out on a date unless her cranky sister Kat does first. Patrick, the out-of-towner, is bribed to take Kat on a date, but of course things go wrong in this comedy of errors.

Heath's favourite scene, and the standout for the critics, comes when he gets to channel his dancing hero Gene Kelly in a routine reminiscent of the *Singing in the Rain* sequence. Patrick Verona dances on the bleachers at the school stadium while serenading Kat, who's on the field, with the Patrick Valli song 'Can't Take My Eyes Off You'. Heath called it his rock star moment.

'We went into a studio and put down the track, then we did the whole classic thing that they used to do in the old musicals. They'd play it back over loudspeakers and I did this dance number up and down the staircase while I was singing the song.

'It was totally choreographed and then I just made it sloppy,' he said.

Julia Stiles had her own insights into Heath.

'Heath and I sparred a lot and laughed even more. He is very much his own person. He's very confident and I loved that he never seemed fragile,' she said.

'We were filming the scene in the car where we had to kiss. Heath was doing a bunch of things that day to try and make me laugh. One of the things he did was grab me and pull me into the back seat, where he made rude gestures. He's sexy, but it's not an "I'm better than you" kind of sexy. He's so much fun to be around, because he doesn't try to play it cool.'

The movie earned Heath $100,000, his biggest pay packet yet, and once filming was wound up he moved out to a modest rented apartment in Beachwood Canyon, a trendy area with a community feel. Heath's apartment was off the winding road that leads up the hills to the Hollywood sign, and not far from a horse ranch where a friend worked. Heath would go up there and ride the horses, or, as he romantically put it, ride them into the night.

He also plugged into the Aussie-posse network of expats. His mate Martin Henderson had moved to the US to look for work. Heath didn't get the chance to do much surfing, but ran, played tennis and went snowboarding. He also bought a black 1970 Ford Mustang Grande, and drove it out into the desert 140 kilometres east of LA to the Joshua Tree Indian Reserve in the National Park, for some peace and fresh air.

Neither of the back-to-back films had been released yet, but scripts were coming his way—although by now he was developing a love–hate relationship with Los Angeles.

'Ask anyone. You want to leave, and as soon as you leave you want to come back,' he said.

Back home in Perth, Heath was the archetypal local boy makes good. Almost without fail, mentions of him in the local media started with the words 'former Guildford Grammar boy', as if that was more important than what he had achieved since. Which for some people it probably was.

10 Things I Hate About You opened in Australia in June 1999, to be followed a month later by the wackier *Two Hands*. With both films to promote, Heath returned to Australia, and for the first time revisited his former school. As keeper of the school's history, Guildford Grammar archivist Rosemary Waller maintains the newspaper clipping files of the newsworthy old boys, of which there are many. They include the much-respected former Chief Justice of Western Australia Sir Francis 'Red' Burt, another former Chief Justice David Malcolm, journalist and former editor of the *West Australian* Paul Murray, test cricketer Brendon Julian, television talk show host Andrew Denton and journalist Piers Akerman. None of the files is as bulky as the one for Heath.

Heath was back in Perth to see his parents—and have some of his mum's hunza pie—before the publicity onslaught. Typically, he just wanted to slip back into the school quietly, partly out of nostalgia and partly to show the other boys that there was life outside Guildford and to inspire them to go out there and grab it. He was twenty, his hair was back to its natural blond but cut in a spiky, punk look, he wore sunnies and was dressed down in the way that was to become his signature style. Kind of grungy but cool. Real local hero stuff.

The boys found it hard to believe that this grown-up Hollywood star had just three years earlier been wearing their uniform and sitting behind desks like they were. His cousin Adam was still there and thought it was great to see Heath again.

He spent a few hours at the school, talking easily with his former schoolmates, and bouncing into Barry Gardner's office for a chat.

'We spent some time talking about his career and reminiscing,' said Gardner. 'To me he was just Heath Ledger, as young and vibrant and excited as ever.'

Heath gave Gardner two tickets for the premier of *10 Things I Hate About You* for him and his wife, Liz.

The opening night was at the Greater Union Innaloo cinema complex outside Perth's city centre, not the red carpet event Heath would get used to in the future, but very Perth. The guests just all rocked up and took their seats. Barry and Liz found themselves sitting behind Heath's parents, Kim and Sally, together for one night only for the premiere.

'We were extremely proud to see him up on the screen. I thought he was great. The film was fun, Heath was dancing and singing, and it showed off his talents and the scope of his ability at that stage,' said Gardner.

The couple was also invited to the low-key party afterwards, held in a reception room in the cinema complex. In among the local industry types and the media were Heath's friends Trevor Di Carlo and twins Ben and Tom Rogers.

As Heath said, 'Good friends I can count on one hand. I have a handful of friends that I value with my life, a core group in Perth. We have been really close since primary school.'

Heath sought out Barry and Liz, giving him a hug and her a kiss on the cheek.

'It would have been very easy with so many people there, with so many of his young friends, for him not to be with us, but he made a point to come over and spend quality time with us. I had to tell him to go out there and mix. He seemed shy,' said Gardner.

Heath came back with a *10 Things* poster, which he signed for them.

His mates were at this point still happy to have their say, although as fame engulfed their friend they became even more private than he did to protect him, rarely again breaking their silence to the media. It was a very close-knit bunch. 'The pressure doesn't get to him at all. When he comes back to Perth we're all on a mates level again. He appreciates home, and he loves talking about old times,' Ben Rogers said at the time.

His identical twin Tom said, 'He wasn't brought up through showbiz like most kids in LA. He's done school. He's been playing hockey since before acting. He's done it his way. It's good to see somebody have a go, and it's a buzz to see him succeed.'

They all had their heads screwed on right, and they knew their friend well. Heath was already being touted as the new Mel Gibson or the new Russell Crowe.

'I reckon he'll be the next Heath Ledger,' said Tom Rogers, knowing his friend was his own man.

Paul Barron, who had produced the series 'Sweat', said the camera loved Heath, but 'he's not getting offered roles because he's a nice guy or just a pretty face. He's a hard-working actor. He's intelligent and professional.'

As for Heath, when he started on the publicity round, he spoke as the self-deprecating professional he would always be.

'I do feel fortunate. I just jumped on it. I jumped on the first thing that struck me. It's kind of like I blinked and said this is my occupation. This started off as a hobby and a love, and now it's that plus an occupation. I think it will always be love and if it stops being love, I'll become a butcher if it makes me happy,' he told Sydney's *Daily Telegraph*.

He had already made a mark as a teenage heart-throb, and no-one was more embarrassed than Heath at the websites dedicated to him. He did not like reading too much about other people, never mind himself.

'I find all of that a little weird, but I just try and completely separate myself from that side of things,' he told Sydney's *Sunday Telegraph*. 'The only time I realise or think about it is when it's presented to me, as in these situations. So I just try and take it as it comes. I don't want to feel overexposed, either.'

While his mates were pleased to see there was not a touch of pretension about Heath, there were some raised eyebrows about whether he had turned new age Californian when he told the *West Australian* how he prepared the night before for a big meeting: 'I'll eat lean, sushi or something.' The sushi was accompanied by a Naked Juice, a green, slimy drink containing herbal and vegetable extracts, and an early night.

Before flying home, Heath went to the Sydney Film Festival Audience Awards at the Dendy cinema, beneath Sydney's Martin Place, where *Two Hands* received the runners-up gong. It was beaten by *Soft Fruit*, a good enough movie, but one which in terms of quality was overshadowed by *Two Hands*, showing how film festival audiences are scared by commercial success.

Confirming there was a huge audience for well-made, home-grown movies, *Two Hands* punched above its weight at the box office, becoming the first Australian film to hit the number one slot in its first week of release since *Reckless Kelly* three years earlier. It outgrossed every other movie including *Entrapment*, starring Sean Connery and Catherine Zeta-Jones, but was knocked off the top spot in its second week by Nicole Kidman and Tom Cruise's *Eyes Wide Shut*.

10 Things was the better received of the two movies overseas. In the UK, it was the *Observer*'s movie of the week, and hailed as the best high school movie in years in other papers. Heath was singled out in the US by reviewers in papers including the influential *Hollywood Reporter*, which said, 'There's also plenty of hunkiness on display in the reluctant tamer of Kat, long-haired, smooth-talking Aussie import Patrick Verona (Heath Ledger).' The independent magazine *Film Threat* called it 'the best teen film of the year'.

While Australian audiences favoured the dark humour in *Two Hands*, it seemed to be lost on audiences overseas, as demonstrated when it screened at Sundance, Heath's second Sundance Festival.

He said, 'At Sundance, there would be twelve Aussies in the audience and a hundred Americans, and the Aussies would be losing it and the Americans would be looking at each other and going, "Was that funny? Did I miss something?" and just kind of chuckling. It's so Australian that Americans wouldn't have an idea what we were talking about.

'Australians have a huge slang which Americans just would not understand. It's not that they don't want to get it—it's just that they haven't lived in Australia and they just can't. It just didn't work.'

Later that year, *Two Hands* was the most nominated feature film at the Australian Film Institute Awards, with eleven nods, only three less than the record held by legendary Australian movie *Newsfront*. It carried off the awards for best film, best direction and best original screenplay, among others. Heath was up for best actor for the first time, but lost out to Russell Dykstra in *Soft Fruit*.

But nothing could dampen his enthusiasm. He had already won the role that would really put him on the Hollywood map.

H

05
THE RIDE
OF HIS LIFE

THE LIFE OF AN OUT-OF-WORK ACTOR IN LOS ANGELES MADE EVEN THE DREADED INDUSTRY FUNCTIONS LOOK GOOD, IF ONLY BECAUSE HEATH COULD EAT ENOUGH TO SUPPLEMENT HIS USUAL FARE OF TWO-MINUTE NOODLES AND WATER. *10 THINGS I HATE ABOUT YOU* FINISHED FILMING IN MID-1998, AND WAITING FOR THE RIGHT SCRIPT WAS WEARING AS THIN AS HIS DIET. HE HAD PLUGGED INTO THE HOLLYWOOD GRAPEVINE AND KNEW WHAT WAS COMING UP, BUT WHAT WAS HOT WAS OFTEN NOT FOR HIM. HE DIDN'T WANT TO DO ANOTHER TEEN MOVIE. DRIVING OUT TO THE JOSHUA TREE NATIONAL PARK, HE'D SIT AND WONDER IF HE WAS BRAVE OR STUPID, DEPENDING ON WHETHER HE FELT HOPEFUL OR HUNGRY, AS HE REPEATEDLY TURNED DOWN SCRIPT AFTER SCRIPT.

'At the start of their career a lot of actors will do anything that comes their way, but even though he didn't have much money, Heath turned down a lot of crappy films. Everything had come so easy for him up until now, and the hardest part of his career was after *10 Things*,' according to a close friend.

Heath wanted to keep the choice to say no.

'I'm in control of my life, not anyone in Hollywood. I know my expectations were high, and I guess I put myself in a class that I wasn't in. But saying no turned out to be a lot more valuable than saying yes,' he said later, looking back on that lean time.

He didn't have a diary and he didn't have a day planner, and would tell interviewers that he was no good at future planning.

'I live completely in the now, not in the past, not in the future,' he said.

But while he had no ten-year plan, when it came to deciding the next step in his career he was calculating his next move as carefully as he did on the chessboard, when he looked laid-back but was always five moves ahead of his opponent. Heath was looking for a dramatic role, something that would stretch him.

'I sat on my arse for a year because I didn't want to get caught in that [teen movie] genre, and it wasn't very good material anyway … I got close to things and then the rug was pulled out from under my feet, usually for reasons like I wasn't a name or I was too young,' he said.

He tried to stay positive, while still seeing life in the fast lane for what it was.

'People always say that Los Angelans are wankers,' he later told Sydney's *Sun-Herald*. 'But basically that hot air is everywhere in the world … I just had to find a good group of friends, my posse. It's a good lifestyle, healthier, no-one smokes. I try to get out and do as much outdoor stuff as I can. I do miss Australia like hell, though.

'I do want to travel. I want to talk to people who aren't polluted by Hollywood, have honest eyes and opinions. That's the danger for actors, only mixing with people in Hollywood. But the one thing I'd say [to other young actors] is that no-one comes knocking at your door. If you really want to do it, you've got to persist and have confidence in yourself.'

It was a very mature attitude for someone still barely twenty.

Heath had his uncle Neil to turn to, but he didn't want his parents to know how bad things were, and it was his best mate Trevor Di Carlo he most often discussed things with. Heath had even considered returning to Australia to try his luck there. Part of it was because he hated auditions, becoming paralysed when faced with a room full of people asking him to improvise.

When his agent put him up for *The Patriot*, he was broke.

'I was hungry at times, it was my last hope,' he told *Vanity Fair*. 'If I didn't get the part I was going to go back home. I had nothing. No money. No nothing. At one point I didn't even want to read the script and go in and meet with them. I had come close to so many great projects that I just had the rub taken out of me.'

Unlike *Two Hands* and *10 Things*, Heath wasn't a shoo-in for the role of Gabriel, the decent, moral son and the patriot of the title. There was fierce competition, with hundreds of actors auditioned for the part until it came down to a hot few, including Elijah Wood, who went on to play Frodo Baggins in Peter Jackson's *The Lord of the Rings* trilogy, Canadian Joshua Jackson, who made his name in 'Dawson's Creek', and Ryan Phillippe. Phillippe, then best known for his role in the horror film *I Know What You Did Last Summer*, and who later married Reese Witherspoon, was the unconfirmed favourite for the part.

Behind *The Patriot* was Academy-Award-nominated screenwriter Robert Rodat and producer Mark Gordon, who had worked with Steven Spielberg on *Saving Private Ryan*. The creative *Independence Day* team of Roland Emmerich and Dean Devlin was also involved, and the movie was developed with the backing of Columbia Pictures. It was as close to Hollywood royalty as Heath had yet come.

Set in the year 1776, with the American War of Independence as the backdrop, the story is about widower Benjamin Martin, the troubled war hero who wants to be left in peace to bring up his seven children on their farm and have nothing to do with fighting the British Redcoats. Gabriel is the idealistic son who drags his reluctant father into the cause. There is action, blood and emotion galore as father and son fight side by side for independence.

'There's an assumption that everyone's patriotic, and not everybody is. This movie is called *The Patriot*, but Benjamin Martin is not a patriot. He knows what war is, and feels that we should avoid it under all circumstances,' said Emmerich.

Gabriel was a complex character; he had a depth to him. He wasn't a boy, but someone 'stepping from the dry stone of childhood to the slippery rock of adulthood. We wanted him to be straddling that line,' said Rodat in Hollywood-speak.

Apart from the script, the other reason so many young actors were lining up for the role of Gabriel was the man playing his father: Mel Gibson, old Mad Max himself. Like most Aussie kids, Heath saw Gibson as a hero because of the Mad Max movies. He was totally in awe. It did nothing to settle his nerves when he turned up to meet Emmerich and Devlin. He had two scenes to read, and was halfway through the second scene when he just stopped.

'I was doing a really bad reading. I said, "I'm sorry. This is shit. I'm wasting your time". I was so in the dumps I just didn't give a shit. I stood up, I shook their hands and walked out,' was how Heath later recalled the nightmare episode.

'I wasn't comfortable being there. I wasn't comfy in my own skin. It had been a long and hard year. I was dead broke. I was starving.

'So I left. I walked off down the hall with my tail between my legs.'

He told them, 'If I could come back and read again, it would be much appreciated.' But he never expected to get the chance.

However, despite the disastrous performance, Emmerich had seen something in Heath.

'Heath did blow that first audition, but you felt in the room when he walked in that everybody was kind of immediately straightening up and saying "Who is this guy?"

'And he has quite an effect on women. We had a lot of women in our company. There was this thing going on with all the women rooting for Heath. Every one of them came into my office and said, "Please cast Heath!" I'd go, "What's wrong with you girls? It's about acting first of all." But they were all in love with him,' Emmerich said.

Two days later, Heath got a callback. He reckoned they either liked him or were curious about what kind of fool would walk out on them. He thought, 'Oh, God, now I've got to prove to them that I wasn't in the right head space.'

He did better second time around, and Gibson was called in from the wings to see if they looked convincing as father and son. Only Australians would appreciate how blown away Heath was to be standing next to Mad Max.

'I'm this far away from my hero, saying, "Hey, you can be my dad",' was how he remembered it.

He'd shied away from being billed as the next Mel Gibson, but now that was exactly what he had to look like.

'I desperately tried to look at Mel and see if I could make my face look like his. They said, "Turn profile, walk together, look at each other, turn", you know, it was silly,' Heath said.

Emmerich was still undecided between Heath and Phillippe and tried to put the decision onto Gibson, who declined to give his opinion. Gibson said it was up to the director.

Heath couldn't sleep for three weeks while waiting to hear whether he had the role.

'It was terrible. It was awful,' he later told journalists in Sydney. 'For every day for three weeks they said, "Tomorrow you're going to know, I promise you".'

He was so tired when he got the good news that he went straight back to bed.

If he was nervous at the audition, that first day on the set in South Carolina in September 1999 left Heath a nervous wreck. It didn't help that he had gallantly given up cigarettes after hearing that Gibson had packed in smoking and couldn't bear to be around smokers.

In the months leading up to the shoot, Heath had time to immerse himself in the character of the brave and defiant Gabriel, reading up on the history of the war and working with a dialogue coach for his first time filming in an American accent.

'I had about four months before shooting to let it sink in, but it never really sank in until the first time I sat down, looked into Mel's eyes and heard "Action!" and "Cut!" Then I started to shake. I went to Dean [Devlin] and said, "You've got to understand, I'm freaked out". I was delusional,' Heath said.

He wasn't a highly strung Hollywood star, just star struck. He confessed to thinking while reading through the script, 'Wow, I can't believe these words are going to be said by Mel in a few months'.

Emmerich could see that Heath was very upset with himself that first day on set.

'He was actually pretty good that day, although you wouldn't be able to tell him that. You could see that he had a reverence for Mel, because Mel is so big in Australia,' Emmerich said.

The crew saw Gibson and Heath go off together, and the next day Heath was transformed.

'He was slugging it out with Mel scene for scene,' said Devlin. 'It was interesting to watch.'

Heath said Gibson put him at ease.

'Mel, he walks to the beat of life,' he said later. Gibson taught Heath how to focus during the take and then relax both on the set and in the industry in general.

'[Mel] keeps his head completely clear. And when he comes on set, he's not walking around stressing about his lines and stressing about his scenes. As soon as he gets on set he talks to everyone, and he's joking and laughing and lively and humorous. And he keeps his head really clean, but you can tell in the back of his mind he knows what he's doing. He's got it all in there.

'I needed that. 'Cause when I got on the set I was so stressed out, I was a wreck.'

He said that once he realised Mel was 'super-relaxed, then it was a walk in the park'.

While filming, Heath called on his experiences with his own dad, Kim.

'The film's similar to what I went through with my father, getting to an age where you feel you had your own opinions and rules in life, taking off, doing it the hard way and not listening to what he has to say,' he explained.

The Patriot was as authentic as possible—despite having two Aussies in the lead roles. It was filmed close to historic battlegrounds, where the action swept across fields and past colonial homesteads. The Smithsonian Institution advised on uniforms and weapons, including rifles, pistols, tomahawks and the mainstay of the armies, flintlock muskets. The cast had to learn how to handle themselves as if it were 200 years ago, and that included firing the weapons.

Their targets were a row of bottles. The muskets were loaded with gunpowder followed by the shot, rammed down with a rod. When Heath pulled the trigger, his finger got stuck and he became the first casualty of the movie.

'The worst thing about it was that the rock was layered with gunpowder that jammed into my wound,' he said. 'I was a real hero, screaming like a girl.'

At the hospital, the wound was cleaned and three stitches put in, and he was straight back on set. It left a small scar, his first war wound.

When you watch *The Patriot*, it is impossible to imagine Elijah Wood or Ryan Phillippe in the role of Gabriel. Heath played his character with a subtlety that made it look as if he wasn't even trying—the mark of an actor at ease with himself. He showed an innate ability to connect with viewers in close-ups.

His co-stars included Jason Isaacs, playing the malevolent British officer Colonel William Tavington, who slays Gabriel. Isaacs went on to play Lucius Malfoy, one of the baddies in the Harry Potter series. There was Nip/Tuck's Joely Richardson, and Heath's love-interest in the movie, Lisa Brenner. She laughed when every morning Heath greeted her with the words, 'Hello, wife.'

While Gibson invited the Carolina Panthers' cheerleaders to brighten up one of the battlefields for Emmerich's birthday, Heath took all the kids who played his younger brothers and sisters bowling one day, treating them to lunch and ice-creams. He brought his camera to the set most days, to indulge his passion for photography.

Mel Gibson was impressed with how Heath handled himself.

'I really like the kid. He is far more mature than his age. He was very measured and very deliberate about his work,' said Gibson.

'I remember what I was like when I was that age. God, I don't think I was capable of some of the more subtle things he did. He was very accurate, precise and subtle in what he did. I think he's got a hell of a future. He's got the right sort of heart and spirit for the whole thing, and he's just going to get better as he goes on.'

Dean Devlin could see comparisons between the two Australian leading men.

'Heath possesses qualities that link him to Mel, and I think that on screen that really comes off as a very believable father and son relationship,' he said.

'If you look at the very early Mel Gibson movies, even when he was very young, he never seemed like a boy. There was something very manly about him, even at a young age. I think that is true about Heath Ledger. He's twenty-one years old, but he doesn't feel like a little boy. He feels like a man. I think they share that quality on screen. You feel that there is a weight to the things they have to say about the cause.'

With the brightness of Heath's star rising, it didn't take much for Columbia Pictures to generate excitement about *The Patriot*. Magazines queued up to feature the next big thing, because Heath's chiselled face on the newsstand sold copies. Among them was *Vogue Australia*, which commissioned a big spread, flying Heath to New York for a session with leading photographer Tony

Amos. Amos's wife, social commentator and former Australian magazine editor Lee Tulloch, recalled the impact as Heath walked into their loft apartment.

'Both of us nearly fell over dead, he was so gorgeous. Not so much because he was handsome, but because of his physical presence—like Mel Gibson was,' she said.

Filming wound up in December 1999, and Heath made it home to Perth for Christmas to see both sides of his family—Kim, Emma and little Olivia, and his mum Sally, Roger and his other half-sister Ashleigh, who was then ten. Three months later he clocked up more air miles when he flew back to help raise money for Perth's Princess Margaret Hospital Foundation's Wear a Bear Day. He was happy to visit patients at the hospital to build the profile of the event, which had raised more than $80,000 through the sale of clip-on bears.

In the US, he had started dating Chrissie Cauchi again. The young, in-demand model was working in New York, and they rekindled their on-again, off-again romance, which they tried to keep low-key.

'I never stopped thinking about her. As soon as I saw her again, she smiled at me and I smiled at her. We looked at each other and couldn't take our eyes away,' Heath uncharacteristically confessed in one interview.

In another: 'The only thing I will say is that I am madly, truly in love and extremely happy.'

With time between movies, Heath moved to hip Greenwich Village in New York, where he rented somewhere in Waverly Place. Here he could hang out with Cauchi, doing the sightseeing thing and finding cosy restaurants for dinner. With time on his hands and a spring in his step, he went to Capezio, the famous dance outfitters, where he bought a pair of tap shoes. In scenes reminiscent of wannabe rock stars singing into a hairbrush, Heath put on the shoes and tap-danced in front of his apartment mirror. Just as with acting, he still shunned lessons.

The Patriot was Heath's first blockbuster, and the premiere was, fittingly, to be his first major red carpet event. There was no-one he wanted to share it with more than his family and his mates, and he flew them out from Perth. The money he made from movies, he once said, brought him and his family and friends closer. His nickname at school had been 'the Pledge', because it rhymed with 'Ledge', but it could also be seen as a recognition of the pledge of loyalty between them all. It was his mates who helped keep him grounded.

'His loyalties were unbelievable, and he was such a generous person,' said a close friend.

He hired his mates pushbikes to get around the back streets of the Hollywood hills.

'He said, "I'm going out for a while", and he came back with portable CD players. He had bought one for each of them, so they could listen to music while they cycled,' said a friend.

There were a few other Aussie actors in town at the time, including Steve Le Marquand (from *Two Hands*) and Ben Mendelsohn, who were both working on *Vertical Limit*. The night before the premiere, Heath met up with them in the foyer of the plush Four Seasons Hotel in Beverly Hills for a few beers. The friends caught up again in the afternoon before the premiere. 'He was very excited and a bit nervous,' said one of them.

Le Marquand gives a spookily accurate, if humorous, view of Australians, actors and otherwise: 'As much as Heath attracted the limelight, he was slightly embarrassed by it as well. Most Australians are crocodile hunters and shearers first, and actors second. That goes for all of us.'

You wouldn't have known Heath had first-night nerves when he turned up on the red carpet at Century City Plaza on the Avenue of the Stars that night. Red, white and blue fireworks lit up the sky, a band played, men dressed in Revolutionary War uniforms marched and girls screamed as Heath appeared—dressed in dark, small, wire-rimmed sunnies, black shirt and very sharp and trendy mid-brown jacket. One reviewer said snidely that he was 'too cool for school', but Heath looked the part.

Everyone who was anyone in LA was there that night, including a few who turn up simply to decorate the red carpet. There was Cher, former 'Dallas' babe Victoria Principal, Tom Sizemore, Matt LeBlanc, Lou Diamond Phillips, Bill Paxton (*Apollo 13* and *Titanic*), who turned up with fellow *Vertical Limit* stars Mendelsohn and Le Marquand, and Charlize Theron with her mum. Much to the delight of the Aussies, they discovered that, being from South Africa, Charlize could talk rugby all night.

The film was greeted with whoops of delight as well as applause, and the party afterwards, in the parking lot behind the cinema complex, was a blast.

'This is all so new to me. This is really the first time it has happened,' Heath told 'Entertainment Tonight'.

By the close of the party, he'd had a kiss from Cher and an invitation to come back to the Playboy mansion. Instead, he retreated to the Sunset Bar on Sunset Boulevard and then, along with about twenty of his mates, went to Roland Emmerich's house.

Gibson could see where Heath was going, and he told him, 'You are going along for the ride, mate. And it's going to be a good one.'

Heath was pleased with his performance and proud of *The Patriot*, and although, as usual, he thought he could have done better, he knew what it had done for his career. A few nights after the premiere, at one of the bars near the Santa Monica beach-front, the Hawaiian-themed Aloha Grill, he was slurping on the restaurant's signature frozen cocktails with some friends. California had only recently brought in a no-smoking rule indoors, so Heath was forced outside for a drag on one of his Camel Lights—despite trying to quit smoking, he had taken it up again after Gibson also relapsed.

'We talked about his career. He knew at that stage that things were going to get big for him, and he was getting pretty excited, although never in a big-headed way,' a friend reveals.

While Heath really didn't give a toss what the often-fickle critics thought, he was gratified that *The Patriot* received good press. *Rolling Stone* called him an Aussie newcomer with 'the talent and looks to become a major star', and *People* magazine said Heath 'shows the most promise as Mel Gibson's strong-willed son'.

Not all the reviews were positive, with one comparing it to the cheesy *The Last of the Mohicans* and others getting movie making mixed up with documentary making, deriding *The Patriot* for not sticking totally to historical fact. But the audiences loved it, and the movie took over $113 million at the US box office and $250 million worldwide, real blockbuster territory.

For Heath, it cemented his position as a fully-fledged teen idol, of which he said, 'I don't take a lot of this all that seriously.'

It also propelled him into the realms of A-list young actors, which he did take seriously, and had already secured him his next movie, his most lucrative to date. Days after he waved his family and friends off at Los Angeles airport, Heath was off to Prague, and the set of *A Knight's Tale*.

Funky Amy Pascal, then the head of Columbia Pictures, had decided Heath was 'the real thing' based on the daily rushes of *The Patriot*.

'You always know when you meet somebody who's going to be a movie star, because they sparkle. And as much as Heath tries to hide his sparkle, it just came through. It was that boyish, sexy, misunderstood, James Dean thing that we are always looking for. He had it,' said Pascal, who was on her way to becoming the most powerful woman in Hollywood.

She believed audiences liked a spectacle, and she was co-producing *A Knight's Tale*. It was a medieval fantasy about the peasant William Thatcher, a young squire who becomes a chivalrous, gallant knight, hiding his lowly background because it is a position forbidden to those not of noble birth.

The movie's writer and director, Brian Helgeland, was familiar with the quirks of Aussie actors. He had directed Mel Gibson in *Payback*, and scored an Oscar for the screenplay of *LA Confidential*, which starred Russell Crowe and Guy Pearce. Pascal set up a meeting between Heath and Helgeland at LAX, with Helgeland flying in and Heath then flying home to Perth during a two-week break in filming for *The Patriot*. This was the sort of audition Heath could cope with, quick and one-on-one.

'[But] we were both dog-tired, and he was certainly jet-lagged. The setting wasn't exactly sparking along,' Heath said.

Helgeland noticed that Heath had a large leather case with him, and asked him what was in it. He thought it was probably every (other) young actor's accessory, a guitar. Heath pulled out a didgeridoo and filled the restaurant with its haunting sounds.

'That's my guy,' Helgeland thought.

He said that of all the actors he'd met, Heath had that movie star quality, a self-possession that comes with an actor having a strong sense of who they are. Something that shows through on the big screen. There was also something else he shared with one of his Aussie compatriots.

'When Heath smiles, it's Errol Flynn. Once every fifty years, a guy like that comes along. For his age, Heath has an incredible manliness about him,' Helgeland said.

He knew Heath could pull off the challenging role of William.

'Ledger's William is the focus. His is a modern archetypal American story of a self-made person who hurdles social barriers. By the time William is ennobled by royalty, he has already been ennobled in his heart. This is a fairytale. *A Knight's Tale* is a tribute to anyone who has accomplished something very far-fetched.'

Prague had built on its reputation for movie making, which stretched back seventy years, to become the Hollywood of Europe. There was the cost—films were half the price of shooting in California—the facilities and the historic city itself, which had survived the communist takeover and emerged fresh and exciting. Prague, along the banks of the Vltava River, was embracing tourism with cosmopolitan bars and cafes—and beer was just 20 cents a pint.

A Knight's Tale was shot in the hills 5 kilometres outside the city on a purpose-built set on the backlot of the Barrandov Studios, which owed a lot to its expansion by the Nazis for their propaganda films in the early 1940s. Its jousting arena was the size of two football fields, and across this Heath (or his stunt double) had to charge on horseback, wearing armour in baking 40 degree heat, holding a lance in his right hand and smashing it into his adversary at nearly 50 kilometres per hour.

'Jousting is tame compared to Aussie sports,' Heath said, recalling his days on the hockey field.

'The set was like a playground for all of us.

'I not only got to act with an amazing ensemble cast, but I rode horses, sang, danced, did sword fighting, comedy and stunts … an actor's dream.'

While the jousting looked dangerous, safety dictated that every lance was made to snap on the slightest impact, their tips made out of balsa wood and dried pasta. Over a thousand lances were broken during the four-month shoot, the most being forty-four on one particular day.

During rehearsals to get his jousting technique right, Heath managed to knock one of Helgeland's front teeth out while demonstrating with a broomstick. Luckily, Helgeland also had a noted sense of humour. While a stunt double did some of the jousting—getting knocked out in one scene which remained in the movie—Heath did all his own sword fights.

The star himself was left bruised and battered on many days after donning the breastplates and body armour, which weighed up to 54 kilograms.

'The armour we had to wear was hot, and you could feel the stuff sizzling on your flesh. The crew were always coming over and pouring water in the gaps between the metal to cool you down,' he later told Sydney's *Sunday Telegraph*.

The knights of yore were like the rock stars or Muhammad Alis of their day, said Heath—and he wouldn't have lasted an hour.

'I don't know how they fought in that heavy armour.

'I wouldn't survive a fucking week. I'd be hopeless … Actually, a week? I'd be dead within the hour,' he said.

'I think it's every man for every hour. William wouldn't have survived in the world of today, and I wouldn't have survived back then. And in 600 years' time, some guy is going to be looking back on what we have now, and shaking his head just as sadly.'

It was hardly an original story, but what Heath liked about the script was that William and his cohorts were guys with contemporary emotions. That was heightened by the 1970s music, with the crowd at the jousting singing Queen's 'We Will Rock You'.

Another Queen song, 'We Are the Champions', was specially recorded by Robbie Williams for the movie, and Thin Lizzy's 'The Boys Are Back in Town' heralds the team's arrival at the world cup of medieval tournaments back in London. The sedate banquet dance sequence, filmed in an ice arena on an island in the Vltava river, morphs into an upbeat number with David Bowie's 'Golden Years'.

A Knight's Tale is the movie where Heath starts to have a real love affair with the camera. While he's dancing to 'Golden Years', there's one scene where he turns and stares right into the lens. Mesmerising.

As the leading man, it was the first movie he had to carry himself, and he was aware the $50 million budget rested on his shoulders.

'I guess I'm a little nervous about driving the bus,' was how he put it to one magazine.

'Before, I got to sit behind Mel [Gibson] and pat him on the back and go, "Hey, keep driving, you're doing a good job. We're all happy back here. Just make sure we get off this bus safe". Now I have to step up and sit in the driver's seat.'

Once again his fellow actors noted how Heath would sit in costume, quiet and alone, fixing himself into the right mind space for his role, usually surrounded by a cloud of cigarette smoke.

The leading man heavily influences the mood of a shoot, and A Knight's Tale was a 'light and happy' set with an easy camaraderie between members of the cast, including Paul Bettany, who played a charming and oft-naked Geoffrey Chaucer; newcomer Shannyn Sossamon as Lady Jocelyn, Heath's love-interest; and Mark Addy (The Full Monty) and Alan Tudyk as his valets, Roland and Wat Falhurst.

'Heath is a joy to be around,' Bettany, who went on to make

Master and Commander with Russell Crowe, told *Vanity Fair* when they sent a journalist and photographer to Prague to capture a day on set for a cover story.

'[His relaxation] comes with being given an enormous amount of confidence at a young age. There's a certain grace in being given a lot of pressure. You've got no choice except to be relaxed. You don't have to fight for anything when so many people have that much faith in you. A transformation occurs that has its own volition.'

It helped that Helgeland got them all together for four weeks before shooting.

'He got us pissed,' Heath confessed. 'We had precisely one table reading, at which we were all blind drunk. But that was a smart move, because this movie is really about friendship. By the end of that month, we really, really liked each other.'

Each movie shoot has its own running jokes, and producer Todd Black was the brunt of one of them on *A Knight's Tale*. He had been unable to make his maid understand that he did not want his jeans ironed with severe creases down the centre of each leg.

'Every time I showed up on the set, Heath Ledger would laugh at me,' he said.

Another thing that cracked them all up was that when they wanted to shoot a scene, the crew had to shout 'Mark, darling!' because Heath's massive horse became too frisky when it heard the usual call of 'Rolling!'

Heath had secured a role as an assistant for his mate Trevor Di Carlo, and the two of them shared an apartment. Every morning they would meet up with the other actors for a coffee, and in the evenings those 20-cent beers and the nightlife helped them all unwind. One night the cast and crew got into a brawl in a Czech bar. Heath was reportedly threatened by three local heavies, and the fight was broken up by Woody Harrelson, said to be handy with his fists himself.

'We drank and partied, I was often hung-over. It was all a romp,' Heath said of time out between filming.

Another diversion was Heather Graham. The actress who had stripped off to her roller-skates in *Boogie Nights* and starred opposite Mike Myers's Austin Powers in *The Spy Who Shagged Me* was in Prague shooting *From Hell* with Johnny Depp. Graham was playing a prostitute living in London in the 1880s, when the streets were terrorised by Jack the Ripper. Like *A Knight's Tale*, the movie is livened up by contemporary music, rap from artists like Snoop Dogg and Jay-Z.

But Heath and Heather had more in common than starring in ye olde movies featuring modern music. He had split up with Christina. Heather was also single after a string of high-profile romances, including her 'Twin Peaks' co-star Kyle MacLachlan and actor-producer-director James Woods. She had just come out of a three-year relationship with Ed Burns, from *Saving Private Ryan*. The proverbial sparks flew when Heath and Heather met one night in a club in Prague, although it took a few months before their affair found its way into the gossip magazines.

She was older than him by nine years, but Heath, then twenty-one, wasn't counting.

'She's my muse,' he later said, rather romantically, demonstrating again that he was a real softie when it came to affairs of the heart.

'She's a beautiful, beautiful girl. We make each other laugh. She's so funny, that's the key. It's fun. It's a good relationship, and a very truthful one.'

Heather called him the love of her life.

'Heath is a great guy ... I feel really protective of him, so I don't want to say too much. But he's an incredible, amazing person and I'm really lucky to know him.'

A Knight's Tale was Heath's first $1 million movie, and he invested in his first home, a Spanish-style two-storey mansion in the hills of trendy LA neighbourhood Los Feliz, with 'jet-liner' views. The five-bedroom, five-bathroom home, which was built in 1925, featured a media room, a detached guesthouse and a period courtyard with an outdoor fireplace, extravagant fountain and vintage tiles. The estate was hidden behind gates. The sale was sealed in July 2000, while Heath was filming in Prague. It was the first and last property he ever bought in his own name, before he adopted the habit of Hollywood stars and put everything into hidden trusts, often with weird names designed to put the prying media off the scent.

One of the first things he did at his first real home was get a state-of-the-art sound system and retrieve his collection of hundreds of CDs from their storage boxes. It was tested on 31 December 2000, when Heath and Heather threw a New Year's Eve bash. Heath flew his family over from Perth, and among the guests were Josh Hartnett, who had just finished filming *Pearl Harbor*, and Heather's friend Molly Shannon (*How the Grinch Stole Christmas*). Johnny Knoxville (who later appeared in *Lords of Dogtown* with Heath) was barman for the night.

Three months later, Heath showed Heather his real home—and gave her a taste of his mum's hunza pie—when he took her with him to Perth on his promotional trip for *A Knight's Tale*, but their arrival on the day of his twenty-second birthday was nothing to be celebrated.

It hadn't sunk in for Heath that he had traded anonymity for fame. In Hollywood, the couple had become one of the hot pairings, not only because of their age difference, but because they couldn't keep their hands off each other. The media was waiting for them at Perth Airport. Having slipped quietly into the city time and again, Heath just wasn't ready for the onslaught now that he was not only a star himself, but had a fully-fledged Hollywood star on his arm in public, engaging in a spot of what the tabloids tagged 'tongue-slurping'.

With Heath wearing a black beanie and his trademark sunnies, the couple arrived in Perth at 12.20 p.m. after flying in from the US via Sydney. They were met by his dad Kim, his sister Kate, who had become his local publicist—and a white Mercedes-Benz that was waiting to drive them to the hotel at Burswood Casino. Heather sat in the back as Heath and his dad collected their baggage. So far, so good. But as the car pulled away from the kerb, Heath leaned out of the back window and swore, and onlookers saw him giving the two-finger sign. It emerged that airport parking staff had told the Mercedes driver the car could not park in the no-standing zone. Kim, who left in another car, didn't help matters by telling the media that the parking inspectors didn't realise 'how big [Heath] was' ... which might have been true, but it all looked like 'Hello, Hicksville' when the media got hold of it.

'M-rated scene as stars arrive'; 'Heath's manners fingered'. They were his first bad headlines, and it stung, especially since he thought they were unfair.

The next day, Kim went into damage control. He told the *West Australian* that a parking officer had called Kate a stupid bitch, and Heath was only defending her.

'Heath's been working eighteen hours a day for eighteen months, and he's buggered and needs a rest,' Kim said. An apology would have defused the drama, but none came from either side.

Airport boss Graham Muir was quoted as saying the parking attendant's behaviour had been unacceptable, 'but so was the behaviour of people using extreme language in a public place'.

Heath, meanwhile, blew off steam celebrating his birthday. There was no Josh Hartnett as celebrity barman, no other movie stars there—just Heath, his usual gang of mates, including Ben and Tom Rogers, and the mini-bar in his mini-suite at the Burswood Resort Hotel.

'Whenever Heath had a party, it was always a good party,' one of the twins told the *Sunday Times*—perhaps because they were identical, the paper was not sure which one of them they had been speaking to and called him simply 'Mr Rogers'.

'We used to run amok; get drunk when you're not supposed to. He's a larrikin just like the rest of us, that's why this [fame] is all so bizarre.'

Heather had given up and gone to bed because of jet lag.

'Her accent's really strong. At first I thought she was taking the piss,' said the Rogers twin, showing how far Heath had moved on from his home town.

Further examples of this were the honours bestowed on him in Western Australia. The international movie star had been named WA's Young Achiever of the Year, winning $2,000 from the Commonwealth Bank and a holiday package from Qantas and Hyatt Hotels. He had also won the Midland Brick sponsored state art award.

Heath was used to walking down the street in Perth with only a few polite 'G'days', but this trip he was learning all about being pursued by the media.

'Most of the time you don't even know that they're there. That's the scary thing. The whole process of being followed around by photographers, on your own or when you are with somebody, is really strange and invading. I'm still working it all out, so I don't let it bother me. I really try and find humour in it all. It really is funny if you think about it,' he said.

But he was lucky that he was still only dealing with the Perth media. Witness one exchange that took place on the Saturday when a reporter with Perth's *Sunday Times* chanced upon Heath and Heather cavorting in the hotel's public pool, all lovey-dovey.

'Their long embraces and passionate kisses while immersed in Burswood Hotel's swimming pool was no acting. They duck-dived, frolicked around the pool's boulders and on the water slide, laughing, hugging and kissing,' gushed the reporter.

'Tiny Heather, in modest two-piece bathers and blonde locks, could easily pass for a schoolgirl rather than the sexy, glamorous, in-demand actress. Heath, rippling with muscles and dripping wet in electric blue boardies, bounded out of the pool at the arrival of photographer Alf Sorbello.

'"I'm on holiday," he told us.

'I requested one picture of the couple.

'Holding out his considerable arms and revealing his large tattoo, he pleaded: "It's a holiday, guys".'

Alf Sorbello didn't get his picture. The reporter agreed to leave the lovebirds alone. Amazing.

What was also amazing about this trip home is that Heath did still manage to just hang out. In jeans, tracksuit top and tousled hair, he drank with Heather at the Como Hotel, ate at Subiaco restaurants, and sampled at Swan Valley wineries. But when they ate fettuccine for the third time at the Café Del Pescatore in Scarborough and it made it into the papers, Heath thought it had reached the verge of being ridiculous, even with his sense of humour.

'I was really unprepared for it. Of all the places you wish to just stay the same, it's your home. You want that to be the same, and it wasn't. I couldn't do anything. It makes front-page news when you eat fettuccine on a Tuesday. I came straight off working eighteen months, and all this was bubbling up while I was working, so when I arrived, bang, it had all changed,' he said.

Heath and Heather tried to blend in while the speed cars threw up dust at the Motorplex track at Kwinana Beach, south of Perth. Organisers offered him a spin around the track for old times' sake, recalling his days as a young go-kart champion. Heath suited up for the occasion and, in good humour, took one of the cars for a spin.

He said of A Knight's Tale, 'We've made a movie about how fame changes you, about how a person can change his stars, alter his future.'

But what he had noticed was how his fame changed not him, but other people: 'It just changes everyone else. It's strange, man. It's invading, intruding.'

He had wanted to spend three months in WA, heading up the coast in an old Kombi van to go surfing, but Columbia had laid down the law: they needed him back in the US to promote A Knight's Tale. He wasn't happy about it, and made that clear, both in media interviews and to the Columbia bosses themselves.

'Next week I'll be doing a fun-loving week of press interviews every day in the US, sometimes fifteen in a day, followed by a fun-loving six weeks touring the world doing press interviews every day,' he told the Sunday Times on his last morning before he flew out, barely disguising his distaste for having to hit the publicity trail.

Amy Pascal had read him the riot act when he whinged about being a salesman for the movie. It just hadn't occurred to Heath that a leading man had to play the leading role on the promotional bandwagon. Once again, he was suffering from what

Steve Le Marquand had described as the crocodile hunter phenomenon, the Aussie cringe at being the centre of attention: Heath would rather be shearing sheep than selling movies.

In the boardroom at Columbia Pictures, he had met with the marketing men and had his first sight of the huge posters of him carrying the legend: 'He will rock you.' After a two-hour onslaught about how they were turning him into the latest 'It' boy, Heath freaked, found a bathroom, locked the door and cried.

He felt like 'a whore', not an actor.

'It was Columbia seeing *The Patriot* and saying "Oh, we can put this kid in this next movie. Let's pump him in this movie and let's create him in the next one, let's create a fucking star so we can sell this movie and rake in the bucks",' he said.

Amy Pascal picked up the phone to Heath.

'Listen, kid, hear this: your career will be over, you'll never work again, you'll never *live* again, unless you do this for me,' was how Heath told the tale.

'I dig Amy now, we've been through a lot of battles and she's cool, but that time was so heavy. In the end I agreed to do part of the promotional tour only, providing they flew my family and Perth friends to America for two weeks.'

Pascal explained that the studio did not see Heath as a product, but that he had a job to sell a movie that was made mostly on his back, 'which is a scary thing the first time you do it'. She stumped up the money and paid for fourteen airfares from Perth to LA.

As those huge posters went up on billboards around the world, Heath admitted he had a hard time living down the advertising tagline. 'I can't tell you how many messages I've got on my answering machine from my friends asking me whether or not I'm going to rock 'em,' he said.

He knuckled down and hit the promotional trail. The day after he flew out of Perth, he met the notorious Sydney media, flipping the paparazzi the one-finger salute at the airport.

But he dropped the cavalier attitude for the press conference later, where he ended up charming the reporters. As he took his seat, there was a pause while the media worked out who would ask the first question. Heath pretended to take that as a sign they were finished, jumped up with a 'Thanks a lot' and made a mock exit. He was never going to become one of those inane celebrities who end up talking a lot but saying nothing. He just didn't talk very much, instead turning the interview on the interviewers, suggesting to the photographers that he swap places with them. Dressed down in red beanie, striped jumper and jeans, he told them he was enjoying life, even if making movies meant enduring publicity tours and being based in Hollywood, where family members sent him fresh supplies of Vegemite. Ah, that old Vegemite line—it always softens the Aussie media up! By the end, he had them eating out of his hand, and had even reduced some to asking for autographs.

He told the *Sunday Telegraph*, 'It's really sinking in now—what's going on, where I am and who I am. I keep on repeating this: I rarely think further forward than a week. I certainly don't expect anything. I just do my job and it's kind of taken me here.'

While his steamroller ride as a Hollywood heart-throb continued, and Heath was named by US magazine *People* as one of the '50 Most Beautiful People in the World'—along with fellow Aussie Hugh Jackman—his whirlwind romance with Heather Graham went ahead uninterrupted. He waltzed her around his old haunts in Sydney, along with some new ones like Hugo's at Bondi and Hemmesphere in the city centre.

Fresh from their Aussie adventure, Heath and Heather strode the red carpet in New York at the premiere of *A Knight's Tale* in May. They smiled and kissed up a storm, she in a clinging red number, he in a blue suit with razzle-dazzle braid around the edges of the jacket. Heath's outfit was even wilder for the London premiere, where he turned up in a three-quarter length scarlet hunting jacket and green hat.

However, when it came to the movie not all the reviewers were as crazy as Heath's dress sense.

The *New York Post* called the movie 'charmingly spirited', and the London *Guardian*'s reviewer said it was silly, with silly lines and a silly plot, but so entertaining that he came out of the cinema with a grin on his face. Heath, he said, was Hollywood's hunk of the moment and, speaking in the manner of Chaucer, 'a lovyere and a lusty bachelor'.

However, another reviewer said Heath looked 'more like a pouty surfer than a pile-driving knight'. Even worse was the one that dubbed the movie 'a dumb rock 'n' roll fairytale even Sir Lancelot couldn't save', and said that Heath looked more like Danny Kaye than Errol Flynn.

A Knight's Tale did well at the box office, taking a total of $56 million in the US alone before it even made it onto DVD.

Like the critics, romance is a fickle thing, and within a month it was goodbye, Heather. Before Heath's next movies were released, there would be another woman gracing his arm, and again she was older than him, this time by ten years.

What was it about this lusty bachelor and older women?

06

SUCH IS LIFE

IT WAS A SECLUDED OLD FARMHOUSE SET WELL BACK FROM THE ROAD IN JANE BROOK, NAMED AFTER THE BROOK THAT FLOWS THROUGH THE SUBURB ON PERTH'S RURAL OUTSKIRTS. THE PROPERTY WAS DIVIDED INTO PADDOCKS AND STABLES WHERE LOCALS KEPT THEIR HORSES. MIKE LEDGER DROVE UP THE LONG, TREE-LINED DRIVEWAY TO THE STABLES WHERE HE HAD SOME HORSES ON AGISTMENT, THE SUN SHINING ON WHAT WAS A WARM SUMMER'S DAY. AS USUAL, AFTER FEEDING THE HORSES MIKE HEADED UP TO THE HOUSE TO PUT THE COFFEE ON. KIM AND EMMA RENTED THE HOUSE, AND HEATH DIVIDED HIS TIME BETWEEN IT AND HIS MUM AND ROGER'S PLACE A FEW KILOMETRES CLOSER TO THE CITY AT MAIDA VALE. MIKE THOUGHT THE HOUSE WOULD BE EMPTY—HE KNEW KIM AND EMMA WERE OUT AND PRESUMED HEATH WAS AT GUILDFORD GRAMMAR, WHERE HE WAS IN HIS FINAL YEAR.

As he pushed open the door, Mike was confronted by a mad scramble of two people springing up. Heath jumped to his feet and, displaying outstanding athletic ability, was three-quarters of the way to his room before he swung around and said, 'Good morning, Uncle Mike.'

The woman was flushed and embarrassed.

'She was red-faced, and I think I might have been as well,' Mike said. 'There was a definite aura of intimate connection, but it really didn't matter as it seemed pretty normal … She was extremely pretty and he was such a good-looking young guy, as we all know.'

Mike knew who she was, but hadn't realised that she and Heath were together. Mike made all three of them a coffee, and kept the encounter to himself. He knew the woman was living with another man, but he also figured it was no-one else's business. It would be years before he said a word about it.

For Heath, it wasn't his first relationship, but appears to have been his first with an older woman. She was eight years his senior, which was a lot when he was just seventeen.

The woman, whose identity will remain confidential, was followed by Lisa Zane (eighteen years older than Heath), Heather Graham (nine years) and Naomi Watts (ten years). In between, Heath was linked to women more his own age, among them Christina Cauchi, actresses Jordana Brewster, Kirsten Dunst and Scarlett Johannson, and Perth model and 2000 Penthouse Pet of the Year Bree Maddox. Maddox, who had met Heath when they were both young teenagers filming 'Sweat', had at the time split from Adultshop.com managing director Malcolm Day.

Until Michelle Williams came along, it took a woman with a few years more experience of life to maintain Heath's interest.

It was easy to understand what the women saw in Heath.

Naomi Watts said, 'Love is love. You fall for the person, not an age. Not a number.'

As well as looks, talent and his sense of humour, Heath was loving and demonstrative, as generous to his girlfriends as he was with his good mates, although Aussie slang did get him into trouble when he moved to LA and called a girl a spunk rat.

'I almost got punched … Americans don't know what a spunk rat is,' he told one interviewer.

His family said Heath was relaxed and natural around women. They said he was never embarrassed to display his feelings, something which Heath said came from growing up around strong women—his mum, sister Kate and half-sisters Ashleigh and Olivia.

'I learned respect for women, and patience. You grow up with these women around you and you learn to wait your turn,' he said.

There was also that Australian-ness which to the amusement of every Aussie actor in Hollywood, Heath included, American commentators tried to pin down.

'The Aussies—even Heath Ledger at the ripe old age of twenty-two—swagger with take-charge manliness,' said one Los Angeles based writer.

'Among male viewers, the Aussies induce a testosterone rush almost as impressive as female viewers' oestrogen rush. When it needs romantic, the industry imports ethereal Brits such as Jude Law, Ralph Fiennes and Rupert Everett. And when it needs rugged and self-reliant, it goes for the rough-hewn Australian.'

Aussies like Heath, Russell Crowe and Hugh Jackman were the macho he-men following in the footsteps of Errol Flynn, Rod Taylor and Peter Finch. They were laconic, and had what one writer called 'slow-burning wit'. Women don't like boring, they like masculine, and Hollywood thought the Australians had it.

'Educated but brash' was how the *Dallas Morning News* in the Texas capital put it. 'They're in touch with their earthy environment, but easily play other nationalities. They greet you with a chipper "G'day, mate", but you know better than to mess with them.'

Top Perth-born Beverly Hills talent manager Rob Marsala said it was because the Australians were more interested in making the movie than in making themselves a movie star. He said Jackman, Crowe and Ledger were liked for being 'normal blokes, not that posing, where's-my-manicure-pedicure kind of guy'—unlike the Americans who had their hair tinted and spent a couple of hours honing their bodies and not their minds at the gym.

Other nationalities might have taken it all too seriously, but the Australians only exaggerated the humour, turning it back on themselves. The late Neal Travis, legendary *New York Post* columnist, was writing about how happy German supermodel Heidi Klum was after four years of wedded bliss with Australia-born hair stylist Ric Pipino. 'What is it with these Aussie guys—Russell Crowe, Heath Ledger, etc.—scoring with great beauties?' he said. 'I liked it better when they were only interested in beer and sheep.'

Travis knew what he was talking about—he was born in New Zealand and started his journalism career in Australia.

Under one headline examining the phenomenon of relationships between younger men and older women—'Lock up your mothers'—Sydney's *Sunday Telegraph* drafted in the CEO of Relationships Australia, Anne Hollands, to try and explain it.

'Younger men in particular seem to be less hung up about being the breadwinner, and perhaps don't have as rigid a view of what their role in a relationship is. And older women can often find it a better match with someone who is comfortable with her being financially independent.'

Heath was mature for his age, having fended for himself since leaving home at the age of seventeen. Entertainment booker Kerry Roberts, who lined up talent for shows from the Logies to the ARIA awards, recognised that trait. She said of Heath, 'One of the nicest of all. He's got an old, wise head on his shoulders.'

Part of the attraction may have been that Heath was self-sufficient and fearless enough to turn down roles in franchise movies, including that of 007 himself. Despite being widely tipped as the favourite to succeed Pierce Brosnan, it was never going to be 'Ledger, Heath Ledger'. Neither was he motivated to don the red, white and blue tights of Spider-Man. He said the role just wasn't for him, and he'd never liked comic books.

'I refused to put on tights and play a superhero. I don't want to be a "mega-dude"—there's too much baggage that goes along with those kinds of roles,' Heath said.

The role went to Tobey Maguire.

'Few could turn down such a high-profile position in this town and survive,' said one Hollywood commentator. Heath, of course, did.

As for Heath, he never thought that deeply about the age of his girlfriends—he just liked the company of older women.

'I don't even think he knew why he dated older women. He was mature beyond his years, and perhaps he just got on better with older women,' said one friend.

Heath's take on it was, 'I know it's weird that I'm such a private person but still date high-profile women, but I can't let the celebrity thing influence my decisions on who I see; that would be unfair to myself.

'I prefer to date older women, because they don't try to act older like younger girls, but because they try to act younger.'

Perhaps it was because they were also less likely to kiss and tell. None of his women have blabbed about their relationship.

Or perhaps they were just more understanding—after meeting Heather in Prague, Heath packed his bags and left her behind to head to Morocco to film *The Four Feathers*.

Like Prague, Morocco had become a cut-price backdrop for Hollywood movies, the setting for films that were once shot in the California desert or in Utah, Nevada or Arizona. For *The Four Feathers*, Morocco was substituting for the Sudan. Heath's character Harry Faversham travels there to redeem himself after walking out on his fellow soldiers and being branded a coward.

Bollywood's Shekhar Kapur, who had directed Cate Blanchett and Geoffrey Rush in the Academy Award nominated movie *Elizabeth*, was fascinated by the themes in A E W Mason's classic 1901 novel. The dashing young army officer Faversham has become engaged to Ethne, played by Kate Hudson of *Almost Famous*, when his infantry regiment, the Royal Cumbrians, is posted to fight in the Sudan. He quits, unable to see the purpose of a war so far from home, and is branded a coward, receiving the four white feathers from three former army comrades and his ex-fiancée. Kapur decided to look at whether the decision not to go to war was an act of cowardice or courage.

Punjab-born Kapur wanted to challenge a classic interpretation of the book—a bunch of British stiff-upper-lip chaps riding off to war in the name of Empire—because his native India had been under British colonial role for ninety years.

'They just did not question colonisation. If you look at the state of the world today, you can trace it back to colonisation,' said Kapur. So he set out to make an anti-colonial movie out of an old-fashioned war melodrama.

'There was an acceptance of the idea that the Western world must go out and conquer other civilisations. It was your moral duty, because the people in those places were heathens, and they needed to be civilised. It was such a colonial story, I decided, why not subvert it?'

Jude Law was signed to play Harry Faversham, but dropped out to make Steven Spielberg's *Artificial Intelligence: AI*.

It is easy to see why Heath was attracted to the man and the movie when Kapur contacted him while he was shooting *A Knight's Tale* in Prague and invited him down to audition. However, it was another audition which Heath just wanted to walk out on, describing it as 'fucking torturous'.

'I had to put myself through the wringer,' he later said.

'I spent eight hours one day with Shekhar, and we shot about 15,000 feet of film. He really scrutinised me. There is a moment halfway through the audition when I was just going to stand up and walk out. I thought, "Fuck this". It was just way too intense. But then I had this vision of a little white feather turning up on my doorstep with a card from Shekhar, so I stuck in there.'

Kapur was looking for a young actor who could portray Faversham as going from being very young to being very wise.

'To be a great actor, what you have to have other than talent is honesty, and you cannot be afraid of exposing yourself. Heath Ledger is honest, and he's not afraid to reveal himself—and that makes him a great actor. His eyes truly, truly express himself,' said Kapur.

'I remember being quite struck by someone who was so young, and yet so much at peace with himself.'

Heath, whose religious beliefs bordered on Buddhism, agreed with the director's take on war.

'Hopefully we're all going to fucking learn our lessons before the clowns—the people running the countries—start throwing nuclear weapons about. I think their brains are about the size of a pea,' he said.

He saw Harry Faversham as courageous for standing up for what he believed in, against the rules of the regimented lifestyle in which he had been brought up.

Filming *The Four Feathers* was more of a physical challenge than *A Knight's Tale*, and once again Heath was on horseback. Djimon Hounsou, who plays the key role of Abou Fatma, the local farmer who helps Faversham, tried to get Heath to go to the gym. He had no luck.

It was also a tough shoot mentally because of the location. There were none of Prague's trendy cafes and bars, and Heath unwound at night by joining the Sudanese drum band that played in the patio bar of the cast's hotel.

'Just bang on bongos for hours at a time. Really therapeutic,' Heath said.

But the band was the sum total of the nightlife, and there was only the one hotel. 'That was it, so we were stuck. That was my life for four months—in my hotel room by myself, and there was nothing else beyond that. It was crazy,' said Heath.

The Four Feathers is famous in his family for the odd shot that revealed that Heath was going to follow the tradition of his dad Kim and other men of the Ledger clan and go bald. They can grow hair on their faces and their chests, but not on their heads. Heath's hairline was already receding, and there is one sneaky shot in the movie that shows a bald patch developing on the crown of his head, something he covered up off screen with a collection of zany head gear.

Kapur thought Heath was handsome, 'but not in a traditional sort of way. He's a bit craggy, but he's very, very sexy'.

The movie featured battles with armies of more than 900. Kapur revealed how he was talking with Heath about making the battle scenes more dramatic and heroic.

'The action guy suggested we shoot a scene where Heath would be seen to fall from his horse and then jump back on, amid a charging cavalry involving a hundred galloping horses,' said Kapur.

'He was going to use a stunt person and make cuts so it would look like Heath. But when no-one was looking, Heath sat down with me and said "Look, I can do it on my own".'

Kapur told Heath, 'You could die.'

'We had just done a scene the day before in which another character says, "I will die if it's God's will". So Heath said to me, "Shekhar, I will die if it's God's will",' Kapur said.

Thankfully for Heath, and the studio's insurance premium, the stunt was a success.

'I got a real kick out of it,' Heath said of the stunt where if he'd slipped for a moment he would probably have been trampled to death.

The cinematography was sensational in both Morocco and at Buckinghamshire in the UK where the movie was completed, and Heath gave it his all. However, despite the best will and intentions of its director, *The Four Feathers* was a box office flop. Kapur laid some of the blame on an unusual reason—too much cash. With $80 million at stake, the Disney money men had their prints all over the film.

'With the amount we had on *The Four Feathers*, it's very difficult to retain creative control. There were meetings, meetings, meetings, when what I needed was to pay more attention to the script,' Kapur said.

The movie just couldn't work out which audience it was aimed at. Heath's female fans gave it a miss, and those likely to understand the contemporary message hidden in the movie would never have seen it, because it was marketed to a teen audience.

The entertainment bible, *Variety* magazine, said of the extravaganza that it was 'a dull rendition of the old warhorse', and that 'performances are uniformly undistinguished, with Ledger appearing rugged and long-suffering, but nothing more'. US-syndicated columnist Jeffrey Wells was scathing of the 'mediocrity' of the movie, and wickedly damning of Heath: 'Ledger's nose is too round and squashy looking for him to be convincing as a nineteenth-century Englishman, and he looks dreadful in a short haircut.'

Heath, however, was proud of *The Four Feathers*, and his verdict on the critics?

'I generally don't give a fuck what people think,' he said, with typical frankness.

He had already moved on to one of his briefest but best roles, in the captivating prison drama *Monster's Ball*.

It came about almost by accident—or fate. Wes Bentley, who was playing Faversham's friend Jack Durrance in *The Four Feathers*, had been cast as Sonny Grotowski in *Monster's Ball*. Bentley's manager, Lee Daniels, had the rights to produce the film, and the plan was for Sean Penn to direct, with Bentley, Robert Di Niro and Marlon Brando playing the lead roles. A producer's lot is probably the worst in the movie-making business, with the job of raising the money—in this case the remarkably low $2.5 million—while actors drop in and out and everyone has their price. Eventually Halle Berry, Billy Bob Thornton and rapper Sean 'Puffy' (now 'P Diddy') Combs came on board with Bentley. Daniels was ready to go, and things got underway.

But as filming of *The Four Feathers* wound up in England, Bentley had to pull out of his role in *Monster's Ball* for family reasons, and it was then the script was handed to Heath.

A monster's ball was a custom in medieval England where the jailers held a feast for the condemned man the night before his death. This was not a death row movie in the manner of *Dead Man Walking*, because it doesn't preach. Combs is the man facing execution, and Halle Berry is his wife, Leticia. Billy Bob Thornton— then still in the middle of his wild marriage to Angelina Jolie, during which they wore samples of each other's blood around their necks—plays Sonny's menacing dad, Hank. Hank is the leader of the death row team, and he and his son live with Hank's dad, Buck, a dyed-in-the-wool racist played by one-time monk, the late Peter Boyle.

It was an eclectic bunch, and Heath said going to work was like being in a kindergarten.

'I did it for those reasons, great people, cool script,' he said.

He just wasn't sure what to call Combs.

'I couldn't bring myself to call him "Puffy", because I knew I would laugh. We all called him Sean. It was very Pythonesque on set, great fun. It was a pleasure to get up and go to work every day,' said Heath.

After the hard graft of *A Knight's Tale* and *The Four Feathers*, it was just what he needed. The whole movie took a refreshing five weeks to shoot, and Heath's part was done in two days. His portrayal of Sonny as a lonely son, desperate for his father's approval but always failing to win it, was the role that took the 'blond' out of his career. It was his best part since *Two Hands*, and made some critics wonder why he didn't choose more of these 'serious acting' pieces, which he professed to covet.

The uncompromising script about damaged souls was written by a couple of out-of-work actors and first-time screenwriters, Milo Addica and Will Rokos, who nabbed themselves small roles in their own movie. They were given access to the Louisiana State Prison for some scenes, including those in the death chamber. One of the most powerful moments in the movie involving Heath comes after Sonny throws up while escorting the condemned man to his death, and Hank confronts his son in the prison toilets.

'They have this fight in there, and we run in and break up the fight,' said Addica, who played one of Hank's death row team.

'We had to do that scene six or seven times. It got to the point where I didn't want to go in and break the fight up, because I was physically getting hurt.'

Heath gave it his all and Thornton said, 'I can't tell you how great a guy that kid is.'

Monster's Ball became the critics' darling and won Halle Berry a Best Actress Oscar in 2002, while Addica and Rokos were nominated for Best Original Screenplay.

Heath's edgy performance in his small but pivotal role was a standout. 'Heath Ledger ... reveals a real strength in his portrayal of Hank's son, a young man with real humanity,' said one reviewer.

By the time *Monster's Ball* was completed in the northern summer of 2001, Heath and Heather's trip to Australia was over, as was their relationship. Heath didn't sit around moping, instead getting his mates together and hitting Los Angeles restaurants and New York nightclubs, where he stayed until the wee hours of the morning. During this time he was linked to a number of younger women, including an unnamed eighteen-year-old American heiress.

His favourite younger woman, however, was back home in Perth—little Olivia. Heath was close to all the women in his family, wearing their initials on the inside of his left wrist. Written in gothic script, the tattoo said KAOS—for Kate, Ashleigh, Olivia and his mum Sally.

'I like to think they stop my own life from falling into chaos,' he said.

However, he had a special affection for Olivia. As well as photography, Heath liked painting. He often said he would like to just spend hours taking photos or painting. One beautiful portrait he painted of Olivia used to hang in the hallway of his Los Angeles homes, and he took it with him when he moved to New York.

While other children took rabbits or goldfish to school for 'show and tell' days, four-year-old Olivia turned up one day with her special big brother. Kim's fortunes had taken a turn for the better since his court battles of a few years earlier, and Olivia went to the private Penrhos Junior School, a former Methodist Ladies' College at Como, south of the Swan River in Perth. Heath's sister Kate had gone to the same school. The young students took it in turns to be class VIP for the day, a privilege that allowed them to bring someone or something special to school. Olivia's turn coincided with a trip home by Heath in early September 2001, and he happily went along to front Olivia's class.

As the youngsters gathered around and sat on the floor in their uniform of green skirts, shirts and ties, the first question was, 'What do you do for a living?'

He told them about being an actor, but what impressed them most was when they learned that he had been jousting in *A Knight's Tale*. Heath spent an hour and a half chatting to the little girls—while the teachers had to chase the big girls away. Word had got around who was at the junior school, and crowds of senior students descended from the other side of the campus. Heath was asked if he wanted to talk to the senior girls, but politely declined and stuck with little Olivia's friends.

Without a celebrity girlfriend on his arm and with no movie to promote, Heath had been able to slip into town a few days earlier, hanging out in the unlikely setting of the car park at Burswood Casino. He was watching the start of the Burswood Casino Classic Rally, in which Kim and Kate were competing in a Mazda RX-7 twin turbo. The three-day race began and ended at Burswood, but took the drivers around the south of the state. Australian motor racing legend Peter Brock was the celebrity driver of the year, helping attract crowds of spectators. (The next race in which Kim followed Brock onto the track was the Targa West rally outside Perth in 2006—the race where Brock's Daytona Coupe slammed into a tree, killing him instantly.)

The reason for Heath's trip home was that there were plans for him to play Australia's favourite outlaw, Ned Kelly. There were three scripts doing the rounds about the nineteenth-century bushranger, and Heath was interested in the one based on Robert Drewe's novel, *Our Sunshine*, which was Ned's father's nickname for him. Heath's mate Gregor 'Gregs' Jordan, who gave him his first big screen role in *Two Hands*, was looking at taking on the formidable job of directing the first Ned Kelly movie since Mick Jagger pulled on the armour in 1970. The producers Working Title Films and Endymion Films were still trying to raise the money for the project, and Heath's name attached to it would help bankroll the movie.

Heath just wanted to chill out.

'We don't live to work, we work to live, you know, but people forget that in Hollywood. I want to hold onto it,' he said.

In Perth, he kept himself healthy, lunching on salads while sipping only lemon, lime and bitters. But at night he had a few beers with his school buddies. Heath wanted to keep it low-key, but he wasn't the only well-known one among them any longer. Ben and Tom Rogers had been rated as two of the top twenty bachelors in the country by *CLEO* magazine, while N'Fa played the black hunk in Arnott's Tim Tam genie ad. Heath could now rib them about their profiles as much as they had been teasing him. They called into the Como Hotel and Claremont's Redrock Hotel, where most of the patrons left them alone. It was much rowdier when Heath took on the job of DJ at Perth's Ambar nightclub, and the party continued on at the Hyatt Regency Hotel.

His dad's girlfriend, Emma Brown, was a huge Madonna fan, and when Heath returned to LA she joined him. He had got her tickets to Madonna's LA concert at the Staples Centre as part of the singer's Drowned World tour. When Emma went back to Perth a few days after the 9/11 attacks, her own world fell apart when she and Kim split up.

Heath used to say that figuring out who he was in life came from studying his parents, particularly his father.

'Most of your life as a young man, I think, is coming to terms with the parallels between you and your father, the mistakes of them, the qualities of them that you have in yourself, and facing them, understanding them, dealing with them in a way that you see fit,' he said.

'You have 50 per cent of yourself in your mother, and 50 per cent in your father, and all the qualities that you have inside, they have in them. And you can see what they've done with them.

'So it's quite an important subject, and it has been to me in terms of finding who I am as a person.'

Like father, like son—women played a big role in both their lives. A month later, Heath was back in the arms of Chrissie Cauchi, and that November she accompanied him to the Melbourne racing carnival, including the Melbourne Cup. Heath was the A-lister all the marquees were trying to nab, but it was Crown Casino who stumped up the airfares and accommodation for Heath and his usual entourage of family and friends. In return, he was one of the famous faces decorating the Crown marquee, and ensured all eyes were on the Members' Lawn when he judged the Fashions in the Field.

He made his own fashion statement in another of the 'trippy hippie' hats which had become a signature of his style along with his sunnies, scuffed shoes, colourful socks—and cigarette hanging out of his mouth. This time he wore a rather staid peaked cap, but made up for it with wild socks displaying cartoon characters. Celebrity hairdresser and social butterfly Lillian Frank professed Heath to be quite one of the nicest, most polite boys she had ever met.

Heath was not part of the racing set, and it was a strange invitation for him to accept, but he did donate his undisclosed appearance fee to the Nuclear Disarmament Foundation. And the trip had other compensations, as he checked out Powderfinger's Melbourne gig, where they performed 'These Days'. Written for Heath's film *Two Hands*, 'These Days' had become one of the band's biggest hits. Heath also visited the shops in trendy Chapel Street, South Yarra, and he attended the AFL grand final between the Brisbane Lions and Essendon. Unfortunately for Heath, his team, the West Coast Eagles, hadn't won a grand final since 1994.

Rome's cobbled streets and hidden piazzas are made for romance, and Heath did not let them go to waste when he moved to the Italian capital to film *The Sin Eater* in early 2002, inviting Cauchi to join him there during breaks in the filming.

The movie, released as *The Order* in the US, reunited Heath with his *A Knight's Tale* director, Brian Helgeland. It started life as a supernatural thriller, a horror movie along the lines of the classic *The Exorcist* and *Rosemary's Baby*. It had a lot going for it, including a $35 million budget backed by 20th Century Fox and locations all over Italy, including Naples, Caserta and of course Rome in winter. Helgeland had brought together other members of the cast that sparked off each other so well in *A Knight's Tale*—Mark Addy and Shannyn Sossamon.

'I'm often asked why I re-teamed with this group. I always reply that it is for the same reason I go home to the same family for the holidays,' Helgeland said.

Helgeland had been working on the idea for a decade after coming across the story of the sin-eaters, who took the sins of a dying person upon themselves, thereby absolving the corpse, through a ritual which included eating bread that had been placed on the body. The movie was almost produced back in 1999 with Antonio Banderas in the lead role. This time it was Heath playing Alex Bernier, a rebellious member of an order of priests known as Carolingians.

As usual, Heath did his homework to get into the skin of his character, taking lessons in Latin catechism, how to wear the vestments in a priestly manner and how to conduct an exorcism.

Bernier is sent to Rome to investigate mysterious events surrounding the death of the head of the religious order. The dead man's body bears strange marks on its chest, which may be a sign that a sin-eater has resurfaced in modern-day Rome. The sin-eater, we later learn, is tired of his job, which had granted him immortality, but can he trick Bernier into taking it over?

The likeable Sossamon, who snared an MTV award nomination with Heath for best kiss in *A Knight's Tale*, was cast as an artist and Bernier's unlikely love-interest. Addy played Bernier's old friend Father Thomas. Heath enjoyed the filming and being back with the *A Knight's Tale* cast, as well as the time spent in Italy. His sister Kate and her boyfriend caught up with Heath and Cauchi in Rome for a holiday.

However, problems began just three weeks into production, when French actor Vincent Cassel walked out on the role of the sin-eater, William Eden. His agent said there was 'an incompatibility of opinions in terms of how the character should be'. He was replaced by German actor Benno Fürmann. One morning, while filming took place on a soundstage, thieves stole $100,000 at gunpoint from the film's production offices next door.

Further problems with the movie proved to be insurmountable. The trade paper, *Variety*, broke the news about the special effects, produced by the London-based Mill Film, which had worked on *Gladiator*. Post-production insiders, who spoke to the paper on condition they remained anonymous, said the effects, which were supposed to depict sins flying out of the human body, looked instead like calamari.

The test audience screamed with laughter instead of fear. 20th Century Fox moved the special effects over to Asylum, a California-based company, and gave them another six months to get it right.

But the early reviews had been the kiss of death for *The Sin Eater*. Critics expected the worst when they were not even given pre-screenings. The movie was dubbed Heath Ledger's 'unintentional comedy,' a dreary horror film and even a stupendous bore.

Reviewers were universal in questioning how Helgeland, who had won an Oscar for co-writing *LA Confidential*, could have made such a brick of the script for *The Sin Eater*. Heath's performance was not as universally panned as the movie, with one reviewer referring to it as 'Hamlet-like'. But even his acting could not redeem a movie that was such a flop it made *The Four Feathers* look like a hit in comparison.

Heath's great-grandfather Sir Frank used to say he put so much into everything that when he was finished each job his 'brains went out the gate' with it. Heath was the same with movies. He gave each of them his all, left them behind and moved on.

This time he was moving on to what was to be one of the

biggest gambles of his career and one which would end up being more than a movie—it would change his life.

Gregor Jordan and Heath had built up an easy relationship since *Two Hands*, one that never faltered, even when Heath became a Hollywood name. The last thing Jordan wanted was to look like he was hanging onto Heath's famous coat-tails.

'Heath became someone it was useful to know. I had something major to gain by being friends with him. So I said, "Hey, look, if we never work together again, I don't give a shit. That's not why I'm hanging out with you". And he said, "Yeah, shit, yeah. Let's just hang out", Jordan said.

'Ned Kelly was an unexpected bonus.'

They hung out snowboarding together and holidayed in Las Vegas with Heath's *Two Hands* love-interest Rose Byrne, who lived with Jordan until they split up in 2001.

Jordan briefly toyed with the idea of Leonardo DiCaprio or Josh Hartnett for the part of Australia's most famous bushranger, but there was really only one man for the role.

'I just thought it was very important to cast an Australian in the role, and Heath was the only guy,' he said.

'Number one, Heath's the right age. Ned was twenty-five when he died. Ned was also a very charismatic guy. When he walked into a room, he'd command attention without even trying. Heath is the kind of guy who just has that thing too. He has lots of charisma.'

Telling the story of a national myth without the usual sentimental navel-gazing was a responsibility not lost on either Heath or Jordan.

'People have been coming up to me at parties, saying, "It's so fantastic that you're making this film", and then they fix you with a stern gaze and say "Don't fuck it up",' said Jordan.

'You get a sense that this is a story that is quite dear to a lot of Australians. So there's a responsibility to do it well, and to not disappoint people. I think we've got a head start with the casting of Ned. If you screw that up, you're dead in the water.'

For an Australian actor, Kelly was the ultimate role and Heath was as nervous as the rest of the cast not to 'fuck it up'.

'Dude, if we mess this up we're going to be selling fish and chips in Byron Bay,' he told Jordan.

Jordan cast actors around the same young age as the Kelly gang, in their late teens and early twenties. There was Orlando Bloom, who was still on the *Lord of the Rings* juggernaut, as the gang's sex symbol, Joe Byrne. History depicts Byrne as the dandy of the outfit in his high-heeled boots, with 'colonial boy charm'. Then there was Laurence Kinlan from *Angela's Ashes* and Philip Barantini from *Band of Brothers* as the third and fourth gang members. Joel Edgerton played Aaron Sherritt, their cohort who turned police informer.

The director sent them off into the cold, windy high country—Kelly country—with nothing but swags, to bond over steaks, beer and billy tea. Kinlan, the only Irishman of the group, had never been camping in his life and was terrified of Australia's snakes and spiders. Heath stayed behind, busy with another star of the movie—Ned's beard.

Heath wanted the beard to be as historically accurate and as un-Hollywood as possible. He said the studio didn't want them to have beards—why hire some of the world's best-looking young actors and hide their faces behind beards? But Heath called in Oscar-winning Jenny Shircore, who had worked with him—and his beard—on *The Four Feathers*. He didn't want to turn Kelly into a contemporary pin-up. They agreed on three looks for Heath's Kelly, who starts as a young Ned with no beard and works up to the full business of a long bushranger beard, which required three hours in the make-up chair.

Heath spent the time during make-up reading and re-reading all 7,500 words of Kelly's Jerilderie Letter, captivated by how passionate and sure the outlaw was about his cause even when his life had been torn out from underneath him. Kelly called the letter 'a little bit of my life'. He dictated it in 1879 after he and his gang held the town of Jerilderie hostage for two days, tied up the police in their cell and stole more than £2,000 from the Bank of New South Wales. The letter outlined the injustices suffered by his family, justified his actions and called police officers 'a parcel of big ugly fat-necked wombat headed big bellied magpie legged narrow hipped splaw-footed sons of Irish bailiffs or English landlords'.

Heath said, 'It really shows very clearly how passionate he was. It also shows the larrikin in him.'

Heath had no boundaries in his own life; he had been allowed by his parents to be a free spirit, and he could see a bit of himself in the anti-authoritarian Ned Kelly, who represented dignity and sticking by family and mates.

'He killed because he had three people shooting at him. It was his life or theirs and fuck that, man, if I was in his position, I'd take them down too,' Heath said.

Jordan said it had been tough for Heath to find the violent side of Kelly, because he didn't have much anger in him at all: 'Heath went through a process on the set where he had to find a darker side of himself. It kind of messed with his head quite a lot … but the thing is, he found it.'

It was a photograph of Kelly taken two days before he was hanged at the Old Melbourne Jail in 1880—when his last words were 'Such is life'—that was Heath's inspiration.

'I looked into that portrait and it's all in his eyes,' he said.

'He is dignified, very proud, and that was enough. I trusted my own instinct and went for it.

'My opinion on Ned will always be a biased one, because I had to play him and I had to feel like him, and so I'll probably defend him to the grave, or something.'

The first person who would shape Heath's future during the Ned Kelly movie was Adam Sutton, although neither of them realised it at the time. Sutton, a shy 28-year-old cowboy, was working as a wrangler with Australian Movie Livestock, with the job of breaking in the horses for the Kelly movie. One morning in the autumn of 2002, Heath, Bloom, Kinlan and Barantini arrived at the company's paddocks up at Spring Hill in the Macedon Ranges north-west of Melbourne for riding lessons. Heath had already spent most of his movies on horseback, and all Sutton had to do was teach him how to shake off American riding habits and make him a credible bushranger, which only took three lessons. Sutton's boss had ordered him not to fraternise with the cast so as far as the wrangler knew, that would be the last time he would speak to Heath.

For the second person, the movie was only meant to be a six-day stint with a weekend in between, but Naomi Watts ended up staying much longer than that.

Heath and Naomi did not know each other before meeting on location, but they shared friendships with Jordan, who was a few steps ahead of them in the romance stakes. He cast Watts to play Ned Kelly's imagined love-interest, squatter's wife Julia Cook, and later said, 'I kind of thought they probably would get together. They are both very, very nice people. I did have a hunch. So it's all kind of in the family.'

He wasn't the only one. Watts's friend, actor and director

Steve Coffey, was also betting there would be chemistry between her and Heath.

'I would call her and go, "I'm checking in", and she goes, "Oh, God, no, no, no". And I would say, "Come on", and then she was like, "Well, maybe …", he said later.

Watts, who had become Hollywood's glitter girl after *Mulholland Drive*, was looking forward to catching up with her friend Rachel Griffiths, who had a supporting role in the movie. By the time Watts arrived, Griffiths had already finished filming her scenes and was starring in the stage play *Proof* for the Melbourne Theatre Company. That first weekend, after Naomi had been filming for a couple of days, Rachel was playing a different role: that of chaperone to Naomi and Heath, as the pair's love scenes spilled off set.

The cast and crew had been together for a couple of months by the time Naomi arrived, and she joined a close, happy group that included Oscar winner Geoffrey Rush as the foppish Superintendent Francis Hare, who hunts Kelly. Jordan had rented a comfortable villa in the Melbourne suburb of St Kilda and the cast would turn up there with wine and beer while he cooked them spaghetti and his signature spicy 'Jordanian meatballs'.

Heath had introduced some of the cast to Aussie Rules when he scored some seats at Optus Oval (now MC Labour Park) in Melbourne to watch his West Coast Eagles play Carlton. Heath was offered a box and asked if wanted to do the coin toss before the match, but he didn't want any fuss and the boys slipped into normal seats to watch the game.

Powderfinger frontman Bernard Fanning made his movie debut on Ned Kelly, and was not allowed to shave or cut his hair before filming a pub scene, in keeping with the theme of beards! Jordan had asked the band to reprise their work on *Two Hands* and come up with a 'traditional' Irish folk song for the movie.

Circumstances had dictated that the climax of the movie, the shoot-out at Glenrowan that sealed the Kelly legend, was one of the first scenes in the can. It set the tone for the rest of the film, because as the actors in their heavy armour walked onto the verandah of the hotel in front of 200 policemen and opened fire, they got a taste of what it was like for the Kelly gang in 1880.

Heath was big enough to stand tall in Ned Kelly's real armour, made out of parts of ploughs, leather and iron bolts, which he tried on while it was in an exhibition at the Old Melbourne Jail.

'The helmet didn't [fit]—my head's too big—but the body armour fits exactly. He was my height and build. But he was skinny because he was starving; I'm skinny 'cause I don't go to the gym,' said Heath. The serviced apartment where he lived during filming coincidentally overlooked the jail, and he could see down into the very yard where Kelly took his last walk.

The armour worn by the actors was as close as possible to the original, and almost as heavy.

'I needed to know what it felt like to try to walk, manoeuvre and see with the armour on. I wanted to feel exactly what Ned felt like when he stepped out at Glenrowan,' Heath said.

The film's armour-maker, Jonathan Leahey, built the suits the same way the gang had done. He set up a forge and hot-forged the suits out of 5 millimetre and 4 millimetre steel, over logs, using the same tools. The helmets weighed 4.5 kilograms each, while the whole suit of breastplate, back guard and apron came in at 32 kilograms, about 13 kilograms less than the original suits. It took four men with tools to get the actors into the armour, and special chairs were made for them to sit on between scenes.

The search for reality brought more problems, because it was the middle of winter and the suits were so cold they couldn't be touched. And they rusted.

Costume designer Anna Borghesi could understand the belief of historians that wearing the armour was tantamount to committing suicide.

'One school of thought says [the bushrangers] knew that once they wore the armour, it would be all over, really—they were basically trapped,' she said.

'The actors couldn't move. On set we found that getting the armour on and off was just the biggest drama.

'So you can imagine being in a pub at Glenrowan with police surrounding the place and threatening to set fire to it, and being stuck in these suits …'

Heath said, 'When we stepped out into the rain with our armour on and dozens of policemen were firing metal pellets at us, it felt like we were there that night in June 1880. I realised how crazy the gang must have been to do it, and that there must have been a real fire in their bellies, that they were fighting for something.'

His scenes with Naomi were shot on bitterly cold days at historic Mount Rothwell Homestead, 60 kilometres south-west of Melbourne, which had changed little since Ned Kelly's day. Kelly probably never had a girlfriend in real life, but he does in Robert Drewe's book. They meet when Ned is a stablehand at the property, and he is with her when he is later accused of killing a policeman. However, she refuses to give him an alibi for fear of losing her children.

'From day one on set, I was really impressed with Heath. He is both a movie star and an actor. There is always something going on behind his eyes—intelligence, warmth or sadness,' Watts said.

Late that Friday afternoon after the couple's first day together on set, the cast and crew were gathered around two small TV screens which had been set up inside the homestead to watch the World Cup quarterfinal between Brazil and Watts's team, England. She was born in the UK, and moved to Australia at the age of fourteen.

Ledger was ready for a beer and wanted to make sure Jordan had ordered plenty in for the night. Jordan had—$300 worth.

Heath and Watts changed out of their muddy period costumes into jeans, T-shirts and sweaters and sat close on the floor in front of the TV set to watch the end of the game, which was won by Brazil.

They all drove back to Melbourne, and it was the next night that Griffiths was spotted sandwiched between Heath and Watts doing the chaperone thing at a nightclub. On Monday when they did their love scene, it was on a closed set.

07
BREAKING TABOOS

HEATH TURNED ON THE IGNITION OF HIS 1970 FORD MUSTANG GRANDE AND DROVE UP INTO THE HOLLYWOOD HILLS, CLEARING HIS MIND. AFTER SO LONG LIVING OUT OF A SUITCASE, IT WAS GOOD TO BE ABLE TO SPEND TIME IN ONE PLACE. HE SHUNNED THE LIMOUSINE LIFESTYLE AND LIVED TO GET BEHIND THE WHEEL OF HIS OWN CARS. THE 'FULL BEEFCAKE, BAD-ASS BLACK' MUSCLE CAR AND HIS EVERYDAY LAND ROVER, WHICH HE JOKED WAS HIS 'LESBIAN CAR', HAD RARELY BEEN OUT OF THE GARAGE OF HIS LOS FELIZ MANSION. HE HAD ONLY LIVED IN THE HOUSE FOR EIGHT MONTHS IN THE FOUR YEARS SINCE HE BOUGHT IT, AND AFTER FINISHING *NED KELLY* HE WAS READY FOR SOME TIME OUT. HE ACTUALLY ENJOYED BUYING FURNITURE AND DECORATING HIS HOME, ALBEIT IN VIVID COLOURS, WITH THE PAINTBRUSH IN HIS HAND AND LOUD AUSSIE ROCK MUSIC PLAYING IN THE BACKGROUND.

The living room mouldings were a famous bright orange.

Heath had quickly worked out that Hollywood was a cruel, fickle place and that the only way to survive was to surround yourself with people who wanted to be with you for who you were, not for what you could do for them.

His friend Gregor Jordan, who often travelled to LA with his London girlfriend Anna and her daughter to stay with Heath, said he was 'very much about family and old friends. He has friends from everywhere'.

Heath shunned the party crowd in favour of 'some good, close friends who are all pretty level-headed,' said Jordan.

Heath was characteristically much more blunt.

'I don't like the party scene. I just wanna sit on my arse and watch movies,' he said—and, of course, play chess. There was no fear Heath Ledger would ever wear out the red carpets.

The Hollywood paparazzi are pussycats compared to their Australian counterparts, probably because they're busier with more scandals per square inch to photograph than they would find in the whole of Sydney. Consequently, Heath found that in LA he could hide away.

'I just live in my own little world,' he said. 'You feel very normal living here. LA is so big and wide that you've got to really hunt someone down to go, "Oh my God, you're that person!"'

For every Heath, Russell Crowe, Cate Blanchett or Nicole Kidman, there are hundreds of Australian actors who toil in obscurity, lost in the Hollywood crowd. Even those who do get a profile can become despondent and disillusioned as they deal with rejection after audition rejection. Heath knew what it was like to be a broke Aussie actor. He had crashed on plenty of couches in his time, including that of his agent Steve Alexander. So Heath's Los Feliz mansion became a home away from home for some of the young actors while they were homeless and couch surfing. Friends said he hated an empty house, and his generosity was well-known around the traps, but never publicised. One of the mates who talked about Heath's kindness was Martin Henderson, who had given Heath a bed in Bondi after they met on the set of 'Sweat'.

After spending time learning theatre in New York, Henderson moved to Los Angeles where he said he was the beneficiary of some 'very charitable friends', including Heath, who handed over his daily expense allowance from *The Patriot*.

'He was a friend who I could call,' Henderson said.

'There was even a point where I was completely broke and I was having to walk to auditions. It was a really tough time for me. He came over and gave me an envelope with some cash in it and it was his per diem from *The Patriot*. And he said, "Here, mate, this might help you out." So we have this special friendship.'

Their friendship grew when Henderson was finally noticed and cast to co-star with Naomi Watts in the supernatural thriller, *The Ring*. At the movie's LA premiere, Watts and Heath stepped out together, holding hands and kissing. The couple was joined on the red carpet by Nicole Kidman, Watts's best friend. The two had met at the casting for a commercial when they were both wannabe actors in Sydney. Heath and Henderson shared a few drinks at the after-party.

Watts, in a barely-there, slashed-to-the-waist dress, gazed up at Heath, who ditched his bohemian wardrobe and scrubbed up well for the night in a black suit. He had even dropped his dark glasses, prompting speculation that he no longer needed to hide his emotions from the world.

'It is a new chapter. I feel like the luckiest girl in the world,' said Watts.

And well she might.

The passion that had been kindled on the set of *Ned Kelly* continued to smoulder on a Balinese holiday. The couple left their luxury villa on the island just two weeks before the infamous nightclub bombing of October 2002 to return to their adopted home of LA where, for a time, they tried to keep their continuing romance a secret. Orlando Bloom often played decoy for the pair, arriving at the city's nightclubs with Heath knowing that once inside the VIP room he would be dumped for Naomi.

Watts, who had been sharing a tiny apartment with a female roommate, moved into Heath's mansion and acquired another best friend—Bob the Yorkshire terrier. Bob hung out with Heath's new cocker spaniel puppy, Ned. While Ned liked to play a bit of football, whereas Bob liked his own company, the two were good mates.

Gentle, smart and with a goofy sense of humour, Watts was good for Heath. She was as relaxed as he was about his scruffy-drama-student attire.

'I love men who are comfortable with themselves and are happy to let their natural beauty radiate,' she said.

'I hate guys who try too hard—with perfect hair, perfect bodies, perfect muscles that line up neatly. Vanity is a big turn-off. Girls can get away with that sort of self-possession, but I don't think guys can.

'I like the just-rolled-out-of-bed, just-happen-to-look-great kind of guy.'

She could even live with the bright decor.

'Yeah, he's got some pretty vivid colours. But as my interior-designer mum says, "No colour, no heart",' she said.

Like Heath, she hated the phoniness around them, and was grateful for the 'Aussie posse' in Hollywood.

'You certainly seek each other out, I think, because no-one's got family in Los Angeles,' she said.

'Like in any circumstance, you yearn to be around like-minded people, people who have had similar experiences. It's not some exclusive "club", like the papers have made it out to be. It's just lovely to have that grounding in a foreign land.'

Watts had grown up in a foreign land—Australia—and was the kind of independent woman Heath was attracted to.

Watts's father had been a road manager and sound engineer who worked for Pink Floyd—it is his maniacal laugh that is heard on Dark Side of the Moon's 'Speak to Me/Breathe'. He left the family when Naomi was four, and died at the age of twenty-nine in 1976. Watts described her mother as a hippie, and when she was fourteen, the family—Naomi, her mum and photographer brother Ben—moved to Australia. Watts decided to be an actor after seeing her mum in a local musical, and had the usual Australian apprenticeship in television series such as 'Home and Away' and 'Brides of Christ'. It was her friend Nicole Kidman who encouraged her to keep going when doors weren't opening for her in Hollywood, until *Mulholland Drive* made her an 'overnight' star.

Kidman and Gregor Jordan were also part of the 'Aussie posse', who tossed aside their superstar status to chuck a few prawns on the barbie.

'The best part of it is, we can sit around talking about riding our bikes as kids and swimming in our neighbours' pools. There is an Australian sensibility where you don't have to explain the joke. You don't end up having to talk about crap,' said Jordan.

'I remember in America people going [he put on a fake accent], "So do all you Aussies have a barbecue when you're together?" and I say, 'Well, yeah. Actually, we do'.'

Heath told the authors of the book *Aussiewood* that 'the

beauty about being an Australian in Hollywood is we've always got this sense of fearlessness that comes from knowing we can always go home'.

Back home in Perth, Heath owned real estate, having bought a block of land while filming *Ned Kelly*. He paid $850,000 for a choice waterfront plot on the banks of the Swan River at Attadale, with views to Dalkeith and the city. The land was destined to become part of his canny investment portfolio, and he had no plans to build on it. He was happy enough, for the time being, in LA.

He later told talk show host and fellow Guildford Grammar old boy Andrew Denton that he had spent this time on his arse, keeping his house clean, doing his washing, playing with the puppies and cooking lasagne.

'I am a lazy bastard,' Heath admitted.

'I had so much time on my hands, I just started cooking. And it's so great—you can just go on the Internet, go to Google and just put in "lasagne", and all of a sudden you've got 100,000 different recipes for a lasagne.'

Heath's agent, Steve Alexander, kept sending him scripts, picking them over before passing on the best of the bunch. Heath would get to see at most about ten out of every hundred that were offered, and rejected most of those. As movies like *The Four Feathers* and *The Sin-Eater* bombed, questions were raised as to why he kept choosing dud scripts.

One Australian producer said the answer was simple.

'There are not that many good scripts going round,' she said, asking not to be identified for fear of cutting her own throat in what is already a cutthroat business.

'People in Hollywood can play silly games. It is a horrible place, like dealing with a pack of chessmen who will do you in while smiling at you. It is a huge game of Russian roulette—I call it

LA roulette—where you can kill your own career by choosing the wrong project. Heath was lucky that he had an immense talent and innate charisma that would see him through this tough time.'

Heath acknowledged the difficulty in finding good work, and chose his scripts based on the fun he would get out of the roles rather than their Hollywood gravitas.

'I get a lot of joy and pleasure out of life, full stop. I work to live and that's the only reason why I work, so I wouldn't think twice about stopping,' said Heath, who was content to just hang out while he waited for something that was going to challenge him.

One of the best scripts Heath read was written by Ehren Kruger, scriptwriter of *The Ring*. It was a fairytale based on the fictional adventures of the German dodgy brothers Jacob and Wilhelm Grimm. In real life, the brothers wrote tales like 'Hansel and Gretel' and 'Little Red Riding Hood'. In the movie *The Brothers Grimm*, they are somewhere between ghostbusters and snake-oil salesmen as they tour villages conning the local yokels into believing they need protection from supernatural creatures. The pair find the tables turned when they have to battle real magic forces. Matt Damon was being talked about to play the other brother and Monty Python naughty boy Terry Gilliam was going to direct it. How could Heath turn down a chance to work with one of his heroes, who was, like him, a Hollywood maverick? Gilliam had made some of Heath's favourite movies, including *Brazil*, *The Fisher King* and *Twelve Monkeys*.

'I love him—he's fantastic, cuckoo in such a beautifully eccentric way,' said Heath.

'He's got such a brilliant mind. I love his movies, am a really big fan, and he's definitely on the top of the list of people I wanted to work with.'

Meanwhile, despite Orlando Bloom's best efforts, it became

impossible for Heath and Watts to keep their relationship secret. Heath could no longer avoid the questions when facing the New York media in August 2002 to promote *The Four Feathers*. Other actors would have had answers ready to deflect such questions, but Heath had no such media training to smooth his edges. What you saw was what you got, as blunt and refreshing as that could often be.

When asked a three-part question about whether the relationship was current, whether it started during the filming of *Ned Kelly* and what attracted them to each other, he gave a three-part answer: 'Yes, yes and something'.

He added, 'That's about it. I just really, seriously, honestly don't like talking about my personal life to anyone, except for the people in it. At the end of the day, why should I give a shit what people think of my private life?'

A couple of weeks later, Heath and Watts appeared together at the MTV Music Video Awards in New York, and later attended the 'Greatest Party of All Time' at world-famous Cipriani 42nd Street, hosted by Heath's *Monster's Ball* buddy, Sean 'Puffy' Coombs, and Madonna's manager, Guy Oseary, CEO of Maverick Records.

Then Watts frocked up to join Ledger for the red carpet ride for *The Four Feathers* before keeping Nicole Kidman company for the opening of *The Hours*. In October, they were joined at the hip for the 6th Annual Hollywood Movie Awards, where Watts won the Hollywood Breakthrough Acting Award.

With Watts away filming *21 Grams*, Nicole Kidman borrowed Heath to join her on the red carpet with her sister Antonia and then brother-in-law Angus Hawley for the Golden Globes. Kidman carried off the Best Actress award for her role in *The Hours*, while Heath deadpanned that people kept forgetting his name, calling him 'Keith Fletcher'.

Watts also had the all-important seal of approval from Heath's family.

His publicist sister Kate said she had met Naomi and 'she's a gorgeous girl'. Not six months earlier, Kate and her boyfriend Nathan Buckey had reportedly been on double dates with Heath and Chrissie Cauchi while he was filming *The Sin Eater* in Rome. Cauchi and Heath had been together at the start of the filming of *Ned Kelly*, where she was seen to spend the night with him at Daylesford's Hepburn Spa Resort. However, Kate said that Heath's relationship with Cauchi was over when he met Watts.

While old blokes have been hanging out with young women for years, there was no hiding from the fact that once again Heath was trashing the trend. Naomi and the 23-year-old Heath celebrated her thirty-fourth birthday hugging and kissing after lunch at celebrity hangout The Ivy, the restaurant featured in the movie *Get Shorty* when Danny DeVito meets with John Travolta.

'Serial Toy Boy: he really likes older women and right now, Heath Ledger just loves Naomi Watts' shouted Australia's *Who Weekly*. The Americans dissed the love of an older woman for a younger man with the term 'tadpoling'.

Perhaps she had more media training than Heath—or perhaps it was her more mature years—but Watts was much more eloquent when answering pointed media questions. There were no pouty moments or monosyllabic answers, even as she tried to deflect questions about their age difference with humour.

'Wait, wait? He's how old? And I'm how old?' she said when quizzed by veteran newswoman Barbara Walters. 'I'm not so good with numbers, Barbara.'

On another occasion, Watts acknowledged the interest of the tabloids in their relationship, but said the attention was odd 'no matter how much you've thought about it or seen it in other people. I don't really think you understand what it is until you're going through it.'

She said she barely noticed their age gap, because 'he's an old soul, that one. He's a very passionate guy. He's always doing something, even if he's sitting still; he's got a million things going on in his mind. Bing, bing, bing, bing, you know.'

Heath was 'wise beyond his years—and that was absolutely evident the minute I met him'.

Naomi Watts could channel the glamour of old-style Hollywood, and there is no doubt that her relationship with Heath boosted his profile. He was the man of the moment, with the tabloids breathlessly following his every move even while he remained aloof and seemingly above it all. He was named *GQ* magazine's man of the year, and made it onto the cover, while Watts's brother Ben took a cover shot of Heath for *The Australian* newspaper's 'Fashion Extra—The Menswear Issue'.

Editor Edwina McCann said, 'It's not just his good looks that gets hearts beating, it's his attitude: cool, calm, collected and tough.' Heath was once again said to be 'spearheading the return of the manly man in Hollywood … more Errol Flynn than Rock Hudson'.

But it was more positive than the usual descriptions of his dress sense, which had him somewhere between 'Kenny on South Park' and a 'faux hippie'.

By the time Heath and Naomi threw off rumours of a split and headed to Melbourne for the world premiere of *Ned Kelly* in March 2003, they were the Brad and Angelina of Australia. The couple even took up a political cause.

A couple of days before the movie opened, the first US missiles struck Baghdad. Within hours of the attack on Iraq, 20,000 demonstrators had poured out of offices onto the streets of Melbourne, bringing the city to a halt. Front and centre beneath the banners was the star power of Heath, Watts and fellow *Ned Kelly* star Joel Edgerton.

Heath had never been politically active, but Prime Minister John Howard's backing of the war had left him 'sickened'.

'We should stand up and be independent of the US decision to go to war. This war's not for human rights, it's for the price of bloody oil. They [pro-war leaders] should be locked up, what they are doing is a crime,' he said, for once not backward in coming forward with the media.

With the forthrightness of youth, he called the Prime Minister 'a dick'.

'The other day, when I called John Howard a dick, I meant it, because he's being a dick, but I sometimes hate it and get really frustrated when I hear actors giving their opinions too strongly. But on the other hand, I think, well, fuck, man, we're in a time where life as we know it could be changed forever, and we could quite possibly be heading into World-War-bloody-Three.

'So I ain't willing to sit back. If I've got the opportunity to get the word out there [I'll use it], because I hate how they don't let the word out. Fuck, we need to be heard.'

His passionate language had Sydney radio announcer Chris Smith reaching for the bleep button when Heath appeared on 2GB.

Heath was unrepentant when talking to Andrew Denton, and angry at accusations that (a) it was a PR stunt, (b) he was grandstanding, and (c) he was a wanker.

'Screw it, man, everyone has their right to their opinion, and that's mine. And, look, I'm not alone, am I?' he said.

'This is the first time in the history of our country that we're an aggressor, and we're not an aggressive nation or people. I'm certainly not, and I'm very proud of my country, and I'm very proud of the people here. We shouldn't be a part of this. It's not a fight for humanity. It's a fight for oil. And screw it and screw them. I think we should all pull out and live a peaceful existence down here.'

But while he was at the protest, chanting 'George Bush go to hell, we won't fight a war for Shell', Heath was making an unintended fashion statement. His yellow T-shirt with the red Shell logo made into the shape of a skull had been made by one of his good mates, Shem Watson.

The anti-war T-shirt was one of many sent down the runway by Shem just a couple of days earlier when his show, featuring gun-toting models and 'hostages' wrapped in bloodied bandages, was one of the most talked about at the Melbourne Fashion Festival. Having his mate Heath kissing and cuddling Watts in the front row did Watson's reputation no harm either. The couple joined a celebrity guest list at Shem's party that night at new bar Kookoo's, staying until 1 a.m., when friends went back to their suite at the Park Hyatt.

Another night Heath and Watts were refused entry to a Melbourne nightclub—because of his tracksuit pants. Once the doorman realised who he had just banned, he changed his tune, but the couple didn't want to trade off their star power. 'Goodbye, it's not worth it,' Watts told him.

Heath was dressed in another of Shem's outfits—this time a sharp black suit—at the pre-screening party for *Ned Kelly*, held on 22 March 2003 in the eerie surrounds of the Old Melbourne Jail, with its sandstone walls and cobbled floor. The gallows above where the party was held made the setting somewhat macabre.

It was a much-anticipated movie, and Heath said he felt ill.

'Self-doubts are a good thing, and I've got plenty of them. I just wanted to paint a picture of a person, and just show he had a heart,' he said.

His family had flown over from Perth for the event.

'The whole "star" thing is not a big issue with them, and that's what I love about them,' he said.

The glitzy premiere was held at the Regent Theatre and the after-party in the theatre's ballroom, where Heath proved once again that he was an unassuming guy who treated everyone as an equal. Some of the actors who played very minor roles were blown away that he took time to talk to them. Joining them for the publicity whirlwind was Adam 'Bushy' Sutton, the wrangler who had broken in the horses and taught Heath how to coach his horse to ride through fire in one of the movie's more spectacular moments. Sutton turned up with a boyfriend on his arm.

It wasn't lost on Heath that the glitz of the movie launch was in sharp contrast to his protests at the Iraq war. In keeping with the anti-war theme, Heath and the rest of the cast flashed peace signs to fans and the media as they moved to Sydney and Perth as part of the massive $2.3 million marketing blitz—one of the biggest ever for an Australian movie. In the midst of all the excitement, Watts's best friend Nicole Kidman won her first Oscar, for *The Hours*.

Asked how he was coping with it all, Heath deadpanned, 'Heineken'.

In his home town, things got a bit out of hand on the red carpet. Heath happily chatted with screaming fans and signed autographs, even taking a photo of himself with the crowds. However, reporters were not so happy. Heath's publicist sister Kate told them they were not to speak to her brother as he walked into the cinema.

'She said to me, "If you don't move now, you'll be shot",' said one local reporter. 'It was ridiculous. For someone so small, she was very aggressive.'

It appeared to be all a misunderstanding, Kate explained.

'Do you know what I actually said? There was one camera crew that was really crowding us, and I said, "If you move out of the way, you will get your shot". As if I'd say, "Get off the red carpet or you'll be shot". It's just ridiculous,' she said.

Unlike *The Story of the Kelly Gang*—the world's first feature-length movie, banned back in 1906 by the censors for its 'romantic' portrayal of bushrangers—Gregor Jordan's *Ned Kelly* opened at number one at the Australian box office. It was the third-biggest opening weekend for an Australian movie after *Moulin Rouge* and *The Dish*, but reviews were mixed.

Reviewer Garry Maddox in the *Sydney Morning Herald* said, 'Ledger stands out. Mixing physical presence with compassion and a rising sense of injustice, he has become the definitive Ned Kelly.'

However in *The Australian*, Evan Williams said that while 'Heath Ledger gives us a stern, brooding Ned, brave and principled in his larrikin way, but with a gentle side, a man whose deeds are somehow mitigated by ill-luck or impulsiveness', the great Australian Ned Kelly film was still to come.

Heath was praised for capturing Kelly's spirit, and the movie praised for its glimpses of Jordan's trademark black humour. On the other hand, the movie was panned for making the murdering outlaw into a saint, and called 'a western with kookaburras and kangaroos'. Then there was the one critic upset that Heath's Ned Kelly was not as political as Mick Jagger's 1970 version.

Later that year it was nominated for nine Australian Film Institute awards, including Best Actor for Heath, Best Supporting Actor for Orlando Bloom and Best Director for Gregor Jordan. However, it took home only two: Anna Borghesi's for Best Costume Design and Steven Jones-Evans's for Best Production Design.

The movie never made its presence felt in the cinemas of the US or the UK, where even Heath's talents could not overcome the cultural problem of translating the Ned Kelly legend outside of Australia.

Writing in *Empire* magazine in London, critic Colin Kennedy said it was 'a wannabe western epic that never quite fills the widescreen, but is quite lovely around the fringes. A bit like Australia.'

One American who loved it was *Titanic* actor Bill Paxton, Steve Le Marquand's friend from *Vertical Limit*, who even made a pilgrimage to the Old Melbourne Jail. Paxton is a Ned Kelly buff who added the movie to his collection of Kelly films.

The fact was that Heath was proud of his portrayal of Ned Kelly, and happier with his work than he had been for a while. He said he had wanted the movie to make audiences talk and argue about the legend, and in that he succeeded. Well might he have said, 'Such is life'.

Heath's pay packet was rising along with his star. He could now command in the region of $15 million a movie, and his financial affairs had been given a revamp by his dad.

The company Kim had formed with Heath in 1997—Act 6 Pty Ltd—was still going, although Heath had quit as a director in October 2002. Kim Ledger continued to have a large say in the management of his son's financial affairs through a new company, HOKK Pty Ltd, set up in June 2002. The name is believed to have come from the initials of family members Heath, Olivia, Kate and Kim. Kim's own finances had continued to improve since the disasters following his handling of Sir Frank's estate, and he was living in the upmarket southern Perth suburb of Applecross, close to his ex-wife Sally and her husband Roger.

One trust that managed Heath's millions was given the cute name, the Thank You for the Trust trust. Trusts have the advantage of almost blanket secrecy, coupled with hefty tax benefits. The tax is paid by the beneficiaries only when the income is distributed to them, while the trust only pays tax on undistributed funds.

It was during Heath's trip home for the *Ned Kelly* launch that he drew up his only known will. Giving his dad's Applecross address as his own, on 12 April 2003 Heath signed the will, appointing Kim's long-time business associates Robert John Collins and William Mark Dyson as executors. Collins was a co-director with Kim of Fella Pty Ltd, trustee of the Ledger Property Trust. Dyson is a chartered accountant who was at the time based in Geraldton, with business interests along the West Australian coast. The witnesses to the signatures on the will were Kate Ledger's boyfriend Nathan Buckey and Hana Rosa, a family friend.

The will opted for a simple distribution of Heath's assets. He left half of his estate to be divided between his sister Kate and half-sisters Olivia and Ashleigh, with the executors to look after the estate until the girls reached the age of eighteen. The other half of his estate was to be split between his mum Sally and Kim.

With Kim playing a central role in Heath's business affairs and his sister Kate handling his Australian public relations, the family had become something of a Ledger Inc. Kim was also involved in business with at least one of Heath's friends.

Shem John Watson, who had designed the T-shirt Heath wore at the anti-war protest, grew up in India as a member of the Children of God religious cult. He hit the fashion scene in late 2002, trading on Heath's name, although he strenuously denied it.

'I met him first and gave him some clothes after,' he said. 'I don't like to elaborate too much on our friendship, apart from the fact that he is a good mate.'

A self-styled 'style delinquent', Shem denied industry rumours that Heath had a financial interest in his fledgling fashion label.

'He's a good friend and he supports the label by wearing the clothes, but he doesn't support me financially—I wish he did,' Shem said at the Melbourne Fashion Festival.

But he was not telling the whole story. Only a week after Shem made this statement, Kim Ledger was outed as the real backer of the label. Company records showed that Kim was one of two directors of Shem's company, Shem Style Delinquent Pty Ltd. The other director was Shem. The company was set up on 20 December 2001 after a mix-up over the spelling of the word 'delinquent': whoever had lodged the company papers six days earlier had spelled it 'Deliquent', so that the company had to be freshly registered with the correct spelling.

Shem quickly attracted a cult following, especially for his Ned Kelly T-shirts, but his light seemed to burn out very quickly. Records show that just two months after the burst of publicity in Melbourne, Shem quit as a director and disappeared from the fashion scene. He said he was heading to LA because it was easy to access Mexico for cheaper manufacturing, but he has not been mentioned in connection with Heath again. Shem quit the company as a director in May 2003, less than two months after it was made public that Kim was one of his backers. Kim has kept the company registered, although no annual returns have been lodged since the end of the 2002–2003 financial year.

That trip back home signalled the end of the current bout of settled domestic bliss for Heath and Watts as well as their dogs, Bob and Ned. Tough quarantine laws stopped the couple bringing their puppies to Australia, but the dogs enjoyed a jet set lifestyle accompanying their gypsy owners around the rest of the world. After a brief visit back to LA, Watts and Bob moved on to Vancouver where Naomi was filming the complex relationship drama *We Don't Live Here Anymore* with Laura Dern—and Bob had his own run-in with the media when he was at the centre of a medical drama.

In June 2003, Heath joined Watts in Vancouver before heading to Prague to film *The Brothers Grimm*. She was on set when Bob took ill and was rushed to the 24-hour Vancouver Animal Emergency Clinic, reportedly because of a drug overdose. The emergency trip to the vet with Bob in a 'listless' state led to reports that he had eaten his way through a bag of high-quality marijuana. The reports were more than just speculation. Heath, whose appetite for dope had never abated, had apparently left a bag of the stuff lying around.

However the spokeswoman for Watts—and Bob—dismissed the reports.

'The dog is very sick,' said Robin Baum. 'He may be suffering from some kind of narcolepsy. Naomi has taken him to hospital about six times now.'

Bob survived, and later that year was with Watts when they visited Heath—and Ned—in Prague. Heath had been showing his co-star Matt Damon around his old haunts in the thriving city, drinking beer, having dinner, bowling every Friday and Saturday night with the rest of the cast and crew.

'That's the sort of stuff that really creates an authentic feeling of brotherhood. Befriending each other wasn't hard. We had four weeks before shooting the film where we were doing accents and horse riding. It was just shaping our characters,' Damon said.

Heath was once again on horseback, his fifth time in six consecutive films.

'I know, I'd like to stop now. I've actually got it written in my contract that I must ride a horse,' he joked.

The sets of the old Barrandov Studios where Heath had filmed *A Knight's Tale* were transformed into a medieval dream world, with forests, a village and a tower like the one in 'Rapunzel'. Here the Mirror Queen, played by Italian actress Monica Belluci, has been hiding out from the plague. Heath and Damon are barely recognisable in their Bavarian costumes, which is how Gilliam wanted it. He liked to have fun with the physical look of characters—his original choice for Jake was Johnny Depp.

'These are very different from their normal characters. They're cast completely against type, which is always a gamble, but when it pays off I love it. The actors love it, and the audience likes waking up and discovering the world is different every day,' Gilliam told *Empire* magazine.

In the movie, the brothers are forced to solve the mystery of why the young girls of the small village of Marbaden go missing. They discover that the 250-year-old Queen is stealing the girls for their youth.

Scene 20 was shot in an inn where Damon's Will has demolished a 1792 Châteauneuf-du-Pape and is ready to relax for the night with the young women at the tavern, while Heath's Jake is not. Italian torturer Mercurio Cavaldi, played by Peter Stormare, sweeps into the room, and a reporter from *Brazil* magazine is there to chronicle the shoot as it runs into take 15, 16, 17, 18. Each time, something interferes which is not always the fault of the actors: someone's shadow, a ray of light. It is Saturday and the cast is ready for their one day off a week. Gilliam takes out his frustration on the back of his chair, breaking it in half with a blow. Then he turns back to the actors and ushers them back to their places for another take. Filming is certainly not all beer and bowling.

Heath said the key to his performance was to eat a 'shit-load' of chocolate to stay hyperactive, like his character.

Gilliam had turned Heath's natural nervousness into an asset. In every interview he did, Heath couldn't stop moving; he crossed and recrossed his legs, brushed his hands across his head, folded his arms across his chest in a protective gesture or flung them around like windmills.

'I sat down with Terry when I first met him, and my hands just go everywhere when I'm nervous or if I'm talking. They go faster than my mind. I was that way in front of Terry. He started giggling. I thought, "What's he giggling about?" He's like, "That's great, what you're doing is great. That's what I want", said Heath.

'I allowed myself to go a little cuckoo once we started shooting. A lot of it came from Terry's energy. I started to mimic him a little bit. Terry gives you the opportunity to step outside of yourself. He dares you to be bad.

'I've always been cast as the hero, but that's always been very boring to me. For the first time I wasn't being asked to tie my hands down. I could express [myself]. So I did.'

When Heath and Damon burst out laughing while watching their latest take on a monitor, Gilliam said that was exactly the reaction he wanted.

'This film certainly is like nothing I have ever done before,' said Damon, whose next job was filming a sequel to *The Bourne Identity*.

Heath described Gilliam as being 'as mad as a mongoose'. 'He's provoked a lot of my stupidity,' he said.

While listening to what the director wanted, Heath regularly came up with one or two of his own ideas per scene.

Lena Headey, who played the beautiful and good huntress Angelika, said of Heath, 'I can't imagine anyone anywhere being able to say no to him. His energy is infectious.'

Terry Gilliam had a $75 million budget, financed by Dimension Films and MGM, and seventeen weeks to finish the filming before getting into post-production.

With filming over, Heath and Ned headed back to Los Angeles. Meanwhile, Watts and Bob were in New York where she was filming the thriller *Stay* with Ewan McGregor—and making clear that she wanted to settle down and have a family.

In a magazine interview published in September she said she was dying to have a child—and so was Heath.

'We'd both like to have kids at some point,' she said, 'but right now we're busy with our careers.'

But before the ink was dry on the page, the couple had split. Watts's friends in Sydney revealed that she had told them it wasn't a big, dramatic bust-up, but more of a drifting apart because they were constantly working in different parts of the world.

Heath's publicist sister released a statement: 'Heath Ledger and Naomi Watts have made the decision to go their separate ways. At this time in their lives, both are busy pursuing careers which are taking them in different directions. They remain close friends.'

But before the ink was dry on *that* announcement, the couple was back together again and heading to Australia for a wedding—not their own.

The details of the marriage between Kate Ledger and Nathan Buckey had been kept so secret that not even the 160 guests knew where it was going to be, in an attempt to foil the paparazzi who were tracking the reunited lovebirds.

Heath and Kate's maternal grandfather, John Ramshaw, told the media that even he didn't know the setting for the ceremony. 'All we know is that a big coach will come and pick us up and take us there.'

The coach, however, didn't have far to go. Kate and her groom had hired out the entire luxurious Empire Retreat on Caves Road at Yallingup, just up the road from the Ramshaw's holiday home at Dunsborough, where the young Ledgers had spent happy holidays. On the Sunday morning Heath joined other men in the wedding party for a round of golf at the exclusive Dunsborough Lakes Golf Club before the 5 p.m. ceremony on the lakeside within the resort, and the reception in a marquee.

Watts, who was going to be a bridesmaid before she split with Heath, wore a mid-calf length floral dress with a handkerchief hem and gold stilettos, and Heath was in what looked to be his staple black suit, the one he had worn to the premiere of *The Ring*.

Kim's side of the family, his brothers and cousins, nieces and nephews, were not on the guest list.

Heath's cousins had not been part of the row between their parents. Only the older ones knew much about it and, even as they understood what had caused it, they didn't have much sympathy for how the grown-ups had torn apart their family. Heath and his oldest cousin Jess had a particularly close relationship, meeting up for a beer at times when he was back in Perth. Jess's dad, Haydn, said Heath never had much cash on him and that one night when the money ran out he paid for the beer by signing autographs. But gradually and inevitably Jess and Heath drifted apart. The younger cousins were excited to have a star in their family and at the same time puzzled about why they were estranged from Heath, who was once 'king of the kids'.

Heath had been shielded from it all by his father, although his sister Kate, being four years older, understood what had gone on. It was a sad situation all around.

However, the whole family had found themselves pursued in one way or another since Heath became a star and 'Ledger' became one of the most famous names in Perth. Anyone with the surname Ledger was asked on a regular basis when they put in work applications or paid by credit card, 'Oh, are you any relation?'

Kim has said that he noticed how old friends came out of

the woodwork, while the cousins got so sick of people asking if they could get Heath's autograph for them that they often just denied they were any relation to him. When Heath was in town, they would be asked if they were catching up with him, and when they answered honestly that they weren't, people thought they were bullshitting to keep everything secret.

Heath's uncle Haydn had a brush with fame when he turned up to an Adelaide hotel on a business trip. He arrived to find the foyer full of TV cameras.

He walked up to the reception desk and asked, 'Do you have a booking for Mr Ledger?'

'Yes, where is he? Is he here?' asked the receptionist as half a dozen other young women suddenly appeared and the cameramen became animated.

At least they had the grace to let him keep the penthouse suite they had reserved thinking 'H Ledger' was Heath Ledger and not the unknown Haydn Ledger.

Watts was hotly tipped to get an Oscar nomination for her role opposite Sean Penn in *21 Grams*—said to represent the weight lost when we die and the soul leaves the body—when Heath joined her in Sydney after his sister's wedding for the Australian premiere of the movie. While Watts was her usual sweetness and light at the party afterwards, thrown by *InStyle* magazine, partygoers thought Heath was just plain rude as he said little, if anything. His behaviour led to speculation that he was on drugs. One guest asked if he was 'stoned or what?'

However Heath and Watts's romance was back on course as they mixed it with friends on Bondi Beach, cuddled in the surf, drank at the Courthouse Hotel in Darlinghurst, and clutched a bottle of champagne and two glasses as they made their way to the trendy harbourside Woolloomooloo eatery Otto. They were regulars at Bondi's Hugo's restaurant, dining once with Watts's close friend Nicole Kidman. Watts used to live in an apartment above the restaurant, overlooking the beach on Campbell Parade.

The usually private Heath threw caution to the wind as he and Watts drove up to Byron Bay to stay with her mum, Myfanwy. Nobody bothered the couple in Byron, where they fit in easily among the town's diverse locals, from mega-millionaires and middle-aged hippies to tradesmen and new-age entrepreneurs. They swam and checked out the windows of real estate agents while spending Christmas with Watts's mum, slipping back into Sydney for New Year's Eve 2004, where they were guests of generous party hosts Deke and Eve Miskin at Sydney's most expensive home, Altona.

Amazingly, they even managed to disappear into the crowd at the Sydney Cricket Ground on 5 January with Kidman and another well-known mate, Russell Crowe. Obviously all eyes were on the pitch, where Australian captain Steve Waugh was batting on the second-last day of his final ever innings. The group wasn't even spotted as they waited outside for about fifteen minutes while their lift was caught up in traffic.

Back in Los Angeles, it was Heath and Naomi's turn to play host to Mrs Watts—for the Oscars. Although she later said that she did not believe film-making should be a competition, Watts was so excited when she heard she had been nominated for a Best Actress award that she picked up the phone and rang her mum.

When the phone rang in Miv Watts's home at 4 a.m., she thought it was someone calling from England who had the time difference wrong and turned over to go back to sleep. When it rang for the third time, she checked her messages. It had been Naomi: 'Muuum, I know it's 4.30 a.m. in the morning, but get your arse out of bed, I've got some really good news.'

Miv Watts told the *Sun-Herald* newspaper, 'Everyone was so completely over the moon about it. My best girlfriend rang me from London and screamed down the phone "You're an Oscars mum!"'

On the night, Watts shimmered on the red carpet in a rhinestone-encrusted Versace gown, while Heath wore what looked suspiciously like that same black suit, as cool as it was. It was noted by the fashion pack that his usually scuffed shoes had been given a lick of shoe polish for the night. He again hid his eyes behind sunnies.

Watts was pipped for the top award by Charlize Theron for *Monster*, and the night belonged to *The Lord of the Rings: Return of the King*. But Watts, her mum, brother Ben and Heath partied well into the morning at all the right places, including at parties hosted by Elton John and *Vanity Fair*, where they rubbed shoulders with Rupert Murdoch, John Travolta and Donald Trump as well as Heath's friends and co-stars, including Matt Damon and Orlando Bloom.

If 2003 had started off quietly for Heath, and 2004 began with him taking a back seat to Watts's career, that was all about to change. Heath was about to stir up both his personal and his professional life.

Veteran western author and screenwriter Larry McMurtry had been working with Diana Ossana to adapt Annie Proulx's short story 'Brokeback Mountain' for the screen when he saw Heath's small but powerful role in *Monster's Ball*. He knew that he had found his Ennis Del Mar.

'I don't give a fuck about image,' Heath told a US newspaper when news about his role in *Brokeback Mountain* emerged.

'This is going to stir things up, and part of me loves that. Let's break taboos, let's be daring. This isn't the 1950s anymore.'

08
NO MORE BLOND BIMBO

IT WAS NAOMI WATTS WHO TALKED HEATH INTO PLAYING THE PART OF A GAY COWBOY. THE ACTRESS, WHOSE OWN MOVIE CHOICES HAD BEEN BOTH EARTHY AND SHREWD, TOLD HIM IT WAS ONE OF THOSE OPPORTUNITIES THAT COME ALONG ONCE IN A LIFETIME. 'IT SCARED ME WHEN I READ THE SCRIPT, FOR OBVIOUS REASONS,' SAID HEATH. 'BUT NAOMI ACTUALLY TAUGHT ME THAT YOU'LL BE REWARDED IN MANY WAYS, SPIRITUALLY AND AS A PERSON, IF YOU FACE YOUR FEARS.' HOWEVER, WATTS COULDN'T TALK HEATH INTO BABIES AND MARRIAGE. SHE HAD MADE NO SECRET OF HER DESIRE FOR A FAMILY. 'MY MOTHER IS DYING FOR ME TO HAVE CHILDREN AND, QUITE FRANKLY, I'VE BEEN DYING FOR IT SINCE I WAS NINETEEN, BUT I HADN'T MET THE RIGHT MAN,' SHE TOLD AMERICAN STYLE MAGAZINE *W*.

'It's interesting. At the age of thirty-five, my career couldn't be going better, but we all know that fertility slows down at this point, so it's about making healthy choices. I really do want to experience having a baby.'

Heath made it equally clear that while he couldn't see anything wrong with having children when he was young, he wasn't ready for them—or marriage—yet.

It wasn't long after they cuddled up on the red carpet at the Academy Awards that Watts moved her belongings and terrier Bob out of Heath's Los Feliz home for the last time. Friends said it had nothing to do with Watts's getting clucky, but that the relationship had simply run its course after almost two years.

'They loved each other but, really, they never got the timing right. Just as Naomi was feeling comfortable about things, Heath wanted to do something else. They were never going to settle down, to use that old-fashioned term,' said a friend.

Watts confirmed that, telling a reporter that while their break-up was sad and inevitable, 'I think deep down we both knew there wasn't a forever plan.'

Heath's womanising was also a factor. After professing that he hated parties, Heath had got off his self-confessed 'lazy arse' and hit the LA night club scene with a vengeance. One night Naomi caught him in a booth at an LA nightclub flirting with Scarlett Johansson, who at nineteen was closer to Heath's age than Naomi was. It led to a public and humiliating argument between Watts and Heath.

Watts had had enough. 'Sources' were quoted as stating that Watts thought Heath was immature and unruly, and that he made her 'look stupid for being with him'. Her publicist, Emma Cooper, who had partied with the couple after the Oscars, finally confirmed the split in May. There was the usual pronouncement that 'the couple remain close friends', which in this case was true. They did remain in touch, and friends said they were both 'sweet' and 'classy' people who had not wanted to hurt each other.

Watts gave some insight into her personal life while promoting *We Don't Live Here Anymore*, the first movie that she co-produced. It is about the adulterous affairs of two married couples, and Watts was not going to be able to escape the subject of the movie in media interviews. She tried to talk about adultery hypothetically, but found herself talking from the heart.

'I have been cheated on. You always fear it. It's horrible,' she said, while refusing to say whether she was talking about Heath.

'I've never been married, of course, but I've been forced to face infidelity and been hurt by it. I know it comes with loss and pain.'

She said she was not the kind of woman who was able to bottle up her emotions when it came to matters of the heart.

'I know what it's like to bottle emotions, and I've definitely been guilty of that at times in my life. But I know if I keep my emotions in I'll explode over the most ridiculous thing. Suddenly it all comes bubbling out and I'll be completely irrational.'

Watts said she learned a lot about herself playing the role of the adulterous wife.

'Passion and sex are at the core of most relationships, but if it evaporates then you are in deep trouble,' she said.

'I have married friends who have gone through infidelity, and they've gotten through it. I've had friends who've had the desire to be with someone else in an animal way, and I think that's completely human. I love it when I hear someone say that they have that desire and got honest with their partner and talked about it, rather than the partner going, "Damn you", and getting all jealous and reactive.

'In some cases, the partner has gone, "Okay, that hurts, but I do understand it".'

Once the hurt of their broken relationship subsided, Watts was able to talk about her friendship with Heath.

'I have nothing but good things to say about my romance with Heath. We loved each other. I'm close with his family; he's close with mine. He's a friend and we'll always remain in contact,' she said.

Watts, who had finally bought her own home in LA after years of sharing places, moved on to New Zealand for her next movie, in which she had the lead role of Fay Wray in Peter Jackson's *King Kong*. Meanwhile, Heath was able to work from home for the first time, filming *Lords of Dogtown*.

In this real-life story he played cigarette and dope smoking Skip Engblom, owner of the local surf shop at California's Venice Beach. Engblom was instrumental in the birth of the modern skateboarding counterculture in the early 1970s, when it merged the skill of wave-riding with the four wheels of a skateboard.

Heath was playing the kind of person he used to read about in *Skateboarder* magazine and *Surfing Life* while growing up in Perth, and it was easy to see why the role attracted him. You see them in every town around the Australian coast—guys both young and older wearing wetsuits pulled down to their waists and carrying a surfboard under one arm as they skateboard down to the beach for a wave.

'If you lived where I did in Australia, you had to surf or you didn't fit in,' Heath said while promoting the movie, again not letting the facts get in the way of his storytelling skills. He failed to mention that while he did surf, he actually grew up miles from the beach.

The movie was based on an award-winning 2002 documentary, *Dogtown and Z-Boys*, a story about a bunch of rebel surfers who caught the waves beneath their local pier as they risked life and limb to dodge the pylons. When a drought emptied backyard swimming pools, the surfers found out which owners were on holidays and moved onto the vertical curves of the pools with their skateboards. As they created an extreme sport out of recreational skateboarding, Engblom was the first to capitalise on its marketing potential. He formed a team called the Z-Boys and kitted them out in T-shirts carrying the name of his surf shop, Zephyr.

Not only did Heath know all about the Z-Boys, but his first skateboard at the age of twelve was one of those designed by the legendary Z-Boy Stacy Peralta, who wrote the *Lords of Dogtown* script.

Heath was meeting part of his own childhood when he caught up with Skip Engblom as he prepared to film the movie. The real, crusty, irascible Engblom said Heath was the only actor he had ever wanted to play him in a movie—and he thought Heath took him off perfectly, mannerisms and all. Engblom still had some of his original 1970s skateboard clothes, and Heath tried them on to find they fit him well.

'Five years ago someone asked me who I thought should play me and I said, that guy in the Mel Gibson movie,' Engblom said, referring to *The Patriot*.

'We have a weird connection that is almost supernatural. Two years later they came to me again, and I told them it had to be him and they said it would never happen. Six months before filming began, I said the same thing. Finally, I told them to get Whoopi Goldberg because if they weren't interested in getting this right person, they might as well get Whoopi Goldberg.'

Amy Pascal, the former head of Columbia who had moved on to become chair of Sony Pictures, was behind *Lords of Dogtown*. She agreed with Engblom, and she persuaded Heath to meet Skip.

Heath said it was particularly challenging to play a person who was still alive.

'I always saw Skip as a success in the way he harnessed this group of kids and gave them the confidence to create,' said Heath.

'He's such a rich character and a beautiful human being to portray, and that was really the clincher for me taking the role.'

In the dope-fuddled, scruffy-haired Engblom, Heath created one of his best roles so far. He was almost unrecognisable with ocean-salted long hair, a handlebar moustache and false teeth.

'I've got such pathetic little wimpish teeth and Skip had such great teeth that I decided I needed a set of fake ones,' he said.

'But then I had to learn how to speak with them because they made me very sibilant and I was whistling all my words.'

The movie was filmed on location in southern California, and was a relaxing shoot for Heath because not only could he indulge his passion for skateboarding between takes, but every night he went home to his own couch, and Ned.

The director was Catherine Hardwicke, who had come to the project with a reputation as a risk-taker—her first film, *Thirteen*, had attracted controversy when it showed young teenagers having sex and using drugs and alcohol. She wanted to make *Lords of Dogtown* as authentic as possible, even hiring many of the original skateboarding gang as technical assistants.

However, when the film was released a year later she was criticised for not taking enough risks with it. Reviewers questioned why it had even been made, because it was too close to the documentary.

Heath's performance attracted mixed reviews, with one critic calling it his best role and Sandra Hall in the *Sydney Morning Herald* describing his hard-living Engblom as 'looking as if he's been pickled in brine and Wild Turkey'.

Another said, 'Ledger was hilarious and eccentric in Catherine Hardwicke's *Lords of Dogtown*, playing a shaggy old-timer on the Venice Beach surf and skateboard scene.'

The critics who said the movie was strictly for the converted were correct. It failed to attract a wide audience, taking just $11 million at the box office against a budget of $25 million. Yet in the video stores of those towns all around Australia where the surfers still skateboard down to the beach, *Lords of Dogtown* remains among the most popular DVDs for hire even today.

Once again, Heath's choice of script had been dictated more by the fun he would have on set than the quality of the movie. It was almost as if having seen the obligations that went with being a movie star, he was scared to become one. While he loved the craft of being an actor and making movies, and understood the importance of box office figures, he had no time for the publicity bandwagon and the 'un-Australian' fawning over LA executives. Talking movies was one thing, talking business another.

'I'm not sure I put thought into how I want to be perceived and how I come across. I have never really concentrated on that,' he said, while promoting *Dogtown*.

'I am ruthless about my attitude towards the industry.

'I don't really care if it doesn't work, or if the movie doesn't make money. It's not my money. To protect my ego or just my wellbeing as a person, I have to not care about it [his image and the industry]. It gives me a licence to pick and choose whatever I want.

'I'm certainly not someone who wants to go out and sell TAG Heuer watches and L'Oreal and all that whole stupid fashion that has come in right now. It's whoring ourselves for millions of dollars.'

Heath was echoing what his mate Russell Crowe had said a

couple of months earlier when he got stuck into big-name actors for 'selling out' to plug big-name brands for the money. They were yet again proving themselves the archetypal 'rough hewn' and brash Aussies, by questioning the celebrity endorsements entered into by many Hollywood actors.

Heath's old art teacher Barry Gardner, who kept in touch with him for several years after Heath left school, confirmed his former student was never into money.

'He never came across as someone who wanted to accumulate millions. His clothes, everything about him, didn't smack of money. He was very laid-back and relaxed about the whole thing,' Gardner said.

But hey, if he was earning it, he might as well spend some of it. In the wake of the split with Naomi, Heath bought himself a Harley-Davidson, having plenty of time to himself now in which to ride it. He took his beloved Harley everywhere with him, including onto the set of his next movie, *Brokeback Mountain*.

If you are seeking real cowboys who look like they have stepped straight off the 'Deadwood' stagecoach, there are only a few places to go. There's Wyoming, home of Annie Proulx and her fictitious *Brokeback Mountain*; Texas, the home of Larry McMurtry, co-writer with Diana Ossana of the movie's screenplay; and Calgary, in Alberta, Canada, where the movie was filmed.

Heath's role as Ennis Del Mar was about as far as you could get from Skip Engblom. After overcoming his initial fears, Heath was keen to make the movie and took a huge pay cut to do it. The entire *Brokeback* budget was only $14 million, less than the pay packet that Heath could earn from a single movie if he chose to. He reportedly did *Brokeback* for just $100,000—the same amount he got for his few days' work on *Monster's Ball*. But he also signed up for a percentage of the gross earnings of *Brokeback*, which proved to be a shrewd move given the runaway success of the movie.

One of the first people he spoke to when he'd read the script was Adam Sutton.

'Bushy,' he said, 'I've just read this script and it sounds a lot like you.'

Sutton, the wrangler from *Ned Kelly*, was the epitome of the lost soul, the real gay cowboy who had not even been able to admit his sexuality to himself. That night of the *Ned Kelly* launch in Melbourne was the first time he had gone out with a boyfriend. He had thought everyone would be looking at him, but found that he was accepted without judgment.

The other man who inspired Heath's Ennis was his uncle Neil Bell, who had looked after him when he was a young actor in LA. Heath drew on what he knew of Bell's difficult early life, when his father was in such denial about Neil's sexuality that he told his son to go to hospital and 'get fixed'.

'[Neil] is really tough, the most masculine guy out there. He had to overcompensate,' said Heath.

But the real inspiration for Ennis came from within Heath himself as he produced a no-holds-barred performance about heartache—as in hearts that truly ache, that really break. It was a film by an A-list director, with A-list stars at the peak of their careers, and it took the backbone of American legend—the Great American Western—and turned it into a beautiful but tragic homosexual love story that broke down gay stereotypes. No wonder the script had been around for a few years without finding anyone to make it, or actors to act in it. It had become known in Hollywood as one of the great unproduced screenplays.

'My cynical view is that we couldn't get the actors because the agencies wouldn't let them go. They thought it would be career suicide,' said McMurtry.

When Jake Gyllenhaal first heard about 'that gay cowboy movie' several years earlier, he wanted nothing to do with it.

'I said, "Absolutely not, I don't even want to read it", said Gyllenhaal, who had gone on to make his name in edgy movies like *Donnie Darko*.

'I was seventeen, and I was scared about tackling the subject. But then years later when Ang called me, I read the script and it was beautiful. I thought I should call those people who called it "the gay cowboy movie" and scold them. It's so much more than that.'

Heath committed to the movie without meeting Taiwan-born director Ang Lee. He had seen two of Lee's previous movies, *The Ice Storm* and *Crouching Tiger, Hidden Dragon*, and knew what Lee could achieve.

'I trusted that story in Ang's hands,' said Heath.

'I loved the script because it was mature and strong and such a pure and beautiful love story. I hadn't done a proper love story [before this] and I find there's not a lot of mystery left in stories between guys and girls; it's all been done or seen before.

'There were so many actors in the past seven years who have been attached to *Brokeback Mountain* yet who have been convinced by their managers, agents, publicists or all three combined not to do it because it would ruin their career. I was approached to make the movie ... and didn't think twice about it.'

Heath flew to New York for the afternoon to meet Lee and producer James Schamus. They met for twenty minutes, had a cup of tea, and Heath recalled that Lee barely said anything.

'Then he stood up. I shook his hand and he left. I was completely confused as to what just happened, completely baffled by him, and then he rang up and said I had the job, and that was it,' said Heath.

The first time Heath met Gyllenhaal was around a table for

dinner with Lee at an LA restaurant. Overcoming his fears about doing the movie had been exhilarating for Heath, and he was excited about the project. The three men hit it off straight away, and Heath and Gyllenhaal were to become close friends.

'It was great working with Jake. He was a very brave and talented actor to work with,' Heath said.

The heart of the movie was Brokeback Mountain itself, and while he toured Proulx's Wyoming and visited McMurtry's Texas, Ang Lee chose to use the mountains around Calgary as the epic backdrop. The scenery could not have been more spectacular, but the final decision was determined by the limited budget. It was simply cheaper to film in Canada than in the US.

'The dramatic core is finding Brokeback Mountain. It is elusive and romantic. It is something that you keep wanting to go back to—but probably never will. For Ennis and Jack, it was their taste of love,' said Lee.

The mountain, away from society's mores, represents a freedom that Ennis and Jack did not feel in their home towns.

'Brokeback Mountain is Ennis and Jack's magical place. It's where they fell in love. They never go back there, which may be unconscious on their parts; it's their idyll and they don't want to spoil it. It's like Jack says, "All we got's Brokeback Mountain",' said Diana Ossana.

A month before shooting began, Heath and Gyllenhaal went to what Jake called 'cowboy training camp' around Calgary.

'[Heath] and Jake needed to feel comfortable and find a chemistry,' said Lee.

Together they got blisters and bloody hands chopping wood, hauling bales of hay, putting up fences, wrangling sheep and riding bulls—but Heath once again drew the line at lifting weights to bulk up. The Calgary Gay Rodeo Association worked as advisers, and its cowboys, who ride the American rodeo circuit, appear in several sequences. Another adviser was Randy Jones, the original gay cowboy in the Village People.

'Heath and I trusted each other enough to take risks. It was wonderful creating an intimacy with him. He made me feel comfortable; he made me want to be present, and that's the best thing you can ask for from someone you're acting with,' said Gyllenhaal.

While the boys were doing cowboy stuff, another star of the movie, Michelle Williams, was on a road trip to Calgary via the biker bars of Wyoming and Montana with the movie's voice coach Joy Ellison. Ellison, trying to capture the accent of a ranch hand from Middle America and to pin down exactly the right voices for the stars, taped people along the way, hiding a microphone up her sleeve in some places where they were wary of city folk, like one particularly roughneck bar in Riverton, Wyoming.

'I held my beer up and leaned my elbow on the bar. Then I just started asking questions about the town and what had changed,' Ellison said.

'Michelle was born in Montana and left at an early age, but she still has that background and so she has a good sense of the rhythms and quality of the speech.'

Michelle, then twenty-four, was born and raised in rural Kalispell, Montana, the youngest of five children. When she was nine her family moved to San Diego, where she became a child actor. When she later chose acting as her career and her mother Carla and father Larry disapproved, Michelle rebelled and left home at the age of fifteen.

Michelle worked out early what it would take Heath until his final film to discover—that playing the baddie was more fun than playing the goodie. She made her name in prime time teen drama

'Dawson's Creek', playing bad girl Jen Lindley until 2003. In 1999, *Teen People* magazine had voted her one of the twenty-one 'Hottest Stars Under 21', an award that made her cringe.

'I don't want to be the "It" girl,' she once said.

Her dad, from whom she is now estranged, said she was always fiercely independent and inquisitive.

'Michelle as a child was frighteningly brilliant. She would ask me things and I would think, "I don't know!" Questions about the universe or God or creation. Here she was, a tiny girl and already asking me questions about the most penetrating subjects,' said Larry, a stock and commodities trader who has lived in Australia since 2006, fighting extradition to the US on tax evasion charges which he denies.

Before filming began in Alberta in May 2004, Ang Lee led the cast and crew in a Chinese good luck ceremony, a tradition he followed with all his movies. He brought them together in a moment of silence in which they lit incense and bowed to the four corners.

However, it did not bring them luck with the weather. The shoot was plagued with sleet, hailstorms, the wind that continually sweeps across the Calgary prairie and the chill air of the mountains. There were no fancy trailers, fancy catering or other such perks, and 80 per cent of the filming was outside in the wilderness. Just getting to the set often involved long drives, or even hikes, with the crew carrying everything with them.

'We really were in cowboy country. So when people would come to be in sequences, they looked the part because they *were* the part. It wasn't a Hollywood production,' said executive producer Michael Costigan.

It was because of the shared hardships that James Schamus, who had worked with Lee on *Crouching Tiger, Hidden Dragon* and

The Ice Storm among other projects, said that *Brokeback* was the most pleasant shoot he had been involved in.

'There was almost an inverse proportion between our lack of money and the abundance of spirit in our cast and crew,' said Schamus.

The rawness of the setting was reflected in the rawness on screen. They were ideal conditions for Heath to create what was then the most complex character of his career: the lonely and conflicted cowboy who falls in love with Gyllenhaal's Jack Twist, a rodeo rider, while herding sheep high up on Brokeback Mountain. Heath's Ennis, a dirt-poor ranch hand, marries Alma because that is what he thinks he is supposed to do. Ennis and Jack then spend the next two decades aching for each other.

'I think Ennis punishes himself over an uncontrollable need— love. Fear was installed in him at an early age, and so the way he loved disgusted him. He's a walking contradiction,' said Heath.

He began to create Ennis by looking at the way he would speak. He wanted Ennis's mouth to be a clenched fist.

'I wanted the words to fight the way out of his mouth,' said Heath.

'I wanted it to be part of the way Ennis sees the world. I wanted the light to be too bright for him and the world to be too loud. But it's also a real ranch hand's face. Even the stiff upper lip. It's something that farmers in Australia do to keep the flies out of their mouths.'

Whether he realised it or not, there was a lot of the private Heath in that role. Although he had been approached to play Jack Twist, he said that he responded more to the painfully shy Ennis.

Watching Heath in interviews, he speaks with a clenched jaw.

'In the past, I've tried so hard to withhold myself, even down to giving a smile,' he has said.

Many cowboys are so shy that they don't know what to do with their hands—like Heath. In real life, Heath hid behind his sunglasses in the same way that the character of Ennis hides beneath his cowboy hat.

Gyllenhaal spotted the similarities: 'Actually, Heath and I as people are really more of the characters that we play.'

Ennis walks with his shoulders slumped and with a slightly bow-legged gait.

'If you spend all day on horseback, and you hop off, you walk around like you still have a horse between your legs. And it affects your shoulders, they fall,' said Heath, getting further into the character.

'I never took an acting class, so I made all my mistakes on film. I get books. I meditate on it. I need a space like this where I can just sit and think and find a voice for the character and visualise it.

'For Ennis, I figured he was battling genetic structure, what had been passed down, his fears, what his father had shown him [as a child]—a murdered old gay ranch hand.

'There's this image he has of what a man should be like, and he's not living up to it. He's basically pretty homophobic. Except the love of his life is another man,' he said.

'That's his story, and that's what I was attracted to about the role: his choices and his lack of choice. That's why there's this violence never too far under the surface with him.'

The movie begins in 1963, but they didn't have the luxury of shooting it in sequence, which, as it turned out, played right into Heath and Michelle's hands. Heath, as usual, wore his heart on his sleeve. For such an accomplished actor, he found it almost impossible to hide his true emotions. Gyllenhaal had spotted something going on between the fictitious husband and wife during the four-week rehearsal period, but it was the first day of filming that confirmed it for the crew.

The script called for a scene of Ennis and Alma having a happy time. It was supposed to be the two of them in a truck doing doughnuts in the snow. However, a lack of snow in the towns led to a change of plan, and it became a tobogganing scene, which had to be shot before the snow melted into the spring air.

'We were knee-deep in snow, and on the fifth take Michelle and I are tobogganing down the hill, we were supposed to fall off, having a fun time, ho ho ho.

'And Michelle was screaming in pain. And I thought she was acting: ha ha ha. "No, I'm really in pain." She's twisted her knee—she was pretty much on crutches for the rest of the shoot.

'And I felt I always had to look after her, after that,' was how Heath described it to *Rolling Stone* magazine.

He accompanied her on the 83 kilometre drive to Canmore General Hospital, where she had X-rays and her knee was strapped.

Anne Hathaway, who played Jake's wife Lureen, could see what was going on between them immediately.

'The first day I was there, we were all sitting having lunch together. Michelle had hurt her knee and Heath was playing with her crutches. Every once in a while Heath would look up and she would look up … I'm sorry, it was just adorable,' Hathaway said.

Jake Gyllenhaal recalled the two being 'googly-eyed' with each other.

'I left for two weeks and came back and they were in love. We were all living in trailers while we were shooting the movie. There were four trailers, and there quickly became three,' he said.

Lee was happy for Heath: 'On the set I push him toward Jake, and off the set he has this great escape the other way.'

Even local actor Larry Reese, the minister who married their characters in the movie, could tell they were falling in love for real as he read them the marriage vows.

'Of course they were falling in love, but that was a secret at the time,' said Reese.

He often shared a ride in the same van as Heath and Michelle on the way to the set and, like so many before him, he found Heath to be down-to-earth and approachable.

'I told him my daughter was a huge fan, and he said, "Well, I will write her a letter", and he did. He went off and found a pen and some paper and he wrote her this really nice note thanking her for being a fan and saying he really appreciated that she liked his work,' said Reese.

'He didn't have an ego—he was as open and curious about my life as I was about his.'

Once again, Heath had mixed business with pleasure and fallen for his leading lady.

'These people are thrown together in emotionally charged situations where they have to get all hot and steamy on set. It is no wonder that so many leading actors and actresses end up having real-life love affairs,' said one experienced Australian producer.

'They're away from home, often on isolated sets, and in many ways it is like a holiday romance. Some of them last no longer than the end of the shoot and remain fairly private; others last a lifetime.'

Heath said that falling in love on set wasn't a cliché he worried about!

'If I cancel out the people I'm working with, I'm never going to meet anyone, because it's hard meeting people,' he later said.

'Inevitably the people I'm surrounded by are the people I'm working with most of the time. That's just the life that we live, so I'm never going to deny myself that opportunity.

'And it is a cliché, but it's not as common as you would think, and it was out of my hands too. It was too good to walk away from.'

That was the off-screen romance.

The first kissing scene of the on-screen romance was also shot out of sequence. It is the one where Jake and Ennis meet up after four years apart and Alma watches from the doorway, unable to comprehend what she is seeing.

'It's difficult, but it's kissing a human being, so fucking what? Once you get the first take done, well—the mystery's out the window; let's get on with it,' said Heath, approaching it in a typical seat-of-the-pants way.

'My biggest anxiety wasn't having to kiss Jake.

'It was a perfect script, and Ang Lee was the perfect director. So the anxiety for me was—I didn't want to be the one to fuck it up. And I was willing to do anything ...'

Gyllenhaal said that Heath almost broke his nose.

'He grabs me and he slams me up against the wall and kisses me. And then I grab him and I slam him up against the wall and I kiss him. And we were doing take after take after take. I got the shit beat out of me. We had other scenes where we fought each other, and I wasn't hurting as badly as I did after that one,' said Gyllenhaal.

Then the camera turns to shoot Alma's reaction, and Ang Lee takes up the story to demonstrate the professionalism Williams brought to her role. She wanted to get the reaction, a split-second look, exactly right.

'And so the guys were down there sort of leaning on each other for her to look at, and she wanted them to start kissing and mess around ... So they started necking, and she was not happy about it. Then they started kissing, and she was like,

"Come on, guys, I need it!" I was very impressed,' said Lee.

'And when I see on the monitor her face, that one moment … again, no dialogue. And it's very hard to show what she thinks. But I just think, for [that] one second it's really worth it.'

The director didn't encourage actors to watch themselves on the monitor, but Heath was an exception.

'He gets better as he gets more self-conscious. He sets himself in a zone and believes in it and keeps refining it,' said Lee. 'Jake sets himself this way and that way, he tries everything, like De Niro. Heath is not like that. He has a specific target within him.'

It was eight weeks into filming before they got around to the first sex scene between the two young drifters, where one thing leads to another in a tiny tent on a mountainside.

Gyllenhaal said they just had to take the plunge.

'The best metaphor I can give is that it felt like we were both like, "Are you ready? Yeah. Let's go", and we dove off the boat into the deep end. It's like when you're terrified of the water—you see a little kid thrown in the water and they're trying to get back to the boat as fast as they can. That's what it was like. But at the same time, when we were there we really went for it,' he said.

'What really tears me apart is, Ennis and Jack are two people who actually found love. If you have love, you should hold onto it.'

Ang Lee said that as actors Heath and Jake were 'pretty brave'. The scene was filmed thirteen times.

'I remember at one point in the first lovemaking scene in the tent, I remember thinking, "This is brave", particularly of Jake,' Lee said.

'The way he pounds. You see in the dark … but I see very clear right in front of my eyes, the detail, and it was very close with a hand-held camera. The whole scene was in one shot.

'So many times you see beautiful lovemaking scenes with a

lot of exposure, or an awkward lovemaking scene, but I think it's very rare that you see it private. And that's what we were shooting for with this story. And I think you see some private moment there [with] actors kind of beside themselves.'

While the lovemaking scene was carefully choreographed, in the same way as is done when between a man and a woman, Heath said that he and Gyllenhaal had to be believeable.

'Part of the magic of acting is, you harness the infinite power of belief,' he said.

The power of Heath's performance was in how he under-played it.

'Heath understood the character better than I did,' said Proulx.

'It scared me how much he got inside Ennis.'

It also took a lot out of him. Heath said the experience was 'incredibly lonely' for him.

'Whether or not Ang created that environment for me to work and live in, or I created it for myself—it's a lonely story, so it's hard not to take it home with you and feel lonely,' Heath said.

Gyllenhaal also spoke about Lee's cold and distant work manner. He said Lee purposely made him and Heath feel uncomfortable, because it was what the movie called for.

Heath described how hard it was for him to come back down after hyping himself up for filming, even with Michelle's support.

'You're affected by whatever you're portraying. Your body has a memory of the experiences you have in life. If you're tricking yourself to feel anger every day, you go home angry,' said Heath.

'Then you get home and you're like, "Argh! Fuck me, why am I angry? I've got no reason to be angry." And you wind yourself down again. But you do carry it. The mood of a film always takes me over.'

With *Brokeback*, he said, the second he lay down to sleep

and closed his eyes, 'I'm going through what happened the whole day all over again. Every take, every single thing: I recollect everything. You don't stop thinking about it, don't stop carrying it around, and that is pretty hard ...

'I feel like a sponge when I'm working.'

He had his Harley with him so he could take off and unwind on long rides through the mountain roads. As well, the Canadians are pretty cannabis-tolerant and, as usual, Heath had plugged into a local supply.

'He was working pretty hard and he found it difficult to relax at night, that's why he used dope. He used to go home and roll a joint, have dinner, roll another joint and then go to bed,' one of his friends has revealed, again stressing that Heath never used any harder drugs.

'The pot helped him relax, it helped him to sleep. It can take a few hours after a shoot before you calm down enough to sleep, then you have an early call the next morning. You can end up tossing and turning with everything running through your mind.'

On the nights they were back in Calgary, Heath and Michelle joined the usual round of cast and crew dinners and parties around the city's restaurants and bars, some of which are parodies of the wild west lifestyle, with mechanical bucking broncos and waitresses in Stetsons.

Adam 'Bushy' Sutton arrived in June, just in time for the Calgary Stampede—the world's biggest rodeo event. The authentic gay cowboy—Adam—was picked up at the city's airport by the actor playing a gay cowboy—Heath.

Heath's acceptance of Adam helped Adam to accept himself. In his book *Say It Out Loud: Journey of a Real Cowboy*, Sutton wrote about their friendship.

'I remember Heath taking a break from filming one afternoon

and sitting down on the grass for a chat. It had been a long, demanding shoot and he was tired, looking forward to it finishing soon. It was no surprise he was drained,' wrote Sutton.

'The word was that he was turning in a good, perhaps truly great, performance. But he was innately modest, and the film was far too risky and unusual for anyone involved to start counting their chickens yet.'

When Heath later watched *Brokeback Mountain* for the first time, he was with Michelle Williams in a cinema alone.

'Once the film was over, we really were unsure about what we'd just seen. We weren't sure whether it was brilliant or terrible,' he said.

'But we were sure about each other's performances, we were like, "You were great", "No, you were great" ... and kind of threw compliments back and forth to each other, but we couldn't recognise ourselves in the film. I think that's just part of who Michelle and I are—we're very similar that way. Watching ourselves is just impossible.'

Always his own most brutal critic, he was never completely happy with a role.

'I still see holes in [Ennis],' he said.

'I never want to feel like I've achieved my goal. It's like Chinese farmers. They never admit that it's a good season. They feel like they'll be punished.'

Heath's Hollywood career of a mere six years had been a rollercoaster of highs and lows as he fought against being typecast.

'People weren't giving me a chance to do anything other than be the blond-haired bimbo, and it was starting to bore me,' he said.

'I couldn't have spent the rest of my life following the paths that were being presented to me, so I had to start creating some for myself.'

He said he took his career and destroyed it, doing what he wanted rather than what his agent, the studios and even his family thought he should do.

'I felt like my career was out of my hands. I wasn't making any decisions; they were being made for me. And so, to a certain degree, I had to go out and destroy my career somewhat in order to rebuild it. At the time, I had studios telling me I was crazy. I had agents on my back, publicists, family members, everyone saying, "What are you doing? You should be this. You should be that. You should follow the dollar. Follow the gloss."

'My life is together, both professionally and socially. But it's been a big learning process, and there is no Yoda—there's no one who points you in the right direction. You've got to figure that out by yourself.

'It's taken a while, but it looks like doors are opening again.'

Steve Alexander, who had become Heath's friend as well as his agent, understood what he had been going through.

'Heath really went through a period of time where he wasn't "the guy". He was hard to get onto the proverbial list. Then he decided he was going to build his career back up the way he wanted it to be,' said Alexander.

'He wanted to take parts that were more complicated and more difficult. He wanted to play characters that he could disappear into, and not the leading man, which might have been an easier path for him. I think that started with *Monster's Ball*, and then, obviously, when he decided he would take on the part of Ennis Del Mar in *Brokeback Mountain*.'

Alexander said that Heath didn't understand what he was creating with *Brokeback*: 'Obviously, at first blush he feared it, which is what made him go towards it. I don't know if he understood completely the importance of what he was doing at that moment, but I think he knew that he was doing good work.'

The movie other actors had shied away from had at last given Heath the opportunity to shock people and show them what he could do. He had gambled and won.

Heath called *Brokeback Mountain* 'a love story for this generation'.

Filming wound up in August 2004 and Ang Lee chose one of Calgary's best-known bars, Ranchman's, for the wrap party. Ranchman's features in the movie as the Childress bar, meant to be in Texas.

'It was the best wrap party I have ever been to,' said assistant director Pierre Tremblay, a veteran of two dozen such events.

Heath had his Harley to take home, as well as a heap of souvenirs and other things he had collected during his four months around Calgary, so he hired a small van and asked Bushy Sutton if he would drive it back for him to LA, all expenses paid. Sutton jumped at the opportunity to do the road trip while Heath and Michelle flew back together.

Heath never let the grass grow under his feet, which was why the unpredictability of an actor's life suited him. *Brokeback Mountain* had been another life-changing experience for him. He had made the movie that would resurrect his career, and met the woman who would be the mother of his child. He had also decided to live in Australia, and around the end of the filming of *Brokeback Mountain*, his dad called to tell him that Heath was now the owner of a house in the Sydney beachside suburb of Bronte.

Or rather, his mum was. Sally Bell had bought the house on Heath's behalf in an attempt to put the media off the scent, but it was just the start of Heath's ongoing struggle with the Australian paparazzi—one that he was never going to win.

⊪

09
THE FLAME, NOT THE MOTH

IT IS A HOT SUMMER IN VENICE, FILLED WITH THE SLOW RHYTHM OF WATER LAPPING AGAINST THE BANKS OF THE CANALS AS THE GONDOLAS SLIP PAST WINDOWS LEFT OPEN TO CATCH THE SLIGHT SEA BREEZE. TUCKED AWAY AMONG THE HAPHAZARD SERIES OF BRIDGES THAT CONNECT THE CITY'S 100-PLUS ISLANDS, A FILM CREW IS GETTING READY TO SHOOT THE NEXT SCENE OF A ROMANTIC ROMP ABOUT LEGENDARY LOVER CASANOVA. THE WOMEN ARE SQUEEZED INTO IMPOSSIBLY SMALL-WAISTED EIGHTEENTH-CENTURY PERIOD DRESSES, THE MEN ARE IN DANDYISH FROTHY FRILLS, HEELS AND VELVET. THERE ARE NO TRAILERS FOR THE STARS, JUST GROUPS OF CHAIRS—AND THE BEST ITALIAN COFFEE. IT WAS NOT ONLY A LONG WAY FROM THE CANADIAN ROCKIES, BUT A LONG WAY FROM HEATH'S PREVIOUS ROLE AS ENNIS DEL MAR. FROM COWBOY TO PLAYBOY.

Heath said he had been 'so wound up' working on *Brokeback*, he needed to unwind.

'I couldn't just go home; I would have gone mad,' he said.

He described filming *Casanova* as a working holiday.

'Casanova was so enjoyable because we didn't have to take ourselves seriously. I'd just come off *Brokeback Mountain* and that was just torturous at times, a really tough, lonely shoot. So to go from Calgary to Venice to shoot this was like a paid holiday,' he told *Empire* magazine.

Sydney was on hold, and Michelle had gone home to New York where she was adding to her reputation as the 'indie princess' with a swag of films waiting to be released—*The Baxter*, a romantic comedy, the drama *Land of Plenty* and the comedy *A Hole in One*. Heath's phone bills, always pages long, became even bigger as he rang Michelle constantly. He was notorious among his family and friends for excitedly calling them at all hours of the day and night from across the world, totally forgetting the time zones.

The cast and crew of *Casanova* had been in Venice for a month when Heath, having wrapped up *Brokeback Mountain*, arrived in August with his mate Trevor Di Carlo. Trevor had once again secured a small role working on the movie, and was sharing an apartment with Heath in the Italian city.

In preparation for the role, Heath was curious to know more about Casanova than just his legendary status as history's greatest lover. He got hold of the twelve volumes of Casanova's journals, read a couple and flicked through the rest to get some historical background for his role. Casanova was a complex and interesting character—he was born in Venice, studied to be a priest, was a bit of a scientist, dabbled in the occult, wrote poetry, composed music, was a gambler and escaped from jail.

'But when I got the script, I realised that information was useless because [the movie] is not historically correct. It's a romp,' he told *Empire* magazine.

The main thing was that it was fun. The script certainly made him laugh.

'I really wanted to not take acting seriously, not take movies seriously; I just wanted to have fun. And I wanted to come home smiling after work, and so by throwing away all the history it allowed me to do that. And it gave me a clean slate, so I just kind of created my own character,' he said.

Sienna Miller, the English actor who was herself never out of the tabloids due to her high-profile relationships, played the tomboy Francesca, an early feminist. She is the woman Casanova falls in love with, but the only woman in Venice who doesn't want him.

Miller and Heath became the movie's clowns, the ice having been broken when he split his tight pants as he lunged during a fencing scene.

'He is completely stupid on set, which I love,' Miller said.

'We play this game of stuffing grapes into our mouths. I've got eight and a half grapes and that's the record. Eight and a half, and walk up to the DP [director of photography] and say, "Can we shoot around this?" So we have hours of fun.'

The director Lasse Hallström had worked with Abba in his native Sweden, and directed the acclaimed *My Life as a Dog*, *Chocolat* and *The Shipping News*, the film of Annie Proulx's novel. He had been looking for an actor ten or twenty years older than Heath to play the infamous lover; someone with more experience of life.

'We needed a sexy guy, and the list was short,' Hallström said. Then he met Heath in January 2004.

'Heath walked in the room, and he was Casanova,' said Betsy

Beers who, with Mark Gordon, produced the movie for Touchstone Pictures, part of the Disney group.

'It was one of those amazing things. He was funny, charming and very, very seductive. But he was also elegant and quite vulnerable.'

Heath wanted to take a more hands-on approach to movie making, and had long held ambitions to become a director. Hallström recognised that Heath could contribute a lot, both on and off the screen, describing him as 'a multi-skilled, multi-talented man'.

'Heath Ledger is a wonderful choice,' said Hallström. 'He has great comedic timing, he is really smart and he has the charm and the looks.'

The production had to cut through layers of bureaucratic red tape to secure permission to film in Venice. There were no trucks to transport cast, crew and equipment around the city—everything had to go by boat. During the summer high tides, they were wading in water two-feet deep. But it was worth it, said Hallström.

'The way Venice is reflected on screen comes across in the performances, and has been a source of inspiration to us. It affects the film, it's more for real with real locations,' he said.

Jeremy Irons, who played the pompous Bishop Pucci, sent by Rome to put Casanova on trial, had worked in Venice before, and reflected on how calm the city was because the only ways to get around were to walk or take a boat.

Heath's Casanova was a more lovable character than in previous versions of the story, which reflected his own personality and his mood at the time. He was never precious as an actor, as Sienna Miller explained.

'A lot of male actors would have come in playing the

greatest lover of all time and had an enormous ego and pouted and puffed their way through it,' she told the media while promoting the movie.

'Heath, being the man that he is and the actor that he is, really sat back and allowed it to be an ensemble piece, which I think is really rare.

'He was great. He really took care of me. He's like kind of my big brother and we had a right giggle on the set. We both don't take life too seriously, and he's just generous and kind. I think he knew that I was nervous, that it was my first big role in a huge film, and he really helped me out.'

Italians, of course, take their eating very seriously, and Heath was happy to oblige with plenty of pasta and wine. There were big cast dinners, and they would seek out restaurants with a piano, so the evenings would end with them all sitting around singing.

There were also the tourists who flood to Venice in the summer. While Casanova was a movie that used very little computer generated imagery (CGI), they could not always shoot around the hordes of visitors and had to 'paint' them out later, especially in the final scene, looking down from a hot-air balloon. Without CGI, the audience would have seen all the water taxis and the tourists taking photographs.

There is a scene where Heath and Miller swing on a rope and leap onto moving horses. Unlike in *The Four Feathers*, Heath didn't insist on doing the stunts himself, instead letting the director rely on CGI.

'It was a lot of fun. But we didn't actually land on the horses that were galloping past. We did a take where I did a sword fight, and it ended with me grabbing a rope and then turning around and running and swinging up in the air, and then letting go and looking back, as if a horse was running underneath me, and kind of landing in a position as if I was landing on a horse, and then I just landed on a mat,' Heath said.

'And then we went back and did the last bit where it looks as if I'm landing. And then they digitally merged the two pictures so it looked like it was all happening at once, but it's not, I was landing on soft, bouncy mats. Great fun, though.'

The time in Venice was the antidote he needed to *Brokeback Mountain*.

'It ended up being a four and a half month guided tour,' Heath said.

'Every day we ended up being taken to the most beautiful parts of Venice to shoot, so essentially it was like filming a movie inside a museum, which was really cool. And, you know, working with great people, great crew. It was a lovely experience.'

One of the more memorable lines in the movie is when Casanova counsels, 'Be the flame, not the moth'. But what might be good advice in love is not the way Heath wanted it to work out in real life.

When filming finished and he moved into his new Sydney home in early December, Heath became the hottest commodity in town, and the paparazzi were the moths to his flame. In LA, he was still one of hundreds of spunky young actors; in Sydney, he was one of only a handful of Hollywood stars. The half a dozen main paparazzi in the city, who make their living from selling photographs of the rich and famous, had dollar signs in their eyes.

Sally Bell had bought the huge, four-storey, five-bedroom house in Bayview Street, Bronte, on her son's behalf the day before its scheduled auction on 3 April 2004, with an offer of $4.45 million. Heath and Naomi Watts had looked in the area while they were in Sydney earlier in the year, but it was his dad who found the house. Heath agreed to the deal after seeing pictures on the Internet. He didn't see the house in person before buying.

However, if Heath hoped to put the media off the scent by having his mum buy the house for him, the ploy had failed before the ink on the deal was dry. The beachside mansion had been owned by the American adult-entertainment entrepreneur Hans Tiedemann, and his wife Hisako was soon telling the media that it had been bought by 'an old lady' on behalf of Heath. The deal was sealed on 3 September 2004.

The first thing he did was get all his friends around.

As Naomi Watts said, 'He had so many great friendships. He had all his Australian friends, who he took everywhere with him. He had a real community.'

Now he was back on home soil, and Bronte, just like his home in Los Angeles, was an open house. His wide circle of friends included people he had met and stayed in touch with from local productions as far back as 'Sweat' and *Blackrock*, as well as high-profile Americans like Sean Penn and Amy Pascal. They were all treated the same.

'He was always introducing you to 3,000 mates whose names you can't remember,' said Pascal.

But Heath's tight-knit group remained the Woodbridge House gang, the mates he went to school with. On his first weekend in Sydney, Heath was out on the Saturday night trying to look low-key in a beanie at Sydney's Gaelic Club, watching his mate N'fa's band 1200 Techniques. Talk about the Guildford Grammar class most likely to make it—when N'fa wasn't on stage, he was a national medal winning 110-metre hurdler.

Bronte is just a couple of beaches south of Bondi, which hadn't changed much since Heath lived there with Trevor at Martin Henderson's place on his journey to the big time. Even the regulars were the same. One of the first people he bumped into was Naomi Watts, home to spend Christmas with her family.

Heath had been invited to an extravagant Rio-themed party for clothes company General Pants and the 'in' rubber thong manufacturer Havaianas at Bondi Icebergs along with Sydney's hip young society, including Heath's friends Deke and Eve Miskin. But after barely fifteen minutes, Heath escaped the crowd with N'fa, seeking refuge across the road at Hugo's, where Watts was having dinner with designer Collette Dinnigan. Heath joined their table for a friendly chat.

There are some stars who would have employed an interior decorator to fit out their new house; who'd have personal assistants go out to buy their groceries. Not Heath. He still had that optimism that, despite his fame, he could live a normal life. He looked for furniture at the Sydney Antique Centre in Surry Hills, and joined the pre-Christmas crowds at the massive Westfield Bondi Junction shopping centre, where he ordered some electrical goods. He was seen coming out of a homewares store with two big red cushions.

Having decided the previous owner's taste was not for him, within a week he had hired a crane to carry away the top-floor jacuzzi and brought in no fewer than three barbecues. He hired his own builders, who were ready to start work in January; in the meantime, with the beach at his doorstep and friends nearby, Heath just wanted to kick back and relax.

But right from the start his every move was chronicled by the photographers who hounded him remorselessly. They knew that a candid shot of the star would sell around the world. He was photographed sitting on the ground cross-legged outside his house waiting for N'fa to turn up before they headed out for lunch at the trendy Aqua Bar down on Circular Quay, then pictured feeding the parking meter with money during lunch, and again taking a dip at the Bronte Beach pool on the way home.

Before the year ended, Heath gave a media interview in which he revealed that he still beat himself up professionally despite what an incredible year 2004 had been.

'I still have far to go. That's what this year was about, pushing myself ... I don't ever want to consider myself a good actor, because, well, I think I'm not. It allows you to be lazy if you start to think you're "hot". I'm not as good as I want to be. I don't think I'll ever be as good as I want to be, but I'll keep striving for it,' he said.

Showing again that he had inherited his dad's love of classy wheels, Heath bought himself a $385,000 royal blue Aston Martin DB7 and paid $8,000 for a sexy reconditioned 1969 Lambretta motor scooter as a surprise present for Michelle Williams, who arrived a few days before Christmas. He whisked her off for a romantic dinner and then to a ballet performance at the Opera House before they flew to Perth to spend Christmas with his family, escaping the media spotlight.

They also managed to sneak up the east coast to the hippie haven of Byron Bay, which Heath had previously visited with Naomi. Byron is known as a mystical place—the only spot on the east coast where the sun sets over the ocean, because of the way the bay is configured. Shops are full of crystals and people wanting to read your aura. It's a famous surfing spot, and the hinterland is full of lush valleys where people go to live alternative lifestyles. It was there that the couple conceived their baby, as Heath later revealed.

'It's very romantic. It's very spiritual,' he said of Byron Bay.

Perhaps the similarity in their ages helped Heath and Michelle's relationship to move on so quickly.

'Very early on in our relationship, we talked about having

babies together. I always knew I would be a young father,' said Heath. He continued on to say that the pregnancy was just something that happened.

'We just fell very deeply into each other's arms. Our bodies definitely made those decisions for us. I mean, the second you acknowledge [having a child] as a possibility, the body just inevitably hits a switch and it happens.'

Starting a family young in life seems to be a Ledger family tradition. Heath's parents were only in their mid-twenties when they had Heath's sister Kate, and Kim was twenty-eight when Heath was born.

While there is no chemical formula for falling in love, Michelle and Heath had many parallels in their lives. Neither took the safe and boring path. They lived bohemian lifestyles, yet they were both grounded, and both became movie stars seemingly despite their best efforts. They shared the good fortune of looks and talent, but neither chose the big-budget blockbusters which could have made them millions, instead building their careers on unpredictability. They remained enthusiastic, and were never cynical.

'I often marvel at it,' said Michelle, 'because I was really young and went to a town full of predators, and I somehow didn't get swallowed up or eaten alive. I marvel not just at the success, but the survival. That's what's most unbelievable to me; what I'm most proud of myself for.'

Her dad, Larry Williams, said both Heath and Michelle were independent.

'They both left home early. They really wanted to create their own world, they both went out in the world by themselves … I bet they both had so many stories to tell each other,' he said.

Michelle describes herself as 'just some nice, quiet girl from Montana', and she looks sweet and meek—but there is a toughness inside her. Larry Williams said she had always been strong-willed, but gave an insight into what made her self-reliant.

'The process of becoming an entertainer is about auditioning two or three times a day, and seeing strangers you will never see again, and they are going to be critical of you, and you are going to do sixty auditions and maybe get two callbacks,' he said.

'And it's very stressful, as a child or as an adult, and you wonder what are you doing wrong, but Michelle learned very early on that it was not a rejection of her.'

While Michelle and her dad are estranged, she is very close to her mother, Carla, and, like Heath, had been brought up to be tactile.

'They do the love hug thing,' said Larry Williams of Carla and Michelle. 'They are always in communication.'

It was Carla who drove Michelle around Hollywood to some of those auditions when she was younger.

'She's mature, an old soul, not the kind to go out and party,' said Carla, who worked in a scrapbook shop and fills scrapbooks with her daughter's achievements.

'She has a strong will, a tough outer shell to take the kinds of rejection actors do.'

She confirmed that her daughter was not carried away with a movie star lifestyle.

'Michelle has remained humble, normal, centred. There's a passion for the work and the actor's life. She loves what she does,' said Carla.

There is no doubt that Heath was itching to have an

independent base in Australia. Since making *Ned Kelly*, he had been talking about plans for an Australian movie, perhaps playing another national icon, the champion boxer Les Darcy.

Another project he had considered was a film about the building of the Kalgoorlie Goldfields Pipeline, inspired by the tales told to him on the knee of his Grandpa, Sir Frank Ledger. Heath had some links to the area himself. He had not only driven out to Kalgoorlie on the way to Sydney years ago with Trevor Di Carlo, but Trevor's mum, Dianne Di Carlo, owns the famous Munty Pub, as it is affectionately known. The pub, with its pressed-tin ceilings and 70-odd years of history, is in the West Australian wheat-belt town of Muntadgin, off the Great Eastern Highway on the way from Perth to Kalgoorlie. Heath and Trevor took a bunch of mates to stay there one weekend, and Heath's signature is still in the visitors' book.

Heath said he was looking forward to telling an Australian story 'in a pair of jeans'.

'I'm looking forward to just telling a contemporary story about youth and about kids my age, and how we interact,' he had told reporters while promoting *Ned Kelly*.

'It's different, a new generation. It hasn't been portrayed correctly, in my eyes, particularly in Australia.'

He would get that chance with *Candy*. Based on the 1997 best-selling novel by Sydney author Luke Davies, it is a bittersweet story about junkie life and two young lovers played by Heath and Abbie Cornish. It was described in one review as a love triangle between the two of them and heroin.

The movie had been on the cards since veteran theatre director Neil Armfield saw Heath in that short but pivotal role in *Monster's Ball*. Armfield had initially resisted Davies's suggestion that Heath was ideal for the role of Dan, the poet in the loosely biographical novel that draws on the author's own experiences as a heroin addict in the 1980s.

Davies said Armfield had based his judgment of Heath on his performance in *A Knight's Tale*, seeing him as more of a star than an actor; a lightweight, not grubby or edgy enough to play Dan. Then he saw *Monster's Ball*.

'It led Armfield to see there was an extraordinary amount, previously unnoticed, going on under the surface,' said Davies, who became another close friend of Heath's during the shoot.

Heath was filming *The Brothers Grimm* when Armfield called him up and sent him the script.

'When Heath was suggested, I immediately thought he was too heroic,' said Armfield. 'Then I saw *Monster's Ball*. I got on the phone and offered Heath the part straightaway. He made an immediate commitment to it.

'He knew where he was. He knew his own power. He had taken his career into his own hands, and started choosing the most quirky, difficult, interesting options.'

Heath signed up even though he was again taking a significant cut on what he could have earned. For example, at around that time Tobey Maguire was reportedly getting $17 million for the sequel to *Spiderman* after getting $27 million for the original—one of the roles Heath had turned down.

Getting the novel to the screen had been a long project, and Abbie Cornish had been in the running for the title role of the artist Candy since producer Margaret Fink first met her in 2000, when the waif-like actor was just eighteen. Fink had first seen her potential in the ABC TV series 'Wildside', when Cornish was just fourteen. In the run-up to filming *Candy*, Cornish had been acclaimed for her role as a sixteen-year-old runaway in *Somersault*, which swept the Australian Film Institute Awards.

'She's going to be huge. She has that spirituality that can't be faked—and she can act,' said Fink.

Fink was just as impressed by Heath when he knocked on the door of her Sydney home.

'Too simple to put it down to that smile, but boy, what a smile. There was energy in that smile,' said Fink, whose production of *My Brilliant Career* in 1979 had launched the careers of director Gillian Armstrong and actor Judy Davis.

Production on *Candy* was due to start in early 2004 until *Brokeback Mountain* put it back several months. Then, in December, Armfield was diagnosed with prostate cancer, and the film was delayed for another eight weeks. Armfield said that Heath, typically generous, filled his house with roses.

It was that delay that allowed Heath and Michelle the time to head north to Byron Bay, and they were almost certain she was pregnant by the time production began in February 2005.

The first few days were very frustrating for Heath because Armfield—who had been artistic director of the internationally renowned Company B at Sydney's Belvoir Street Theatre since 1994—was a stage director first and a movie director second. His style was to bring the cast together in a circle, as he would for a theatre production, and have a script read through. Geoffrey Rush, who was playing the gay junkie supplier and father figure to Candy and Dan, was a seasoned theatre actor and understood this process, but Heath mumbled his way through the read and then, as Armfield described it, 'sat on the floor like a naughty boy in the classroom, the ADD kid in the corner'.

Armfield kept a diary which revealed how uncomfortable Heath was.

28 February: 'Heath fidgety after lunch—clearly unhappy— Geoffrey brilliant and enjoying himself. Heath says he doesn't

want to rehearse with all those others, commenting on each other's characters and plucking at the mystery. I say it's good to talk—it helps to explore the ground, the landscape, and to consider the rhythms that might be played.'

The next day, Heath didn't turn up.

1 March: 'I call Heath and suggest we find some time in a cocoon together (after a troubled night, I realise I just have to spend time with him). We have a great talk in corner of rehearsal room—we just have to learn to respect each other's needs.'

Heath said, 'Abbie and I were the naughty kids in class who sat at the back. We didn't want to give too much. It was slightly superstitious of us both. We didn't want to capture our performance in rehearsal. We were nervous about it, because we were not sure we could repeat it in the shoot.

'Neil backed down and let us work in our own patterns.'

The movie begins part of the way into the relationship between Dan and Candy. He is already a heroin addict, although his addiction appears to be under control, and she graduates from sniffing heroin to shooting up because she wants to share everything with him.

'I wanna try it your way this time,' she says.

Their relationship deteriorates as their addiction grows until they are living off her earnings as a prostitute.

'When you first meet Dan in the film, he's knee-deep in addiction. He's a regular user of heroin, and a poet. He looks at drug use as poetic and romantic. Candy's curiosity towards drugs is born through him. He's attracted by the way she wants to dive into his world, to share his experience,' said Heath.

'Heroin ends up binding the two of them together, and destroying them as a couple. They go to hell and back. *Candy* is also the story of their rebirth.

'The prospect of shooting a film using my own accent—which I haven't done for eight years—was very attractive to me. It gave me a sense of freedom—being able to mumble, to breathe in my own accent. I was able to improvise more freely.'

It was while promoting the movie that Heath publicly admitted for the first time that he had smoked dope, although he played it down.

'I've smoked pot before, and I know what it feels like to be high. But I've never been addicted to anything other than cigarettes, although that's quite a fuckin' addiction,' he said.

To play the part of Dan, he had to learn how to use harder drugs. Luke Davies could give them some direction from first-hand experience, but Heath and Abbie Cornish also went to a drug session with 'junkie Paul'.

'We met a guy who'd been addicted to heroin for, like, twenty years. And he took us through the steps of how to shoot up. He took a prosthetic arm with veins and blood bags and showed us how to find the vein, and the angle to slip the needle in,' said Heath.

'They're designed to teach nurses how to find veins, but they have one here to teach people how to inject safely.'

Heath filmed it with a video camera and, very proud of his work, he gave one copy to Geoffrey Rush, one to the art department and one to Neil.

Armfield said he had no idea how good Heath was until they started filming and Heath showed how much he knew about his craft.

'Heath's relationship with the camera was so instinctive, so private,' said Armfield in a newspaper article he wrote about the production.

'But I was fearful that he wasn't showing enough, wasn't

letting us into the soul of the character. "We need to see your eyes," I'd say. "You need to show more!"

'He was frustrated. "I'm showing you!"

'We went outside so as not to fight in front of the crew. I said, "Why don't you trust me?" He said, "Well, so I'll show more— let's go and do it again. But I guarantee you'll use the earlier take." We did.'

While the whole film is confronting, Michelle's pregnancy made one scene difficult for Heath to deal with. It was when Candy's baby is stillborn.

'I'd just found out Michelle was pregnant with our first child, and that was four weeks before we had to shoot that scene. So it was strange. I didn't want to jinx our own pregnancy, and having to hold a little prosthetic, bloody, dead baby in your hands … it was very uncomfortable,' he said.

'It's supposed to be uncomfortable. I'm not sure whether or not we should have seen as much as we did, but that's not really up to me to make that call, obviously. But yeah, it was definitely difficult to shoot.'

For the film to work, Armfield said that Heath's character had to remain likeable despite his appalling drug-driven, selfish behaviour, and Heath achieved that.

'Heath touched [Dan's] thread of optimism and skewed nobility, this core of love that holds the whole picture together,' said Armfield.

It was Luke Davies's first time on a set. He said that after working on the screenplay for seven years, he was amazed to watch Heath transform it.

'We spent years fretting about really important lines of dialogue that carried information that got you from one place to another. It was, "We've got to find a way of expressing this, there's no way we can lose that", and we lost it because Heath Ledger would do something with a twist of his face or a glance of his eye,' Davies told the *Sydney Morning Herald* while promoting the movie.

'That's why actors are so great,' he continued, 'and why they earn so much money. They take away the anxious necessity to find the right words.'

Cornish found Heath to be 'free and so spontaneous within his work, which is refreshing. I learn to just be within it, let it happen.'

Unusually for Heath, there were no stunts and no horse riding—but he did manage to knock himself out in a shower scene, and wore a scar on his knuckle to prove it.

Armfield described Heath as a nightmare for sound recordists on *Candy*, just as he had been on *Brokeback Mountain*. They kept asking him to speak up, but Heath told them, 'I shouldn't have to speak any louder than I would to be understood by the person I'm with.' He was correct.

Towards the end of the movie, Heath went for so much realism that he actually injected on camera. It is the scene where his character starts using again after being clean.

'There was a shot that we had, a tight shot of my arm, and I slipped the needle in and pulled back until you saw the blood, and then they went off it onto my face,' he said.

'I actually injected. It had water colour and sugar in it to make it look watery brown. And then we found out that was the difference between a [Mature] rating and an R. The penetration. When it looked like it was going in and it didn't really go in, that was okay.'

The scene was dropped to gain *Candy* an M rating in Australia.

At night, Heath went home to his house at Bronte—and Michelle. He had his friends, a pregnant girlfriend, and he was high on life. His happiness was palpable.

Luke Davies recalled one night when they all went out to a nightclub in the seedy district of Kings Cross.

'He seemed quite literally beside himself with love for her, unable to contain his excitement,' said Davies, in an article for *The Australian* newspaper.

'I remember one night, in an almost empty nightclub, watching him sweep her to her feet and swirl her around an empty dance floor, much to the relief of a bored DJ. It was a completely private moment; he wasn't doing it for the benefit of others, those of us settling into our seats or buying a round. He wanted to dance with Williams.

'He seemed to carry that same I-can't-believe-I-can-feel-like-this grin from *10 Things I Hate About You*. I had the odd sensation watching them that their experience at just that moment was a little more intense than mine. I almost felt the need to avert my eyes: that pure joy again.'

Meanwhile, his house was coming together as he wanted it, solid and blokey and a lot like his Spanish-style home in LA, with dark timber and white walls.

He had bought a dining-room table and chairs built from black, recycled oregon. In the open-plan lounge, from where he could hear and see the waves crashing, he had dark leather chairs and a trendy, beige retro couch with wooden arms and a slash of his favourite colour orange running through the middle. A DJ's turntable had been built into the sideboard, and the room contained two of his beloved chess sets. He liked the room to look lived-in, with shelves full of books including *The Complete Works of Shakespeare* and Tolstoy's *War and Peace*, plus his eclectic collection of CDs, including those by Macy Gray, REM, U2, Nick Drake, David Bowie and Bob Dylan.

Heath was pretty nifty with a hammer and screwdriver and

liked to do building work himself, but there were some things he could not do, even if given the time. The house remained a work in progress, with builders knocking down internal walls to open up the amazing views. A black Lacanche chef's oven was added to the remodelled kitchen, and concrete floors were polished. There was a theatre room, with sound-absorbing chocolate carpet and a framed 3.5-metre screen. The main bedroom included an open bathroom, with a tub facing the ocean. It was clear that Heath intended to live there for many years.

But the paparazzi were driving him mad. Heath never mastered the art of dealing with them. Nicole Kidman was another target they revelled in pursuing, but unlike Heath she wasn't living in Sydney, and made only brief visits. The 'paps' didn't bother the other Hollywood stars in town, Hugh Jackman and Russell Crowe. Jackman was unfailingly polite, and Crowe deliberately always wore the same daggy pants and tops so photographs of him one day looked the same as those of the day before, having worked out that shots like that are worth nothing. But some of the photographers knew that if they kept goading Heath, he would explode and give them a shot that could make them thousands.

They followed him to the beach when he went for a swim. They were there when he had a coffee with friends in one of the little cafés, and again when he and Michelle just wanted a private moment, sitting in the park opposite the house or on a rock overlooking the ocean.

It didn't help that the house was not built for privacy. Just as its three levels looked out over Bronte Park and the beach, so people could look in. The rear was all glass, and even its previous owner, Hans Tiedemann, had commented that he didn't think a celebrity would like to live there. Heath got the builders to cover the windows with a dark tint to try to thwart the long lenses of the media, and had the house painted a dark shade of grey—from its old 'pooey beige' colour—perhaps in an effort to merge into the background.

But while pictures of Heath sold newspapers and magazines, the paparazzi would remain camped outside. He had graduated from his one-finger salute to throwing eggs at them, which only made things worse. He looked like a whiny brat.

'When someone takes a photo of you and your girlfriend outside your house, it makes you feel like you're being assaulted; it's the equivalent of getting shoved in the chest,' said Heath.

'If anyone does that to me, I see red. You don't stop and go, "OK, just calm down".

'My family will ring me up and say, "Why don't you just smile and give them their shots and walk away? Why do you have to retaliate?" I'm like, "Because I want them to know that they can't just sit outside my house. I will throw an egg at them. This is my space, it's my house."'

The anger spilled over on the first day of filming, when the *Daily Telegraph* reporter Vanessa McCausland and a photographer turned up at Mascot to record the event, along with other media. Heath was unnecessarily rude and offensive, spitting at the *Daily Telegraph* car, making his trademark middle-finger gesture and hurling abuse, calling the media 'fucking cunts' and 'pussies'. Then he hid behind his skateboard.

Perhaps he was just in character as Dan the junkie, in his baggy pants and Castro hat, because a couple of days later he was all smiles when the media turned up at Alexandria Town Hall to capture the scene where Dan and Candy get married.

But the more aggressive paparazzi kept on his tail until they got their pound of flesh. It happened on a street in the gritty inner-west suburb of Newtown, on the second-last night of filming. A small crowd had gathered to watch.

As Armfield recalled in his diary: 'It had been a hard day, and we were desperately short of time and were covering the scene in a single, choreographed shot.

'We were on our third—and best—take and from the crowd came the flash of a camera, a man called out "Flash" and walked away fast up the street. The take was ruined.

'In the confusion—had a lamp blown?—nobody knew what had happened except Heath. He bolted up the street after the photographer—Guy Finlay—shouting abuse. Finlay screamed, "I'll see you at home, Ledger." It was only Heath who had the speed and courage of reaction.

'I was ashamed to have stood there in stunned incomprehension. I wish I'd chased him too. I wish I'd smashed his camera.'

Davies, who was there that night, claims Finlay said, 'You're a fucking dweeb, Ledger,' and then got in his car at the end of the street, put his high beam on and his hand on the horn.

On the way to his car, the stocky Finlay, one of Sydney's more robust photographers, stumbled and fell to the ground, later claiming he had been assaulted and spat on by Heath.

A year later, out of the blue, Heath rang the editor of the *Daily Telegraph*'s gossip section, Fiona Connolly, to set the record straight.

'It's Heath Ledger here,' he said, his deep voice and trans-Atlantic accent confirming for Connolly that it was indeed him on the phone on this quiet Sunday morning.

She thought she was going to cop it from him, because the newspaper had called him just about every epithet it could come up with, including 'Ledger the lout', 'potty-mouthed grump' and 'high-strung hooligan'. The paper believed that his behaviour towards the media, however much he was hounded, more than justified the labels. There were even more stories of assaults on photographers which the paper had not reported.

But Connolly recalls Heath being polite and softly spoken.

'I'm calling to apologise. I've been out of line and I want to talk about that,' he said in a whisper, explaining that Michelle and their new baby daughter were asleep.

The previous week, the newspaper had reported that a photographer claimed Heath and his uncle, Neil Bell, had tried to spit in the face of paparazzi photographer David Morgan. Both men had denied the claims.

'It's disgusting and it's awful. I would never in a million years do anything like that,' Heath told Connolly.

'I'm not some sort of dirty spitter.'

He said he had just wanted to return to Australia and live a nice quiet life with Michelle and their baby, and recognised that would not be possible unless he dealt with the media intrusion a bit better.

'That's been my problem. It's not necessarily a tantrum thing, but it's a really bad way in which I've handled myself in the past. I can admit it's a little out of line to pull the finger out, and I'm trying not to do that anymore,' he said.

'I'm trying to bite my finger these days.'

He again denied he had spat at the newspaper's car on the set of *Candy*.

'I felt really embarrassed by that too, because it just didn't happen ... It's disgusting to spit on anyone,' said Heath, during a 20-minute conversation.

Connolly was impressed that he had the courage to call.

'It was a conversation ... not about an upcoming film with his publicist listening in, but between a bloke in a pressure cooker and someone he obviously thought might be able to help,' Connolly said.

'In a way, it did. I stopped thinking of Ledger as a young punk with too much money and attitude [and saw him more] as a shy guy with a short fuse and too much attention—at least, more than he could deal with. I never wrote another bad word about Heath Ledger, not because he wooed me with his phone call, or because of the anguish in his voice, but because he really did "learn to deal with things a bit better".'

Candy was released to impressive reviews in Australia, and played to a standing ovation at the prestigious Berlin Film Festival, which is considered to be as influential—if not as flashy—as the annual Cannes Film Festival. Heath, Cornish and Armfield charmed the film media in Berlin.

But in America, *Candy* was seen as too much of an art movie because of its subject. However, Heath's performance as a heroin addict was so convincing that when he died there was conjecture that his life may have come to resemble Dan's, as people cast about for clues to his death.

The suggestion angered his friends.

'It was acting; it was what he got paid to do. Nobody said that about Abbie Cornish,' said his friend from *Two Hands*, Steve Le Marquand.

'I played an armed robber in *Two Hands*, but I had never been in jail.'

Producer Margaret Fink saw nothing in Heath's life that in any way reflected what he portrayed on screen.

'He didn't even drink much when we were shooting. He was a conscientious performer,' she said.

'Ledger was no victim. He wasn't a River Phoenix or a Marilyn. That's not who he was.'

HEATH
LEDGER
DATE 14·07·95

PEOPLE WEREN'T GIVING ME A CHANCE TO DO ANYTHING OTHER THAN BE THE BLOND-HAIRED BIMBO, AND IT WAS STARTING TO BORE ME ... I FELT LIKE MY CAREER WAS OUT OF MY HANDS. I WASN'T MAKING ANY DECISIONS; THEY WERE BEING MADE FOR ME. AND SO, TO A CERTAIN DEGREE, I HAD TO GO OUT AND DESTROY MY CAREER SOMEWHAT IN ORDER TO REBUILD IT ... I COULDN'T HAVE SPENT THE REST OF MY LIFE FOLLOWING THE PATHS THAT WERE BEING PRESENTED TO ME, SO I HAD TO START CREATING SOME FOR MYSELF ... AT THE TIME, I HAD STUDIOS TELLING ME I WAS CRAZY. I HAD AGENTS ON MY BACK, PUBLICISTS, FAMILY MEMBERS, EVERYONE SAYING, 'WHAT ARE YOU DOING? YOU SHOULD BE THIS. YOU SHOULD BE THAT. YOU SHOULD FOLLOW THE DOLLAR. FOLLOW THE GLOSS.'

MY LIFE IS TOGETHER, BOTH PROFESSIONALLY AND SOCIALLY. BUT IT'S BEEN A BIG LEARNING PROCESS, AND THERE IS NO YODA—THERE'S NO ONE WHO POINTS YOU IN THE RIGHT DIRECTION. YOU'VE GOT TO FIGURE THAT OUT BY YOURSELF ... IT'S TAKEN A WHILE, BUT IT LOOKS LIKE DOORS ARE OPENING AGAIN.

PEOPLE ALWAYS FEEL COMPELLED TO SUM YOU UP, TO PRESUME THAT THEY HAVE YOU AND CAN DESCRIBE YOU. THAT'S FINE. BUT THERE ARE MANY STORIES INSIDE OF ME, AND A LOT I WANT TO ACHIEVE OUTSIDE OF ONE FLAT NOTE.

To the Ledger family.
Deepest sympathies for the
loss of your beloved son.
Our thoughts are with
you always.

10
OLD MAN RIVER

NOBODY RECOGNISED THE TALL, TATTOOED GUY IN THE RATTY JEANS OR BAGGY SHORTS AND THONGS WHEN HE RODE THE NEW YORK SUBWAY, SHOPPED FOR GROCERIES AROUND HIS BROOKLYN NEIGHBOURHOOD AND CARRIED HIS OWN WASHING TO THE LAUNDROMAT. 'I REALLY APPRECIATE BROOKLYN BECAUSE, QUITE FRANKLY, NO-ONE GIVES A SHIT,' SAID HEATH, REVELLING IN THE ANONYMITY AFTER THE FISHBOWL OF SYDNEY. 'THE BEST THING ABOUT BROOKLYN IS, IT'S REMOVED. I JUST LIVE A REALLY NORMAL LIFE. I KEEP THE HOUSE NICE AND TIDY AND CLEAN, I GO SHOPPING AT THE SUPERMARKET, AND I COOK. I COMMUTE ON THE TRAIN BACK AND FORTH, IN AND OUT OF TOWN, AND I SIT AND OBSERVE ALL THESE PEOPLE AROUND ME, ALL THESE LIVES AND THESE STORIES.

'It's really stimulating, and I feel like I'm really living for the first time. It's wonderful.'

He had three movies screening on consecutive nights at the upcoming 62nd annual Venice Film Festival—*Brokeback Mountain*, *The Brothers Grimm* and *Casanova*—but it was his biggest production that was causing 'just huge amounts of excitement'.

'I can't wait to meet my child,' said Heath.

'We've been preparing, yeah. We're both fit and happy and healthy, and that's all you can ask for.'

The rumours that had begun when Michelle was seen attending evening pre-natal yoga classes in Bondi and reading baby books on the beach while Heath was filming *Candy* were confirmed only when the couple could no longer hide the secret. They stepped out with Michelle's tummy bulging and a big diamond ring on her engagement finger at the Los Angeles premiere of *The Brothers Grimm* in August 2005.

Despite his years in the spotlight, Heath hadn't prepared himself for the media interest in his baby, earning comparisons to an orang-utan after one on-camera interview a few days later, with Australia's *Sunrise* program. He exhibited bizarre behaviour, peeling and eating an orange and answering in monosyllables. It was at the tail end of a round of those quick in-and-out, conveyor-belt interviews that actors have to do, and Heath was supposed to be doing his job and promoting *Lords of Dogtown*. It was his bad manners that became the story, not the movie. The headlines were all about his rudeness.

The next day, he wrote to the reporter, Katherine Tulich, apologising for his behaviour, as he had done before. Blaming dehydration and inexperience, Heath also gave a candid insight into his personal life, and a public glimpse into his softer side. Coupled with that telephone call to the *Daily Telegraph*, it showed he was *trying* to do the right thing by the media even if he didn't always get it right. Unlike other celebrities, he hadn't devised thousands of ways of parrying unwanted questions, something which worked both for him and against him.

Dear Katherine Tulich and all at *Sunrise*,

I am yet to see this interview in which I so rudely avoided questions and proceeded to peel my lunch throughout, but my family being of course affected by the backlash of insults and slander concerning my ways came to me and explained what has been spoken of lately in the Australian press.

I would firstly like to apologise for my lack of enthusiasm to answer questions in the interview. It was one of about sixty television interviews I completed in that sitting, and it sounds like you landed the dud.

I remember peeling that orange and eating it through an interview. In hindsight it probably wasn't a polite thing to do. I was just hungry and dehydrated.

In terms of talking about my private life, you also caught me way back when I wasn't prepared to expose stories about something so special and wonderfully private happening in my life.

I guess a part of me wishes that I'd never have to and that maybe I could protect this special time. I was dreaming. In the end, everyone of course finds out and I'm forced into talking about it.

I'm sorry you were asking me these questions so early and I hadn't figured out a way to speak of it in public. It's something I need to learn.

I'm writing this letter mainly for my family, who have to sit back and hear these insults knowing that I'm nothing of the sort, and in fact at the happiest and most exciting time of my life.

I'm just figuring out how to play this "game". Once again,

I apologise for my terrible interview skills. Next time I'll peel you a slice!

Yours sincerely,

Heath

It was a regrettable incident which obviously played on his mind, because he brought it up again a few months later.

'It was the worst thing I could have done,' he said.

'When it was aired, they had people calling in asking, "Who does he think he is? He should get off his high horse."

'Australians are the world's greatest at cutting you down to size, and I'd better not forget it. I just have to remember not to take myself too seriously.'

But at the time, he just wanted to get back to his new home. Williams had been living in Brooklyn for some time. She had family nearby, and the couple decided to move there, away from the Hollywood hype and the prying paparazzi.

'Heath fell for it as soon as he spent some time there,' Williams said.

They rented a townhouse while Heath had his Los Feliz home on the market. It sold for close to its US$2,795,000 asking price—almost double what he had paid for it five years earlier—to Tony Kanal, bass player for top-selling group No Doubt. Kim Ledger later recalled that Heath had been such a generous host that there had been thirty sets of keys out there to be handed in before the house could be sold.

Heath felt the people of Brooklyn were 'mellow', which was what he needed at this time. In a nesting mood, he bought a corner brownstone close to where the couple had been renting, in the newly hip and leafy area of Boerum Hill. With his quest for privacy now a priority, it was the Thank You for the Trust trust that was listed as the owner of the US$3.5 million house, along with a Jeff Gillman, who was also co-trustee of the trust.

The 1860s house had been completely renovated by its previous owner, Sydney-born actor and nightclub owner Nell Campbell, known as 'Little Nell' and famous for her role as Columbia in the stage production of *The Rocky Horror Show*, and in the later film version. Heath's spacious new four-storey home had the high ceilings that brownstones are known for, thick walls and enough room in the three-car garage for his cars and Harley-Davidson. There was a deck on top of the garage, and a walled-in backyard garden. Just 200 metres away from their affluent street, the area became rundown, with graffiti, derelict buildings and public housing, but that was part of its boho charm.

It was a precious time for Heath and Michelle as they not only got ready for the baby, but got to know each other better. They were still starry-eyed, having met just over a year earlier, during which time Heath had filmed both *Casanova* and *Candy*. One day Michelle wrote 'Old Man River' on his right forearm, and Heath got a local tattoo artist to make it permanent in ink, adding to his body art, which had grown since the original 'KAOS' inside his left wrist.

It would have been fitting to think that 'Old Man River' referred to the words of the famous song, because Heath could be seen as someone who 'mus' know sumpin', but don't say nuthin'. He jes' keeps rollin', he keeps on rollin' along'. But it had more to do with where Heath was at that time of his life, and was inspired by two of his favourite tracks—'Old Man' by Neil Young, and 'River Man', by an artist with whom he admitted he was obsessed, the late Nick Drake.

'It's got a few meanings,' he said of the tattoo.

'They all have many meanings, and I usually get tattoos

when I need to be reminded of something, but the answer I'll give you is that it has nothing to do with the song [Old Man River], I just felt there was something eternal about the phrase, and I feel that I'm at a stage in my life now where life is just about to really speed up and flash by, and so I feel like I am on old man river paddling on a little row boat. That's my answer for today.'

Michelle quickly saw what most of his friends knew: that beneath his all-male, all-Aussie public image, Heath was very vulnerable, which is why Drake held such a fascination for him. He believed the English singer and songwriter was a 'very mysterious figure', and planned to make a movie of his short life—Drake died at the age of twenty-six, overdosing on anti-depressant medication.

On a more upbeat musical note, Heath had called his friend, American musician Ben Harper, as soon as it was confirmed that the couple was having a daughter.

'Heath Ledger called me up and said, "Ben, I'm having a baby, and you need to write a lullaby for my baby girl",' said Harper, who obliged with 'Happy Everafter in Your Eyes'.

At home, Heath and Michelle stuck some early ultrasound pictures up on their fridge. Heath was amazed that the baby's features were already formed: 'It's just two little nostril holes and then the shape of the lips—it's Michelle's mouth. It's so bizarre. These little porcelain lips that are exactly the same shape as Michelle's. It's just adorable.'

He was such a doting dad-to-be that he even wrote a list of things he wanted to say to his child.

'I just need to meet her. I need to hold her,' he said.

He was cooking up a storm, looking after his girlfriend who was 'eating for two'.

'Italian is my forte,' he said.

'I'm into hand-making pasta now, hand-making gnocchi and fettuccine. There's flour everywhere in my kitchen. I like making a mess.'

He and Michelle read literally dozens of baby books, and went to hypno-birthing classes before rejecting the technique, with Heath quipping, 'I don't think we'll be throwing Michelle into a trance.'

They opted for a natural birth with a doula, a non-medical assistant.

When the baby arrived on 28 October weighing 2.83 kilograms, it was Michelle who had picked the name, although it was appropriately Australian.

'I came up with it on the subway one day. It just fell from the sky and into my head. And I love, love the Roald Dahl book *Matilda*,' said Michelle.

'I didn't think about it at the time, but then afterwards, I was like, "Yeah, that's the girl I want: reads lots of books and makes things move with her eyes." That'll be my daughter for sure.'

Kim Ledger confirmed the birth a few days later, saying his son was thrilled by the arrival of Matilda Rose.

'Heath is the cluckiest guy you'll ever meet. He's totally wrapped up in Matilda,' said Kim.

Heath said that like most new fathers, he had never felt so useless as after seeing Michelle give birth.

'For man, birth is the realisation that you're just a hopeless, useless specimen of life and witnessing this innate, primal strength within women can be such an intimidating experience,' he said.

'When you come out of the birthing experience, you actually have a better understanding of how and why men have over-compensated in society by creating battles and wars and steroids, and why they go to the gym. It's because we want to be strong and tough, and we're not. And it's this endless quest to kind of find this strength that can equal women's. Experiencing those nine months with Michelle was incredibly humbling, and I just relinquish all kinds of respect and power to her. She's incredible.'

It didn't take long for the realisation to sink in that babies were hard work, but that the rewards were more than worth it.

'It's going great,' he said, when Matilda was four weeks old.

'It's exhausting, but it's a pleasure waking up to your daughter.

'My life right now is … I wouldn't say reduced to food … but my duties in life are that I wake up, cook breakfast, clean the dishes, prepare lunch, clean those dishes, go to the market, get fresh produce, cook dinner, clean those dishes and then sleep if I can.

'I love it. I actually adore it.'

While his family might have expected Heath to choose his best mate Trevor to be godfather, the intense nature of filming *Brokeback* had forged a powerful bond between Ledger, Williams and Jake Gyllenhaal. Heath asked Jake to be godfather, while Williams asked her 'Dawson's Creek' pal Busy Philipps to be godmother.

'There was never an issue with Trevor over that. Heath explained it to him, his loyalties were unbelievable,' said a family friend.

Matilda's godfather showed his sense of humour: 'Heath and I made love,' said Jake, 'and they ended up having a baby.'

Heath had lived out of a suitcase for years and never really taken root anywhere, but Matilda's birth appeared to go some way to settling his inbuilt restlessness.

'The level of synchronicity that's in my life now, with me and Michelle and now Matilda, had meant it's become everything to me—the most important thing I do,' he said of his new role as a family man.

'My child smiles up at me in the morning and that's it—I feel connected to life; this is what it's all about.'

His professions of happiness were euphoric, almost over-the-top.

'Before I felt I was floating through life, like a ghost—I may not even have existed—and now I feel physical and grounded, and life now is about as real as it gets. There's something very cosmic about the experience of parenthood. Suddenly you get the right perspective and priorities,' he said.

'Becoming a father definitely exceeds all my expectations, but I was always expecting it and a lot from it. It's marvellous—and the most remarkable experience I've ever had.'

His neighbours in Boerum Hill started turning up with casseroles, Heath told *Rolling Stone* magazine. But all of them respected the couple's privacy, and none of them sneaked pictures for which they could have earned thousands. Nor did they sell stories to the media. Heath appreciated that they treated him as just one of them.

'It was very sweet,' he said.

'I made a big feast for them, and we got to know each other.'

He said moving to Brooklyn was the greatest decision they had made.

'We really blend in there. We're friends with all our neighbours, and they come around with lasagnes, and we go to community dinners,' said Heath.

He and Michelle were never going to be into selling 'first pictures' of their baby to the glossy magazines, so when she was sixteen days old, they casually took her out for her first stroll. As Matilda slept in a sling around Michelle's chest, the couple shopped for antiques in Brooklyn, rugged up against the cold and holding takeaway coffees.

He showed a new maturity when he later spoke about how they had decided to deal with photographers wanting to get a picture of Matilda.

'At this point it's about trying to leave her in the dark. Like, if we're out somewhere and there's a camera, trying not to whip her away; trying not to let our anxiety and our panic merge into her,' he said.

'It's important, we're just trying to breathe and keep her relaxed, and keep her unaware of anything uncomfortable in our lives, because it's unfair for that to affect her.'

With no nanny and no family around for those first few weeks, Michelle said it was a unique time.

'The first six weeks of our daughter Matilda's life was this incredibly insular, protected time. It was just he and I and her, living in our new house in Brooklyn. No nanny, no help—not really even any family. A couple of friends came through, but we were really committed to forming a bond just between the three of us,' she said.

'And then that bubble got broken with work. *Brokeback Mountain* was going to come out, and the press stuff started rearing up. But those six weeks were just blissful.'

The first time Ang Lee saw the baby he felt he had helped create, he was thrilled for the couple.

'The baby keeps staring at me. Michelle said she doesn't usually stare at people like that. I said maybe she remembers I am the reason she came into existence,' he said.

Excitement had been building about *Brokeback Mountain* since the Venice Film Festival, where the world got its first glimpse of Ennis Del Mar and Jack Twist. Heath, whose face was on a dozen billboards above the canals and palazzos because of his three high-profile movies, had to tear himself away from Michelle a month before Matilda was born to put in an appearance.

He turned up in his well-worn black suit, tie askew, looking his usual dishevelled self, joining Jake Gyllenhaal, Anne Hathaway and Ang Lee as they took their seats in the Palazzo del Cinema for the highly anticipated premiere of *Brokeback*.

When the lights went up at the end, the audience knew it had seen something extraordinary. The movie took the prestigious top honour, the Golden Lion award, beating out the favourite, George Clooney's slick, black-and-white *Good Night, and Good Luck*, and was already being tipped as an Oscar contender.

Receiving the award, Lee described the movie as 'a great American love story' that is 'unique and so universal'.

Asked which of the three movies he preferred, Heath was diplomatic.

'Well, they were all important for me,' he said.

'I mean obviously *Brokeback Mountain* was an obstacle I felt I could never climb, I could never defeat, that it was too tough, but ultimately decided to do it. And with that I came out with a real sense of accomplishment, which was something that I lacked in the movies that I've done before. I'd never felt that [I'd] accomplished anything.

'But then in both *Brothers Grimm* and *Casanova* there was a lot to enjoy. *Brothers Grimm* was the first time I've been let loose [to] use my kind of frantic energy and twitching and nervousness and clumsiness, and Terry Gilliam is very good at allowing you to do that. He sets you free and creates an environment where you can feel safe enough to be bad—he lets you be bad and he lets you be big, which is fun.

'And with Lasse on *Casanova*, he created such a lovely atmosphere on the set, with such a great group of people, cast and crew, that it really helped the film.'

The eleven-day Venice festival attracts foreign and art-house movies, and foreign movie legends like Roman Polanski. While *Brokeback* was the talk of the event, there was still the question of how mainstream audiences would respond to a western about gay lovers. After all, this was no pistol-packing, John Wayne, right-wing, gunslinging adventure.

In a post-Venice review in the influential trade journal *Variety*, Todd McCarthy described the film as 'an achingly sad tale of two damaged souls whose intimate connection across many years cannot ever be properly resolved', and said it was 'marked by a heightened degree of sensitivity and tact, as well as an outstanding performance from Heath Ledger'.

London's *Daily Telegraph* said that despite spending the movie muttering to himself, Heath's performance 'has a cumulative, moving power. *Brokeback Mountain* takes its own sweet time unfolding, but its emotional impact is extraordinary.'

It would be the end of November before the general public got to see it, after the film had done the rounds of the film festivals. It opened in LA on 30 November and New York on 6 December 2005, part of the pre-Christmas Oscar rush—to qualify for an Academy Award the movie must have screened in the US before Christmas. Heath and Michelle's Brooklyn neighbours were among the first to see it when Heath gave them tickets to the star-studded New York premiere.

Sure enough, *Brokeback Mountain* challenged a few conventions in the American wild west, where a few testosterone-fuelled locals got all het-up.

'They've gone and killed John Wayne,' one Wyoming cowboy was reported as moaning.

Christian fundamentalist groups protested, and some cinemas in Washington and Utah banned the film, with West

Virginia considering a ban, leaving the other cinemas laughing all the way to the bank as audiences flocked to see it anyway.

Nor did the people of Childress, location of a famous bar scene in *Brokeback*, get to see the movie. It didn't play in the town's one theatre, the Lone Star 4, because of its content.

'We're a real small community with a lot of church presence,' said Vince LaCario, owner of the Lone Star.

'I'm afraid it would shake up some turmoil.'

Heath thought it was all too much hype.

'The fact that it's controversial is a little silly. Whether or not it's controversial is relative to the kind of person you are,' he said.

'I don't think the topic is controversial at all. It got a little out of hand, but I am glad the movie has transcended the gay cowboy title, and people are just seeing it as a beautiful love story.'

He labelled the bans as immature and unnecessary.

'I think it's proven to have the opposite effect. All of the American states, besides the odd one here and there, have ended up seeing it. It seems to have proven everyone wrong,' he said.

Then he put his foot in his mouth—again.

'I heard that West Virginia was going to ban it, but that's a state that was lynching people only twenty-five years ago, so that's to be expected,' said Heath. The last lynching in the state was in 1931.

But *Brokeback Mountain* was already on its way to becoming a phenomenon. Academics and wild west historians came out of the closet, so to speak, to reveal that homosexuality had been an unspoken norm on the American frontier. The *London Times*, which devoted a serious feature to the topic, discovered a 1948 paper on rural homosexuality by Alfred Kinsey. Kinsey, who was famous for his work on human sexuality, noted that a fair bit of it went on among the older males in western rural areas, although the cowboys and lumberjacks themselves were often deeply homophobic. But the fact was that women were scarce, and men were plentiful.

The Village People's Randy Jones said gay cowboys were for real. He revealed that when Heath and Gyllenhaal asked for advice about the love scenes, he told them 'to keep their hats and boots on in bed. The boots are for traction.'

Countless websites devoted to the movie appeared almost overnight, and Gyllenhaal's line 'I wish I knew how to quit you' entered popular culture.

The movie changed the way Heath was seen as an actor, catapulting him into the stratosphere. The *New York Times* reviewer Stephen Holden said Heath 'magically and mysteriously disappears beneath the skin of his lean, sinewy character'.

'It is a great screen performance, as good as the best of Marlon Brando and Sean Penn,' said Holden.

Annie Proulx was expansive in her praise of Heath's portrayal of Ennis Del Mar.

'Heath Ledger erased the image I had when I wrote it,' she said. 'He was so visceral. How did this actor get inside my head so well? He understood more about the character than I did. This isn't nice for a 70-year-old woman to say, but it was a skullfuck.'

The US film critic Peter Traver called Heath's 'magnificent' performance an acting miracle.

'He seems to tear it from his insides. Ledger doesn't just know how Ennis moves, speaks and listens; he knows how he breathes. To see him inhale the scent of a shirt hanging in Jack's closet is to take measure of the pain of love lost.'

The *Wall Street Journal* pinpointed Heath's fight to overcome his bimbo image when it said, 'The triumph is that of Heath Ledger, a young Australian who has been known until now as a hunky heart-throb. He's certainly handsome enough here, but in a touchingly bleak, self-contained way.'

The *New York Observer* best summed up everyone's surprised reaction to the movie, albeit in tongue-in-cheek fashion: 'The tales of crusty Manhattan critics spending two hours weeping in the screening rooms are flooding the city; while at a screening yesterday a few could be heard sniffling, one of New York's most jaded reporters admitted afterward that he found it impossible to be cynical about the film—and this admission was somehow even more shocking than tears.'

The Golden Globes are seen as an indicator of the Oscars to come, and Heath was nominated for a Golden Globe as Best Actor. Michelle was also nominated for Best Supporting Actress, Ang Lee for Best Director, Larry McMurtry and Diana Ossana for Best Screenplay—and *Brokeback* for Best Movie.

Inevitably, promotion for the film was tied into two things— gay cowboys and babies. On screen, Heath played a man who couldn't admit his love; off screen, he couldn't stop talking about Michelle and Matilda.

'Every day I fall deeper and deeper in love with both my girls,' he said.

Children do tend to bring a different perspective to life, and hitting the publicity trail with Matilda only a few weeks old took its toll on Heath and Michelle.

'Five weeks after you've had your baby, the mother shouldn't get out of her pyjamas, let alone get out of her house and into the spotlight and answering questions and taking photos,' said Heath.

'I mean, the poor thing is just completely exhausted. I am too, but men aren't allowed to complain, because we're really hopeless and useless. We really do nothing in comparison to what the mothers have to go through.'

He was up by 5.30 a.m. every day, and didn't even mind that a new baby had turned his internal clock on its head.

'The one thing I realised is that before Matilda, we were just sleeping in too long. We were missing out on so much of the day. I get much more done now; I feel more focused,' he said. 'I actually need to go to bed at 9 p.m. now, I feel it in my bones.'

Michelle said she saw herself in a new role—that of the mother of Matilda.

'The difference between the day before I gave birth and the day after is like the old me and the new me,' she said.

'I knew having a baby would work some magic on me. I feel different in my body, and in my mind. And I don't think work will be like therapy anymore—my acting will be more about my characters and less about me.'

The trio joined Michelle's family in Montana, where Heath was hoping for a white Christmas, before being back at their Bronte home in the new year for a summer holiday.

Heath said his hope was to spend as much time in Australia as possible.

'I want to introduce Matilda to the ocean,' he said.

There was a nursery waiting back at Bronte for Matilda, and the house was beginning to look more and more like home, with surfboards and baby gear littering the garage, vying for space with Heath's treasured 1975 Volkswagen Kombi van. The Kombi is the quintessential Aussie pop-top campervan for those endless-summer-style surfing road trips, and Heath was doing it up. He had it painted khaki green and the windows tinted dark among other expensive modifications including a state-of-the-art sound system.

Heath turned the garage into a makeshift film studio for his directing debut, for his friend N'fa's single 'Cause an Effect', the title track of his EP, which was released in April 2006. Heath shot and directed the music video over a day during his stay in January, and edited it later in New York with help from film industry contacts.

He came up with the idea of making N'fa into a voodoo character to convey emotional repression.

'We've been good friends since we were kids, so when he asked me if he could shoot the video, I was like, yeah, sure,' N'fa told Sydney's *Daily Telegraph*.

'The ideas were all his. He ran them by me, but I was like, "Whatever, man, I'm stoked you're making my video".'

Most of the renovations to the Bronte house had been finished, many of them aimed at improving privacy with screens, video surveillance and alarm system, and a rooftop pergola.

The couple planned on staying in Australia for a while, and Heath was upbeat about the future. He told the *Sun-Herald* at the time how *Brokeback Mountain* had changed his life in more ways than one.

'I mean, it's given me an incredible amount of synchronicity. I have these two girls that I fall deeper and deeper in love with daily, and that is, hands down, the greatest gift that I've been given from this. I'll forever be grateful,' he said.

The usually private star even opened up about how being a father was changing the way he looked at life.

'I think you have a certain level of responsibility to "man-up", so to speak. Fatherhood or parenthood is ultimately the most selfless act you can participate in, so in order to be so selfless you have to be healthy-minded and healthy-spirited in order to focus in wholly on this other person and making them happy and safer,' he said.

'So you're forced into ironing out any kinks. That's certainly the way I'm approaching parenthood. I'm not sure if it's the right way, it's just my way.'

He said he had given a lot of thought to how he came over in interviews, saying he wanted to take more control of his image, rather than leaving it to the media to speculate.

'I'm feeling the need to explain myself clearly these days, as opposed to the past where I was more protective and deflective and defensive about my private life, because that just gave everyone else the opportunity to fabricate their own answers to who I am and what my life is,' he said.

'Now I've brought this very special child into my life and I have this very special girl in my life, I don't want them to be misrepresented, or my love for them to be misrepresented either.

'I'd rather explain the way it really is than let other people guess. So you just learn to deal with it, relax with it, be more diplomatic about it, and then hopefully it will relieve you of that stress. Which it has, because I care less about it now, and care more about just being happy with my own family.'

He and Michelle were like a mutual admiration society.

'She is beautiful, she's gorgeous, and I'm so proud of her in this film. She is an incredibly talented actor, and she really shines in this movie—I think she gives the best performance in the film. I'm incredibly proud of her,' he said.

'Michelle's ability to dive deep within her soul never ceased to amaze me. She's a brilliant actress.'

Michelle spoke about how Heath and Jake Gyllenhaal knew their craft.

'My hat is off to both of them; Heath was totally supportive, selfless and helpful [in our scenes together],' she said.

She was referring to Heath as her husband, but neither of them was talking of a wedding.

'I had a few fantasies about a husband and a wedding when I was a little girl. But I'm really happy with things the way they are right now,' Michelle had said at the Toronto premiere of *Brokeback Mountain*.

Heath continued the theme: 'I really don't feel like I need a piece of paper to validate the love I have for her. She's my soul mate, and we couldn't love each other any more.'

For a time, life in Sydney was almost normal, and there appeared to be an uneasy truce between Heath and the paparazzi. He joined mate Russell Crowe and his son Charlie in a box at the Sydney Cricket Ground watching Australian captain Ricky Ponting work his way towards a century against South Africa. He tried to slip into the Flickerfest short film festival at Bondi Pavilion, even approaching the media, who were there covering the event independent of Heath, and asking, 'Where can I buy a ticket?' Of course, as soon as organisers knew that Sydney's hottest Hollywood star was there, they ushered him inside without making him put his hand in his pocket to pay.

Michelle slipped out to go shopping at Bondi Junction and, following the family's decision not to pass on their anxiety regarding photographers to their daughter, was even polite to one of the photographers when he snapped her in the food hall at the David Jones store.

The Australian premiere of *Brokeback Mountain* in Melbourne on 10 January 2006 was a triumph, with over a thousand fans turning up despite the rain, and Heath displaying his new public congeniality.

But he hated the red carpet experience, wherever he was, full stop.

He described it as 'like diving into an Olympic pool, swimming the length underwater, then emerging gasping for breath. It's so noisy that it's quiet, you can't hear; the flashlights are so blinding that it's dark, you can't see.'

So picture the scene three nights later at the highly anticipated premiere of *Brokeback* in Sydney when suddenly, out of that dark, came streams of water aimed at Heath and Michelle. As the couple stopped to talk in front of the bank of photographers, even shaking hands and joking with one of the paparazzi, three grinning rogue photographers led by Peter Carrette fired water pistols at them.

'Hey, hey, what are you doing?' said Heath, putting up his arm to protect himself before ushering Michelle inside. Both of them were soaking wet.

Carrette and his employees Pierre Smithdorf and Guy Finlay—the photographer who had disrupted the last night's filming on *Candy*—said they had staged a 'joke protest' to teach Heath a lesson.

'He keeps spitting at us and kicking in car doors. It is just bad manners, real brat pack sort of stuff, and we are sick of being treated that way. We are not dogs,' said Carrette.

It was an idiotic stunt, but Heath's reaction to it was out of all proportion. He carried on regardless during the premiere, but when he got home to Bronte, he cried.

Kim Ledger said the water pistol episode broke Heath's heart.

'Heath had to go into the cinema and introduce the film soaking wet,' said Kim.

'He cried all night, and he rang me and said, "Dad, that's it—sell the house".'

Kim counselled Heath to give the decision forty-eight hours.

'Two days later he rang me back and said, "Dad, it's been forty-seven hours and fifty-seven minutes—sell the house",' said Kim.

For the past two mornings Heath had woken up to a line of long lenses. Carrette had sent a bunch of flowers to Michelle to apologise, and then turned up with every other photographer to see if she accepted them. She didn't.

'Some [Australian] paparazzi chant at me, "Can't you take it, Heath? You shouldn't be in showbiz if you can't take being followed and photographed. You need us, Heath." No, I freakin' don't,' Heath said.

'The thing is, I can't find anything that interesting about my life. Why follow me around with a camera?'

Less than two weeks after moving back into his luxury home with girlfriend and new baby, and two days after the water pistol soaking, Heath quit Australia for good. Unless he was going to live in a house hidden behind high walls, or a high-rise apartment without balconies, there was no other way he was going to be able to escape the paparazzi.

'I felt so stressed and disheartened. I wanted Michelle to love Australia, but we couldn't live like that,' he said.

'It sucks that I can't live in my own country. We were pursued like aliens.'

For Carrette and his gang, the stunt totally backfired, because it meant they lost one of their biggest cash cows, the man who had helped them make thousands of dollars in photographs.

Australian cinemas were not as wary of showing *Brokeback Mountain* as the American chains had been, but the movie did open on limited screens after a decision by distributor Roadshow, which categorised it as art-house and therefore not suitable for some of the more working-class suburbs.

In the cinemas of Perth, the movie attracted a mixed reaction from Heath's extended family, just as his first gay role in 'Sweat' had. Like many people who didn't even know the star, they had to get over the shock value. His uncle Haydn had to walk out when things began to heat up between Ennis and Jack, and his uncle Mike didn't get past the kissing.

'I have seen it completely since and thoroughly enjoyed it, but yes, there was an initial shock because it was hard to detach myself from Heath,' said Haydn.

Heath's uncle Mike said, 'In the first instance, the kissing is a bit overwhelming, but once you put out of your mind the fact that he's our nephew you enjoy his talent and the story even more.'

Heath was devastated at leaving Australia behind, but the move was good for his Academy Award chances. He was needed back in LA to keep up appearances as part of the run-up to the announcement of Oscar nominees.

Los Angeles Times columnist Tom O'Neil said Heath's absence had been noted.

'His shyness is hurting him. He is pulling out of public appearances, and it's been widely noticed. He's been pulling back when he should be campaigning,' said O'Neil.

When Heath's publicist rang them at 5.30 a.m. New York time, shortly after the early morning announcements in LA, to tell them they had been nominated for his-and-hers Oscars, Matilda had already woken them up three times during the night and they had only just closed their eyes again.

'We gave each other a little kiss and fell back asleep,' said Heath.

He was as tough on himself as ever: 'I never really have great expectations for my work or the movies I'm on. It's a wonderful surprise.'

But as laid-back and egalitarian as Heath was over the fame and award business, even he had to admit to feeling good about the nomination that propelled him into an elite group of actors.

'I think it's a great honour to be in a movie that's been well-received,' he said.

'Michelle and I definitely don't really sit around worrying about it. It's also a little surreal; kind of a strange concept to me that one performance or one movie can be compared or compete against another. It's an award season of opinions, so it's full of a false sense of success and failure.'

By the time the 78th Academy Awards ceremony came around in March, *Brokeback* had already carried off a slew of heavyweight prizes. Heath was named Best Actor by the New York Film Critics Circle, and *Brokeback* took Best Film and Best Director honours. At the British Academy Awards, *Brokeback Mountain* won Best Film, Best Direction and Best Adapted Screenplay, and Jake Gyllenhaal won Best Supporting Actor.

But Philip Seymour Hoffman, who played *In Cold Blood* writer Truman Capote in the film *Capote*, was firming as the favourite to take the Best Actor Oscar away from Heath, after edging him out in other top awards including the Screen Actors Guild awards—a ceremony which Heath stuffed up with more odd behaviour.

He and Gyllenhaal had to read a blurb from an autocue to introduce *Brokeback Mountain*. Most of the 5,798 voting members of the Academy of Motion Picture Arts and Sciences who would decide Heath's fate at the Oscars were probably watching the ceremony, either in the audience or at home. Bizarrely, Heath got a fit of the giggles, and he stood there on stage with his body slumped and his left hand on his hip. It was widely interpreted as a gay spoof.

Yet again, Heath was prompted to apologise for his immature behaviour. He called the *Los Angeles Times*.

'I am so sorry, and I apologise for my nervousness. I would be absolutely horrified if my stage fright was misinterpreted as a lack of respect for the film, the topic and for the amazing filmmakers,' he told the newspaper.

He said that his stance, with his hand on his hip, was normal for him.

'I've stood like that since I was a kid. You can ask my mum. It's nerves, I guess. I'm a very fidgety person, always moving, never able to sit or stand still,' said Heath.

He blamed it all on panic, saying he had asked Gyllenhaal while they were all sitting at the table who would be introducing the movie.

'I leaned over and asked Jake and he said, "*We* are! Didn't you get the script?" I said, "*What?*" I thought it was a script for the Directors Guild Awards a few nights earlier,' said Heath.

'I'm nervous under any circumstances in front of crowds.

'I am not a public speaker and never will be. I was so nervous before the DGA Awards backstage that my jaw was jittering and I could not get the words out. I'm just not one of those naturally funny, relaxed actors who enjoy the spotlight and are so good at it. And this was really weird, because we were basically introducing ourselves; like, here's this brilliant cast and guess what, it's us.'

He said he got the giggles: 'How can you say all that stuff— "two brave cowboys"—with a straight face? It was just so surreal.'

With Hoffman also taking the top prize at the British Academy Awards, the Independent Spirit Awards—which are the art-house equivalent of the Oscars—the LA Film Critics Association Awards and the Golden Globes, it at least it took the heat off Heath for the Oscars on 5 March. He knew he was up against it with Hoffman's performance, and said he already felt a sense of achievement.

'We've already done our job. The success for us is that Annie Proulx … wrote us all letters approving of our performances. That was the best feeling, pleasing her. To do that was about as successful as you could get.'

Michelle's mum, Carla, said she got the best job—babysitting her four-month-old granddaughter for the night as Heath and Michelle stepped out for the ultimate red carpet moment at Tinseltown's Kodak Theatre.

At least Heath was among friends, with his ex, Naomi Watts, as one of the presenters along with fellow Aussies Russell Crowe, Eric Bana and Nicole Kidman. His dad Kim was in the audience, hoping to see his son win. As for Heath, he said, 'I'm looking forward to it—and it being over so I can relax.'

Brokeback Mountain was widely considered to be the front-runner for the Best Picture Oscar, and was also up for another seven nominations, for Best Actor, Best Actor in a Supporting Role, Best Actress in a Supporting Role, Best Director, Best Original Score, Best Adapted Screenplay and Best Cinematography. Heath turned up looking the part in a tux and bow tie—although his hair could have done with a brush—but walked away empty-handed when Hoffman took the top award. Of its eight nominations, *Brokeback* won only three—Best Director for Ang Lee, Best Original Score for Gustavo Santaolalla and Best Adapted Screenplay for Larry McMurtry and Diana Ossana. It lost for Best Picture to the LA-set crime drama *Crash*, which pulled off one of the biggest upsets in Oscar history.

If Heath felt let down after the huge build-up, he didn't show it as he headed off to the glitzy Vanity Fair party at Morton's restaurant with a cheeky two-finger salute over his shoulder to the photographers. There he mixed with the rest of the guests including Kidman and husband Keith Urban, Madonna, Joaquin Phoenix, Lindsay Lohan and Mick Jagger, who had met Heath after inviting him to the party for the launch of one of his solo albums a few years earlier. Heath made a beeline for one of his other favourite singers, the rapper Eve, grabbing her hand and chatting for a while.

Heath and Michelle quickly moved on from the disappointment, snuggling up at the basketball match between the LA Lakers and the San Antonio Spurs, but Larry McMurtry couldn't hide his disappointment that *Brokeback* didn't win Best Picture.

'Perhaps the truth really is, Americans don't want cowboys to be gay,' he said.

Annie Proulx, however, wanted to have the final say. In a passionate piece in the *Guardian* newspaper a few days later, Proulx wrote what she acknowledged was a 'Sour Grapes Rant'.

'When Jack Nicholson said best picture went to *Crash*, there was a gasp of shock, and then applause from many—the choice was a hit with the home team since the film is set in Los Angeles. It was a safe pick of "controversial film" for the heffalumps,' she said.

'None of the acting awards came *Brokeback*'s way, you betcha. The prize, as expected, went to Philip Seymour Hoffman for his brilliant portrayal of Capote, but in the months preceding the awards thing, there has been little discussion of acting styles and various approaches to character development by this year's nominees.

'Hollywood loves mimicry, the conversion of a film actor into the spittin' image of a once-living celeb. But which takes more skill, acting a person who strolled the boulevard a few decades ago and who left behind tapes, films, photographs, voice recordings and friends with strong memories, or the construction of characters from imagination and a few cold words on the page?'

Brokeback Mountain went on to become the fifth-highest-earning western of all time, taking $175 million at the global box office and adding to Heath's bank accounts, as he had taken a share of profits.

As for Heath, he put his house in Bronte on the market as it was, without moving Matilda's baby things from the garage floor, or taking the Lambretta he had bought Michelle, or moving his and Michelle's clothes out of the wardrobes or their books from the shelves.

Just months after saying he wanted to spend as much time as he could in Australia, Heath walked away and closed the door on that part of his life.

⊞

11
WRESTLING
WITH
HEARTACHE

AMERICAN MUSICIAN BEN HARPER HAD JUST BROUGHT OUT HIS DOUBLE ALBUM 'BOTH SIDES OF THE GUN' AND WAS PREPARING FOR A WORLDWIDE TOUR WITH HIS BAND, THE INNOCENT CRIMINALS, TO SUPPORT ITS RELEASE WHEN HIS MATE HEATH LEDGER GAVE HIM A CALL. 'HEATH RANG AND SAID, "COME OVER, I HAVE A PIANO FOR YOU", SAID HARPER. HARPER AND HIS ACTOR WIFE LAURA DERN, WHO HAD STARRED WITH NAOMI WATTS IN *WE DON'T LIVE HERE ANYMORE*, HAD JUST MOVED INTO A NEW HOUSE, AND THEY FOUND A SPOT FOR THE GRAND PIANO. 'I'VE BEEN PLAYING IT A LOT. I'M VERY EXCITED ABOUT BECOMING PROFICIENT,' SAID HARPER.

The gift was both a sign of Heath's wonderful generosity to his friends and his growing interest in music—as well as playing the didgeridoo and guitar, he was learning to play the piano himself, and wanted to spent more time directing music videos, following on from the first one he had done for N'fa.

'I think that music became more important to him because he could do something creative without it costing him his privacy. He could be more in the background. He could be in charge, but invisible,' said Michelle.

After the drama of quitting Bronte and the Oscars, Heath had spoken about taking time out for twelve months to let Michelle work.

'I'll be Mr Mum. It's something very important to me,' he said.

Heath told *Newsweek* magazine of his plans: 'As a dad, I've been trying to work as little as possible, to devote myself to Michelle and Matilda. All you can do is give your child an infinite amount of love and space and creativity, and defend her from pains and keep her fearless.'

He seemed content with their new, humdrum days, when he and Michelle would wheel Matilda down to the shops near their Brooklyn home in her baby Wallabies jumper, a gift from Aussie friends. He described his life in the suburb as like living on an island, so insulated was it.

'It's the usual stuff,' Heath said, 'very simple things. If we need laundry, we pay the laundromat. If the house needs food, I go get groceries. At the end of the day, we put her down and it's mum or dad time. We'll watch a movie, or go and have a date.'

And he spoke of their dreams for a big family: 'Six, that's close to the figure we're talking about. We feel like it's ideal. That's like our magic number.'

Heath also spoke about taking two years off to indulge his

twin passions of painting and photography—or his dream of moving to Europe.

'I have kind of been living out of bags for the past thirteen years,' said Heath. 'Home is like, Earth. I don't care where I land. I am actually thinking of going to live in Italy. The food and the wine are great. That's it, really. Oh, we have a couple of plans; we have a few places up our sleeves.'

Their Brooklyn brownstone was only two blocks south of the Smith Street shopping district, and Heath liked to walk Matilda down to the French-inspired Bar Tabac, where he would order two beers.

'The old ladies would fawn over his daughter. They had no idea who he was,' one barman said.

Heath and a group of friends would turn up at one of the several bars in Brooklyn where patrons can have a beer and play a rowdy game of bocce. Bocce New York style was a lot different to the game as played in a peaceful Italian village square.

Early mornings would see Heath down at Manhattan's Washington Square Park playing chess, winning a couple of dollars, losing a couple of dollars and having fun at the game he had played since a kid. It was about the only time that he sat still.

One of the regulars, Earl Biggs, sixty-three, said Heath got into good-natured verbal duels with his rivals.

'Heath would just come around and jump into a game. People walking by didn't bother him,' Biggs said.

'We'd talk trash talk at the chess table ... We'd say things to him like, "How can you make that move! How can you make a move like that!!!" And he'd just laugh.'

Heath and Michelle even came to a kind of truce with the local photographers who wanted pictures of their little girl. In a flower store one day, Heath saw that they had been spotted by a photographer. He grabbed a flower and ran outside.

'If I give you this flower, please, please, please do not take a photo of our daughter,' said Heath.

'He didn't want to take it, but eventually took the flower and put his camera away and jumped in his car and left us, which was really nice of him.'

With others, Heath did crafty deals so that he owned the copyright to the pictures that were released, as is done with many so-called 'candid' shots of movie stars. He was trying to beat his paranoia about being photographed, while at the same time still fiercely protective of both his girls.

Heath had joined Abbie Cornish in February 2006 to promote *Candy* at the Berlin Film Festival. With *Brokeback Mountain* under his belt and the energy of a new baby daughter in his life, Heath showed that he was not only on top of the world—he was prepared to play the leader of the western world.

'I can generally identify with everyone. I could totally identify with George Bush if I had to,' he told the media, despite the personal stand he had taken against America's intrusion into Iraq.

'I can be sympathetic towards any person and figure them out enough to play them and love them as human beings. I know how to breathe and so do they, so that's at least one way I can relate to them.'

But he couldn't love the Sydney paparazzi. When *Candy* premiered in Australia in May, Heath didn't make the trip to Sydney to appear on the red carpet. While his publicist cited 'other commitments', his no-show was widely interpreted as a result of the water pistol soaking he endured at the *Brokeback* premiere.

Candy producer Margaret Fink hit out at the paparazzi 'jerks'.

'Why would he want to come out here when people behave like that towards him? He was quite rightly infuriated,' said Fink.

It was his fear of the Australian paparazzi that halted plans by *Candy* director Neil Armfield and Heath for him to perform on stage as Hamlet.

Heath decided he just didn't want the stress, preferring to stay in the comfortable cocoon of life with Michelle and Matilda.

With no base in LA since Heath sold his Los Feliz mansion, the family had been forced to stay in hotel suites whenever they visited the west coast for work, so they decided to look for a new house there—a place where they could hide away, where they didn't have to walk through a crowded lobby whenever they wanted to come or go.

'Whether we like it or not, we go in and out of LA all the time,' said Heath.

One hotelier, Jeff Klein, revealed how Heath was perved at by an elderly gay man, who had seen him in *Brokeback Mountain*, while he stayed at Klein's Sunset Tower, a landmark art deco place. The man was an event planner who Klein was hoping to do business with. Heath dealt with it with his innate sense of humour.

'Ledger passed by us in the lobby and with all the confidence that only someone truly comfortable with their sexuality could muster, he winked at the event planner, who just about fainted. Needless to say, I snagged the very lucrative event, thanks to Ledger's flirtatiousness,' said Klein in a blog.

In Sydney, Heath's Bronte house had sold for $7 million, around $500,000 short of the asking price, but still a massive profit for Heath, even taking into account the extensive renovations. In the first ten days after the 'For Sale' sign went up, 16,390 people had logged on to the house on the website www.realestate.com.au to have a virtual look inside. Heath had also sold his Aston Martin in Australia, and gave his Kombi van to his friend Trevor to look after.

Cashed up, he and Michelle found their new home, hidden

away in the Hollywood Hills—a place called 'The Treehouse' because it was built around a hundred-year-old sycamore tree. The house was behind walls, protected by a security gate, surrounded by high hedges and overlooked half an acre of woods—and unlike the Bronte house, could not be seen by the lenses of photographers. The $2.3 million house was on Woodrow Wilson Drive in a celebrity neighbourhood that attracted music industry types.

They bought it from talk show host Ellen DeGeneres and her Aussie partner Portia de Rossi, who had fully renovated the house just two years earlier in what a real estate agent called 'a Zen meets 1950s modern feel'. The concrete and teak house, built in 1951, was open plan, with giant outdoor terraces for entertaining. The main bathroom had a Japanese theme, with floor to ceiling glass on two sides overlooking fern gardens, and there were giant bronze Buddhas throughout the home.

Again, the house was bought by Heath's Thank You for the Trust trust, and this time LA lawyer Layne Dicker was listed as the co-owner. It was the first place Heath had bought since Kim Ledger had handed over control of the burgeoning multi-million-dollar empire earlier that year. Kim said they had discussed it while he was in America for the Oscars.

'We both agreed that Heath should handle things; it was one of the reasons I went over there,' said Kim, who said it had brought him and Heath closer than ever.

'Heath has Michelle and Matilda in his life now, and it's right for him to have charge of his own destiny.'

Kim had arranged for Heath to deal directly with the team of accountants, lawyers and banks that handled Kim's affairs. Heath's sister Kate had also stopped handling his media, which took a lot of pressure off their relationships.

'It's great because when Heath rings up me or his sister, we talk about family matters rather than business,' said Kim.

Unlike Heath's expansive Los Feliz mansion, The Treehouse had just two bedrooms and two bathrooms, but it fit his life at that time.

'Michelle and I really appreciate small spaces now. Our lives feel smaller. We're far away from everything else. It helps us survive,' he said.

Comedian Will Ferrell rented the place next-door, while Kirsten Dunst and Matthew McConaughey lived nearby. When Heath and Michelle threw a housewarming, DeGeneres and de Rossi were there, along with Aussie sports reporter Lee Furlong and her friend, Olympic swimmer Ian Thorpe. By all reports, it was a rowdy night and Heath showed that he was a good neighbour by taking around champagne to the people next-door the morning after.

DeGeneres was impressed with Heath's eye for decorating.

'I love buying houses and fixing them up, and Heath and Michelle lived in a house that I did. But Heath had such amazing taste—in art, in furniture. He loved that place so much. And I think he loved what I made, and then he made it better,' she told *Interview* magazine.

They had met when she persuaded Heath to appear on her TV talk show earlier in the year, and they did a memorable scene in a bobsled in front of a backdrop that made it look as if they were doing a run down a mountain. Heath, who had appeared nervous and typically did not know what to do with his hands during the interview, was hilarious as he ad-libbed in the back of the bobsled, juggling oranges, reading a book and napping while they were supposed to be racing dangerously. He was transformed when he was able to play someone other than himself.

He even laughed, which was unusual for him in an interview situation.

'When he walked out the first time, I could tell that he was uncomfortable,' said DeGeneres. 'But I thought he was very cool in a very unaffected way. Heath clearly could become anything he wanted to become—you can look at his body of work and see that he's an incredible actor. But he didn't try to be something that he wasn't. And I appreciated that.'

Heath and his little family appeared to slip seamlessly into their part-time LA lifestyle. As usual, he had a community of friends, many of them Australian, including Ian Thorpe, who had moved in five minutes up the road from Heath in Laurel Canyon, and had been drafted in by Heath and his friend from *Ned Kelly*, Joel Edgerton, for their Sunday soccer games in a local park.

'I couldn't ask for better timing in my life,' Heath said. 'Any hype of excitement around work doesn't mean anything. Having this child has taken any pressure off my shoulders in terms of what people think of the movies. It doesn't matter.'

Surrounded by Heath's Australian friends, who dropped in to stay with them whether in LA or New York, Michelle had become an honorary Aussie.

'Our love for each other grows. We had a really good relationship [before Matilda] and we still love, respect and are patient with each other. Even with all the new demands, pressures and challenges, we still work really well together, and it doesn't break us.'

And Matilda, he said, was 'adorable and beautifully observant and wise. Michelle and I love her so much.'

But not even Matilda could tame his restless nature for long. Heath found it impossible not to do a million things at once.

'He was good at sports. He was good at directing. He was

good at painting. He was good at taking pictures. He was good at building things,' said Michelle, who had to live with his hyperactive nature.

'It could be infuriating to a lot of his friends—I mean, he had a talent for everything that he put his mind to, pretty much, so he didn't know limits. Maybe he had never been told that he couldn't do something, so everything was possible for him.'

She later revealed the downside of a mind that never stopped. For as long as they had been together, Heath had battled insomnia.

'He had uncontrollable energy. He buzzed,' said Michelle.

'He would jump out of bed. For as long as I'd known him, he'd had bouts with insomnia. He just had too much energy. His mind was turning, turning, turning—always turning.'

In fact, he was so wound up that the only way to slow down was to smoke dope, as he had done from his schooldays and which friends said he did throughout his life. 'Every time I saw him,' said one.

A secret tape which later emerged of Heath at a Hollywood drug party confirmed this when he was filmed admitting his own drug use. The heavily edited video, shot through the window of a room at celebrity hangout Chateau Marmont after the Screen Actors Guild Awards in January 2006, shows Heath full of guilt at even being at the party.

'I'm going to get serious shit from my girlfriend,' he says.

'We just had a baby three months ago. I shouldn't be here at all.'

Michelle was said to be in their Chateau Marmont bungalow asleep with Matilda at the time. The video was obviously a set-up, but while other people in the room are apparently snorting cocaine, there is nothing to show Heath using hard drugs.

WRESTLING WITH HEARTACHE 239

But he tells his companions, 'I used to smoke five joints a day for five years'.

It might go some way to explaining his bizarre giggling on stage earlier that evening, when he was introducing *Brokeback*.

Being back in LA without any pressing movie commitments allowed Heath to develop his twin interests in music and directing.

He had been on the outskirts of an art collective and production company called the Masses since it was launched in 2002 by a friend of his, Matt Amato. It was a loosely formed group of alternative musicians, directors, writers, photographers and producers, drawn together by an interest in telling stories in different ways.

Amato and Heath had met back when Heath first arrived in Hollywood on the arm of Lisa Zane. Zane had been sharing a Spanish-style apartment on South Orange Drive with Amato and Amato's then boyfriend, artist Andrew Campbell, for years, and eighteen-year-old Heath moved in. It was a full-on welcome to the LA scene.

When Heath got his first video camera, Matt Amato said he taught him how to edit the footage on equipment in a studio in his apartment, which the collective dubbed Orange Avenue Studios. The studio was still on the go when Heath wanted to do more work on the other side of the camera and teamed up with Ben Harper to direct a music video for Harper's track 'Morning Yearning'.

Harper was someone else Heath had got to know when he was just fresh in Hollywood. They met at the El Rey Theatre, the art deco live music venue, in November 2001 when they were both on the invite list to the party to launch Mick Jagger's solo album 'Goddess in the Doorway'.

The two men became closer through Naomi Watts and Laura Dern, with the two couples attending the 2004 Sundance Film Festival together when *We Don't Live Here Anymore* was showing— but their friendship outlived Heath's relationship with Watts.

Ellen DeGeneres recalled the day that Heath and Harper made the video, and the way he never stopped.

'He and Michelle came over to the house once, and they were really late because he was directing a Ben Harper video. He was coming straight from that, and he was telling us about it, and how much he loved it. And then we played poker and he proceeded to take all of our money,' she said. 'He was good at everything he did.'

While Heath was editing the Ben Harper video at Matt Amato's apartment, it became clear to him that without any corporate structure, and with little cash flow, the collective was floundering. He came to the rescue and offered to set up an office for them.

'He said, "I want everything that's in your office at home to be there",' said Amato.

Heath invested both time and money into the collective, becoming one of their directors. Their office was in Hancock Park, Hollywood, and Heath's involvement helped the group both create a structure and start paying staff, like Sara Cline who became the Masses' executive producer.

'The company started as a dream,' said Cline.

'Heath kind of came in and made that dream a reality. We were all, literally, living the dream of working in a collective of artists, where everyone had great respect for each other's work and talent, but we also had this great force behind us to actually make things happen.'

Heath's vision transformed the Masses. He brought in wild-life film-maker Tristan Bayer with the intention of making a documentary on the controversial anti-whaling group the Sea Shepherd Conservation Society, and their charismatic leader, the self-styled pirate Paul Watson. Heath planned to produce the documentary and shoot some of the footage.

'He wanted to be on the boat with the video camera in his hand, ramming the Japanese boats, swimming with the whales. He wanted to be part of the crew,' said Bayer.

Heath had also started working on an animated video for the alternative rock band Modest Mouse, which showed whales fishing from a boat and harpooning humans to feed to their offspring.

Masses designer, the Italian artist Daniel Auber, said Heath wasn't the company's boss, but more of a patron of the arts.

'It felt like that, but in a really natural way. It was completely spontaneous—and so much fun. The Masses was a shelter from the bad side of Hollywood,' said Auber.

So Heath was immersed in music and directing when he began his next movie—as a young Bob Dylan in *I'm Not There*.

'Music, on so many levels, has affected my life, and still continues to … particularly a voice singing, songwriters, poets, Dylan, whoever … to me it's such a pure expression of a song from the soul that deeply connects to mine,' he told *Cinema Confidential*.

'It's always been a key that unlocked or enabled me to express anger or pains of any sort. So it's always been a wonderful excuse or door opener for me in terms of being able to express, creatively and personally.'

While they didn't seek out his-and-hers parts in movies, Michelle had been cast as Coco Rivington, the Edie Sedgewick-like underground ingenue who hung around Dylan when he was in his wild, electric and drugged-up years.

Michelle liked smaller, indie films with roles she could put her own spin on.

'Where do they come from?' she said of her characters. 'It's an absolute culmination of everything in your life until then, of poetry, of music, of other films, interviews, essays; it's like everything comes together.'

Like Heath, she shunned Hollywood-style action flicks.

'I think I would do really bad at it. Acting with an alien or acting with a gun … I'll read those scripts, but I just can't see myself there, and I don't think I would serve the story better than anyone else could. That's just not for me right now,' said Michelle.

In director Todd Haynes's strange biopic, there are six Dylans, each one reflecting a part of his personality, and none of them called Bob Dylan, or even Robert Zimmerman. All had been cast. Christian Bale, who had worked with Haynes before on the movie *Velvet Goldmine*, about glam rock in the early seventies, played Dylan in his early folk years as a character called Jack Rollins; Marcus Carl Franklin played Dylan as a black boy growing up in the south who names himself after his hero Woody Guthrie; Richard Gere played him as a kind of Billy the Kid character; Ben Whishaw, as a French symbolist poet; and Cate Blanchett was outstanding as the electric Dylan, and the only one of the actors who actually gets to look like Dylan. Michelle Williams played the Blanchett character's lover.

Irish actor Colin Farrell was cast as the 'Robbie Clark' stage of Dylan's life: 'the media superstar, a charismatic, swaggering figure who parties with celebrities, wears look-at-me-but-leave-me-alone sunglasses, and watches his personal life collapse under the pressures of his public persona'.

In his role of 'Mr Mum', Heath was going to be accompanying Michelle and Matilda to Montreal, where the movie was being shot, so he thought he would see if there was a spare acting role going.

'I said to my agent, "Is there something I can do on it? I'm going to be there anyway, looking after Matilda",' said Heath.

When Farrell had to drop out to go into rehab for addiction to prescription drugs, Heath was hired to play Robbie Clark.

The movie was shot between July and September 2006. Heath and Michelle set up home in an apartment in Montreal, travelling to and from New York as each of them was needed on set, and trying to make sure one of them was always with Matilda, who was by then walking and 'babbling as if we should understand her', Heath told a reporter.

'She's such an awesome, beautiful little girl that Michelle and I hate spending five minutes away from her, never mind five months, so [the work] has to be really, really worth it,' he said.

Like the other actors playing an aspect of Dylan, Heath received his section of the script bound separately, with a CD of the music of Dylan's that was pertinent to that time in his life. Dylan gave his blessing to the movie, and authorised Haynes to use his songs—there are thirty-eight of them on the soundtrack, twenty-three of which are Dylan's recordings. The actors weren't told to impersonate him, but to use his cadences, looks and styles.

'Essentially, Todd dissected Bob, and I was like an amputated limb,' said Heath. 'So I was just concentrating on one arm of Bob Dylan, essentially.'

Heath always got nervous, excited and anxious before beginning a new movie.

'I go into a movie thinking that I'm hopeless, and I don't know how to do it anymore, and I've forgotten it,' he said.

'And this time I hadn't worked in a year and a half, so it was worse. But Todd's such a wonderful man, and I was only working twelve days, so I was put to ease pretty quickly.'

It was the first time Heath worked with the man who would be his Batman co-star, Christian Bale. In the movie, Heath's Dylan character Robbie Clark makes his name playing Bale's Dylan character Jack Rollins in a movie. Heath filmed his scenes before Bale did his. Heath was, he said, faced with 'playing an actor portraying a Dylanesque character, and not being sure what Christian was going to do'. Or, as he put it, 'Who was I playing when I was acting?'

'I stressed out a little too much,' he said.

Heath didn't hide the fact that he was having trouble sleeping, and it became obvious that he was also plagued with crippling insecurities, possibly because he was so hard on himself: he never thought he was good enough. One stage of filming, when Michelle had returned to Brooklyn with Matilda, was particularly trying for Heath, who hated being alone.

'The night before we were going to shoot a scene, he started to have a real panic about it,' Haynes revealed.

'He had to call Michelle in New York, who talked him through relaxation methods to try to get him asleep. He said he was just curled up in a corner holding one of Matilda's stuffed animals, and he slept about an hour and came on set,' said Haynes.

The list of directors that Heath would have liked to work with was pretty exclusive—Federico Fellini, John Cassavetes, Bob Fosse, Stanley Kubrick and Terrence Malick. As for Haynes, Heath was attracted by his 'wildly ambitious and incredibly creative' approach to movie-making.

'You get a sense that he's really reinventing film,' said Heath, displaying a wide-eyed enthusiasm for it all.

'The crew are working 20-hour days, and they don't complain, and afterward they all meet up in the camera truck for an extra hour to drink beer and watch the dailies, because they're so blown away with what he's doing. They're saying, "Fellini's been resurrected". It's really sweet, everyone's trying to pour themselves into it … because they believe in him. It's feeling like the world's most expensive student film, in the most beautiful possible way.'

In turn, Haynes was impressed with Heath's input on set.

'He loved the idea of being around like-minded, creative people and doing work as a group. He [was involved with] this company, the Masses, which was kind of a troupe of people who did communal creative work, and I think he thrived in that.'

Heath's fascination with Haynes's work grew as he saw how each section was filmed in a different style—for Heath's Robbie Clark section, the inspiration was Jean-Luc Godard.

'[Godard] favoured static shots. He would intercut long angles that would hold, and let action play within them, with these tight close-ups. His framings are so beautiful, so clean and spare,' said Haynes.

Montreal's Museum of Fine Arts stood in for New York's Metropolitan Museum of Art for some scenes, and for Paris's Louvre in others. Haynes found it tough to get permission to film inside the museum, and admitted to pulling every string and using every connection he had.

'We finally got the okay after Heath posed for a photo with the museum director,' said Haynes.

When *I'm Not There* was released in November 2007, Haynes's abstract treatment of Dylan's life received rave reviews.

'It's brilliant, demanding, exasperating; it's undramatic but absorbing, more enigmatic than revealing, up itself and wildly inventive. It's fun, confusing and some of it is just plain obscure. He's not there? Well, where the hell is he?' said the *Sydney Morning Herald*'s critic Paul Byrnes.

Rolling Stone loved it: 'It's a feast for the eyes, the ears and the

Dylanologist scratching around our minds and hearts. And, get this, never once does Haynes mention the name of the mesmeric changeling at his film's centre.'

Almost universally, reviewers singled out Blanchett's Dylan character for praise, but many, including the *Times* in London, recognised the contribution of the other Dylans.

'Everyone takes on a name, job, and demeanour that is only inches away from the musician's public life. Christian Bale, Ben Wishaw and Heath Ledger are unspeakably brilliant as various shades of Dylan,' said James Christopher.

'They wrestle with Nixon, fame, drugs, Christianity and celebrity, more often than not in ravishing black and white. They are mostly trapped in ghastly interviews. The television footage is extraordinary.'

As usual, Heath was his own harshest critic.

'I can't say I was proud of my work. I feel the same way about everything I do. The day I say "It's good" is the day I should start doing something else.'

When *I'm Not There* started filming, Heath and Michelle were apparently living happily in Montreal and New York, deeply in love and enjoying their 'awesome, beautiful little girl'. By the time the film premiered, Michelle was avoiding the after-party because Heath was going. What had gone wrong?

In December 2006, Heath was alone when he flew to Sydney for the Australian Film Institute Awards. It had been a vintage year for Australian film production, and *Candy* was one of four exceptional movies nominated for the top award. It was vying for Best Film with

Ten Canoes, the first feature-length film in an Aboriginal language; *Kenny*, a mockumentary about a philosophical plumber who installs portable toilets at outdoor events; and *Jindabyne*, set in the New South Wales Snowy Mountains town of the same name, which follows the ripple effect of a murder.

Heath had been nominated for Best Lead Actor and his *Candy* co-star Abbie Cornish for Best Lead Actress.

He turned up with his sister Kate as his date, and showed how good a sport he was when he was single-handedly mobbed by comedian Magda Szubanski as he was being interviewed on the red carpet. Szubanski then turned up onstage in the character of Sharon Strzelecki, who she played in the TV comedy 'Kath and Kim', to present the News Limited Readers' Choice Award—which went to Heath. He was laughing, and clearly having a good night.

Heath missed out on the Best Lead Actor award, which went to Shane Jacobson, who played the plumber in *Kenny*.

'It's like comparing Mr Ed to Phar Lap,' said Jacobson of his surprise win. 'I feel like a poodle in a room full of lions.'

But Heath was soon back up onstage receiving an award that was being given for the first time, the AFI International Award for Best Actor, for his role as Ennis Del Mar in *Brokeback*.

'Oh, God, this film won't go away,' he joked, when accepting the award.

'The best thing I got out of it was my two girls. I made out with Jake Gyllenhaal, and I got a daughter.'

Ten Canoes won Best Picture while *Candy* took only one award—Best Adapted Screenplay for Luke Davies and Neil Armfield.

Australian acting friends who caught up with Heath at the awards said he was 'on cloud nine'.

'He was so much in love with Michelle and Matilda. He was telling me that I should do it, have kids,' said Steve Le Marquand.

A week later, Michelle and Matilda joined Heath in Perth for the evening wedding of Kim to his long-term partner Ines, an event that was kept so secret that not even the kitchen staff at the reception venue knew who they were cooking for. Heath turned up with a camera to capture the event for himself.

In hindsight, Heath's gushing comments about Michelle to friends at the AFI Awards may seem strange, given that just two months later it emerged that their relationship was in deep trouble.

The *New York Daily News* quoted sources as saying that Heath had gone out by himself on Valentine's Day 2007 to Teddy's nightclub in Hollywood's classy Roosevelt Hotel, where he was 'surrounded by women', and that Michelle was furious.

'They had a huge fight and they're not speaking,' said a source.

But the evidence is that it was Heath who wanted to keep the relationship going, and Michelle who could no longer cope with his highs and lows. It seems that he did not want to admit even to himself that it was all going wrong. He wanted it to work.

Michelle's publicist Mara Buxbaum, who also represented Heath and, later, Kim Ledger, denied a report in *US Weekly* magazine after Heath's death that Michelle had tried to drop Heath off at a Malibu rehab clinic in 2006.

While that report is unsubstantiated, someone close to the couple has confirmed that Michelle had told Heath to clean up his drug-taking, although whether that was just his dope-smoking or rumoured cocaine use remains unclear.

'His drug problem was out of control, and she told him it wasn't good for Matilda, and it was not good for her, and he had to clean himself up. The ball was in his court. She would have him back only when he got himself under control,' said the reliable source.

The couple didn't confirm their split until August 2007.

Michelle's father, Larry Williams, who was still stuck in Sydney because of his US tax evasion charges, said his heart went out to them at this 'hugely difficult time of their lives'.

'We've known about their troubles for a while, but it's always a very difficult thing in life when these things happen,' Williams told Sydney's *Daily Telegraph*.

'I know Heath and Michelle still care about each other deeply, and are very committed to being great parents to their daughter.

'You can never be stunned by what happens in Hollywood. I learned that when we were dealing with Michelle's career when she was younger. Michelle was grown-up at sixteen, and, just like Heath, her life has had an extremely fast pace to it.

'But they are both very talented artists, and they live with their hearts. I feel tremendously for her, and for him, and hope they will find what they want in life.'

Michelle later revealed how hard the split had been for her.

'Going through a break-up is a really humanising experience. It just strips you to your core. You're nothing but feeling, nothing but emotion,' she told UK *Vogue* magazine.

'There's no difference between my break-up and anyone else's. I really only look back on [the relationship] with love, because of my daughter. I can't regret a single second of it because of this little hell-raising cherub sleeping in the room next to me. She's bigger than any heartache could ever be.'

Matilda was the spitting image of Heath, and the light of his life. He took it hard when he moved out of their Brooklyn home into an apartment, because it ripped apart the life he had loved.

Michelle bunkered down with Matilda to try and work through what had happened. The only bonus was that without her more famous partner, she got some breathing space from the paparazzi.

'Obviously so much has changed for me in the last few months that I don't really have an idea of what my life is going to be,' she said.

'I thought I knew certain things, and it turned out that I didn't, so I don't really try and anticipate so much anymore. I'm not making any bets on the future.'

Like many people after a break-up, she re-evaluated what was important to her, and how to deal with the future.

'I love domestic life,' she said. 'There's been a lot going on in my personal life and part of me is ... I don't know. I shouldn't talk about it, but it's like I'm re-emerging back into the world or something.'

Publicly, Heath said nothing about the reasons for his split from Michelle, which he had taken very hard, while privately he was hoping their relationship could work again. He turned for support to the friends who knew him best—his Aussie mates—who joined him in New York as often as they could.

He missed the grounding that having Michelle and Matilda had given him, and spent as much time as possible with his daughter, trying not to be just a weekend dad. He took her places like Manhattan's Children's Museum, where he mucked in with her at the sand table and in the PlayWorks area. For her second birthday on 28 October, the couple got together to host a party, with all Matilda's little friends receiving roses with their names on them. A source told the media there was no frostiness between the couple.

Seemingly as a way of coping, Heath tried to keep busy, putting more of his energies into the Masses, flying to LA regularly.

'His life turned on a dime all the time, which taught me a lot about living in the moment,' said Sara Cline.

An example of his impulsive behaviour was his suggestion one day, out of the blue, that they all go camping.

In an article for *LA Weekly*, one of Amato's friends, Randall Roberts, quoted Cline as saying, 'Heath just kind of came in one day and said, "Let's get an RV and go to Mexico".

'I said, "Heath, we have a company to run, and those are working days." And he said, "But it's our company, and we can do whatever we want".'

Then he called back to say perhaps they should leave a few days later, less traffic, more time to arrange it. But Cline told him, 'Heath, by Wednesday you could be in another country.'

She rented a campervan and at the unearthly hour of 3 a.m. on a Saturday, Heath, Cline and ten friends drove out of LA.

Over the next week, they camped on the beach, surfed during the day, and cooked and talked through the night.

'It was free,' said Cline.

'We had only ever existed in LA together, and there was always a sort of nervous energy to Heath in the city. Every time he'd walk down the street, he'd get recognised, and he felt maybe a little restricted by that. [Mexico] was a place where nobody knew where the fuck he was, and it was very liberating for him. And I think it was liberating for all of us.'

Roberts said that Heath would turn up at the Hollywood office on his yellow Ducati with a full-face helmet on so he could ride around unrecognised.

'Upstairs, he'd sit on a balance ball in front of a work station and edit, take meetings at the grand conference table ... make a move on one of the ongoing games of chess, listen to music, talk and watch movies,' said Roberts.

Heath was constantly experimenting with his video camera, filming himself from every angle he could, 'making faces, learning how he looked from different angles. He practised a lot of shit on me because I was his video chat buddy when he was making his coffee at work,' said Matt Amato. 'He probably did the Alexander technique a dozen times in front of my face on video chat, where he would morph into the Joker.'

Heath had signed on to play the Joker in July 2006, and was going to be filming in 2007 at the same time Michelle was due to be working on the thriller *Incendiary* with Ewan McGregor in the UK.

Before he began work on the Batman movie, *The Dark Knight*, Heath threw himself into yet another project. He teamed up with Ben Harper to further extend the Masses with a music label, Masses Music Co. And he wasted no time in signing up the label's first act, Grace Woodroofe, making the announcement on 9 February 2007 at the opening of the latest hot Hollywood venue, the Edison Lounge. The seventeen-year-old teenage singer-songwriter from Perth had gone to high school with Heath's half-sister Ashleigh, which brought her to his attention, and Heath 'fell in love' with her voice.

'Heath's really into music and he knows what he's talking about. He's my manager, but he's more like my big brother,' said Woodroofe, who described herself as an 'indie blues' singer.

Heath directed and shot her first video clip, which was a cover of the David Bowie song 'Quicksand'. The backdrop for the filming was the Edison, which had morphed from downtown LA's first private power plant.

'Ledger created a surreal, curious little psychodrama, filled with vivid reds and greens. Each cut feels perfectly executed and moves along with a carefree confidence,' wrote Randall Roberts in *LA Weekly*.

Heath planned to move on from directing only music videos and had been juggling plans for a feature film that involved his passion for chess—an adaptation of Walter Tevis's 1983 novel *The Queen's Gambit*. As well as everything else that had been going on in his life, he had been working for about a year on both starring in and directing the project.

The Queen's Gambit had a script written by veteran Scottish screenwriter Allan Shiach. Shiach, who works in the movie business under the name Allan Scott, had co-written the classic thriller *Don't Look Now*, which starred Donald Sutherland and Julie Christie. He became used to having email discussions with the insomniac Heath at 5 a.m. New York time.

He said that Heath had set himself a personal goal before beginning filming.

'One of his reasons for being interested in *The Queen's Gambit* was the fact that he was a very, very advanced chess player. He was, in fact, very close to grandmaster, and he said to me he thought he would try and go for grandmaster before we started shooting the movie,' he said.

Tevis's other works include *The Hustler*, *The Colour of Money* and *The Man Who Fell to Earth*, all of which have been famously filmed. *The Queen's Gambit* follows the life of Beth Harmon, who grows up in a Kentucky orphanage where the children are given tranquillisers to keep them quiet. Harmon learns to play chess with the janitor and becomes a chess prodigy, but ends up addicted to prescription drugs.

Shiach told *Scotland on Sunday* that they had asked Ellen Page, Oscar-nominated star of the surprise indie hit comedy *Juno*, to co-star.

A haunting section of the script, which appeared in a British newspaper, read, 'There is noise coming from everywhere in the house. Her suitcase lies open on the bed, clothes spilling everywhere.

'There are at least a dozen bottles of tranquilliser pills lying in suitcases, stuffed into every corner, each with Mexican labels. She opens one of these, grabs a bottle of liquor, and drinks direct from the bottle to swallow two pills.'

Shiach said they were waiting for Page to confirm her acceptance of the role, and were planning to shoot in North America and Russia in 2008.

It would have been yet another challenging departure for Heath.

'I don't really like to do the same thing twice,' he said.

'I like to do something I fear. I like to set up obstacles and defeat them. I like to be afraid of the project. I always am. When I get cast in something, I always believe I shouldn't have been cast. There's a huge amount of anxiety that drowns out any excitement I have toward the project. Pretty much any time I've signed on to a movie, I've tried to get out of it.

'It feels like it's necessary to put myself down. It inspires me to focus more and work harder.'

Those years of avoiding being typecast had been worth it. Heath's next role would leave no doubt that he had taken that blond hunk image and ripped it to shreds.

'Some people find their shtick. I've never figured out who "Heath Ledger" is on film: "This is what you expect when you hire me, and it will be recognisable", he told the *New York Times*.

'People always feel compelled to sum you up, to presume that they have you and can describe you. That's fine. But there are many stories inside of me, and a lot I want to achieve outside of one flat note.'

12
THE MAN WITH THE MASK

WHEN *THE DARK KNIGHT* DIRECTOR CHRISTOPHER NOLAN SAW WHAT HEATH WAS CREATING WITH THE JOKER, HE TOLD THE CREW, 'YOU KNOW WHAT? PUT IT ON A STEADICAM, PUT IT ON A HANDHELD, AND LET'S SEE WHAT THIS KID DOES.' WHAT HE DID WAS CREATE ONE OF THE MOST RIVETTING AND HAUNTING PERFORMANCES IN CINEMA HISTORY. NOLAN AND HEATH HAD BEGUN CREATING THE JOKER BEFORE THE SCRIPT FOR NOLAN'S FOLLOW-UP TO *BATMAN BEGINS* WAS EVEN FINISHED. NOLAN HAD GONE BACK TO THE ORIGINAL JOKER FOR INSPIRATION FOR THE CHARACTER'S RESURRECTION. TO ONE GENERATION, THE JOKER WAS CESAR ROMERO, WHO WAS MORE AT HOME AS A LATIN LOVER AND ROMANTIC LEAD.

He played the arch villain as an almost lovable prankster in the campy 1960s film *Batman: The Movie* and the TV series 'Batman'—but refused to shave off his famous moustache, which is faintly visible beneath the Joker's white make-up. To another generation, he was Jack Nicholson, who hammed it up for his flamboyant portrayal in the 1989 Warner Bros movie *Batman*, directed by Tim Burton.

But the character of the Joker was originally inspired, strangely enough, by German actor Conrad Veidt, who is best known for playing the Nazi major Heinrich Strasser in *Casablanca*. The creators of the Joker—artist Bob Kane, writer Bill Finger and artist Jerry Robinson—used as inspiration stills taken for the 1928 silent film, *The Man Who Laughs*, with Veidt wearing make-up and sporting a maniacal grin. A legend was born in 1940.

Unlike Bruce Wayne, who was motivated to become Batman through witnessing his parents killed as a child, the Joker has never had one basic background story throughout his years in 'Batman' comics. There have been several reasons given for how his face came to be disfigured and how he got his name, including that he was once a stand-up comedian. Also unlike Batman, the Joker's real name has never been revealed. It gave Heath a blank canvas on which to create his own version.

'I was looking for someone who was fearless,' said Nolan.

'I knew that I needed a fantastic actor, but I also knew that I needed someone who wasn't going to worry about comparisons to any other actors who had played the role. I met with Heath before we even actually had a script. We talked about ideas for who the character would be in this movie as opposed to his previous appearances in movies, and we both saw it in the same way.'

From a gay, introverted cowboy to a homicidal maniac whose chaotic life terrified audiences—Heath conceded that most people would have thought him an unusual choice for the part.

'It's definitely going to stump people,' he said.

'I think getting the role was tougher for other people to comprehend than it was for me. I wouldn't have thought of me either, but it's obviously not going to be what Jack Nicholson did.'

Nolan, a father of four whose previous movies included the psychological thrillers *Memento* and *Insomnia*, had wanted to work with Heath in the past, but nothing had come of it.

'The first time I met him, I remember him explaining to me that he wanted to take his time as a young actor. He didn't want to be thrust centre stage before he achieved what he wanted to achieve,' Nolan told *Entertainment Weekly*.

'To be perfectly honest, that's a line I've heard from a lot of young actors. But he's the only one that I then paid $10 to go see do something really extraordinary—which was *Brokeback Mountain*.'

Nolan denied rumours that Robin Williams and Sean Penn were on the shortlist for the part of the Joker.

'Heath was the only one on it. I knew he was it from the start,' he said. 'The guy had serious nuts.'

Heath knew the role was a career risk because whatever he did would be compared to Nicholson's Joker.

'You couldn't touch what Jack Nicholson did. It would be a crime. When Chris came to me, I'd already seen *Batman Begins*, and I really liked it. I already knew the world which he had created. I instantly knew of an angle. I instantly knew a way into this character, a way to create a character to fit into this world,' he said.

Heath also liked to scare himself with the parts he chose.

'To endure as a person, as an actor, you need to be fearless somewhat, and push yourself, and dare to be bad. Don't be afraid to fail,' he said while filming *The Dark Knight*.

Nolan had taken the Batman story back to its grim roots in

Batman Begins, and Heath's Joker was never going to be a popcorn interpretation.

'It's going to be more nuanced and dark,' said Heath, in what turned out to be an understatement.

Christopher Nolan worked on the script with his brother Jonathan and David S Goyer. They were so paranoid about anything leaking out that Heath had to read the script at one of their houses and leave it behind. They even had a codename for the movie, to keep it under the public radar—*Rory's First Kiss* (Rory is Christopher Nolan's son's name) or 'RFK'.

Heath and Nolan worked to create a villain inspired by punk influences like Sid Vicious and films like *A Clockwork Orange*—the movie in which Malcolm McDowell was said to have 'perfected nutterdom'. Heath's Joker was going to give him a run for his money.

'Heath and I talked a lot about the abstractions of the character, of the underlying philosophy of the character and what he represents in the story, and what that tone would need to be. But then it was really up to him to go off and figure out how he was going to make something that he understood had to be iconic somehow,' said Nolan, giving Heath freedom to go away and create a monster.

'But he also understood that it had to be human and recognisably human, because ... an individual whose only real pleasure, only real amusement, comes from tearing down the structures around him—that's a very human form of evil.

'So he has to be human as well as iconic. Heath put a lot of time and energy into figuring out a very complex way of achieving this.'

Four months before filming began, Heath started keeping a Joker diary, a book in which he saved ideas for the Joker's inner thoughts, upon which to build his character. It included a list of sick things the Joker would find funny, like AIDS. For a month, he locked himself away in a hotel room in London working out who his Joker would be, calling Nolan with updates.

'So he was talking to me about how he'd been studying the way that ventriloquist dummies talk, and things like that. I'd be sitting on the other end of the line going, "Well, that's a bit peculiar". But what I'm really hearing is an actor really invested in trying to come up with something very unique,' Nolan told the website About.com.

'I ended up landing more in the realm of a psychopath,' Heath told *Empire* magazine, 'someone with very little conscience towards his acts.'

In that hotel room, Heath worked on the sinister voice, the macabre laugh and gestures like the facial tic. He also came up with a specific walk: a hunched over gait, chin held low.

'The physicality reminds me of the great silent comedians,' said Nolan. 'It has a bit of [Buster] Keaton and [Charlie] Chaplin about it.'

Heath grew his hair long, and created the idea of the crazy, blotchy white face himself with white greasepaint, a thick splatter of mascara and red lipstick. Then it was over to the professionals to make the garish make-up work. In the finished version, the slashed lips and scars look almost like infected wounds.

'We gave a Francis Bacon spin to [his face],' said Nolan.

'This corruption, this decay in the texture of the look itself. It's grubby. You can almost imagine what he smells like.'

Heath told *SFX* magazine that the clown mask was made up of three pieces of silicone, making it feel as if he barely had any make-up on at all, and taking only an hour to apply. The technology had taken two years to perfect.

'It's not a prosthetic. This guy created these silicone pieces and they stamp them on. It's a lot quicker, and super-flexible. You hardly even know it's on your face. If it were a prosthetic, I'd have to have my whole neck and jaw done,' he said.

Make-up artist John Caglione Jr described the process of creating the Joker's unique look.

'Heath would scrunch up his face in specific expressions, raising his forehead and squinting his eyes, and I would paint on the white over his facial contortions,' he said.

'This technique created textures and expressions that just painting the face a flat white would not. Then I used black make-up around Heath's eyes while he held them closed very tight ... After the black was on, I sprayed water over his eyes, and he would squeeze his eyes and shake his head, and all that black, drippy, smudgy stuff would happen.'

While Heath's Joker was staying in his traditional purple suit, costume designer Lindy Hemming gave the look a fresh edge using a mix of influences including Vivienne Westwood, Johnny Rotten, Iggy Pop, Pete Doherty and Alexander McQueen.

'Once I knew the Joker was going to be played by Heath Ledger, I wanted the costume to have a younger, trendier style than previous versions,' said Hemming.

She came up with a style that she said 'has a somewhat foppish attitude to it, with a little grunge thrown in', making the Joker a bit of a dandy.

The pattern on his shirt was based on one Hemming found in an antiques stall, and the shoes were from Milan. The material for the Joker's tie was specially woven to Hemming's specifications by exclusive British clothiers Turnbull & Asser.

'Heath wanted it to be thin, so it's a sixties tie, but in a Turnbull & Asser fabric. I dare say it's the weirdest tie that Turnbull

& Asser has ever made,' said Hemming. 'When Heath came in and we showed him all the bits and pieces of the costume, he thought it was fantastically original and just went for it.'

Now it was up to Heath to pull it all together and create the ultimate screen maniac.

'Everything about what he does, from every gesture, every little facial tic, everything he's doing with his voice—it all speaks to the heart of this character,' said Nolan.

While the lead character was Christian Bale's Batman, it was the Joker who was the centre of the movie.

'He's just an absolute sociopath, a cold-blooded, mass-murdering clown, and Chris gave me free rein. Which is fun, because there are no real boundaries to what the Joker would say or do. Nothing intimidates him, and everything is a big joke,' Heath told *Empire* magazine.

When the cameras started rolling in April 2007, the first scene Heath and Christian Bale filmed together was in the interrogation room.

The caped crusader and the grinning Joker are facing off across a table. The actors, like their characters, were totally alone inside the room for at least part of the scene.

'The cameras were outside and there were mirrors surrounding us,' said Bale. 'So the two of us were eyeballing each other, and any way we looked we would see reflections of these two freaks just sitting at this table together.'

It was his first chance to see how Heath was playing the Joker—and Heath's total commitment to the role. It was also a very physical scene.

'The more he beats the Joker, the bigger the smile on the Joker's face becomes, so he realises he's just satisfying the Joker with this violence,' Bale told reporter Paul Fischer.

'Heath, man, received some heavy bangs and bruises from that scene, and he loved every second of it.

'He just adored it, and he was egging me on for more as the walls were buckling in from doing that scene. He had total commitment to it, he created this really iconic villain, portrayed the Joker in a way that he's never been portrayed before—far creepier, far more anarchic than anything we've seen.'

Gary Oldman, who played Commissioner Jim Gordon, said he could tell from day one how special Heath's Joker would be.

'You can think of people like Jack Nicholson in *One Flew Over the Cuckoo's Nest*, Al Pacino in *Dog Day Afternoon* ... There's certain landmark performances where you just think that they just fly. And Heath has done that here. He's just tuning in to a radio station—he's got a frequency that none of us can hear,' said Oldman, who played Sirius Black in the Harry Potter movies.

'Sirius Black might scare six-year-olds, but he doesn't scare nine-year-olds. It's hard to scare kids these days. Heath does. He scares everybody. This is one of the most frightening performances I have ever seen put on film.'

Oldman, a huge fan of Malcolm McDowell's *A Clockwork Orange* performance, spotted where Heath had drawn some of his inspiration from.

'It was the scene after we capture the Joker, and he's in a holding pen, sitting with his back against the bars,' said Oldman.

'And Heath is sort of looking at me, kind of under his brow, and then he just starts clapping. I remember going over to him between takes and saying, "You know, you remind me of Alex from *A Clockwork Orange*". And Heath said, "Yeah, yeah, yeah. Funnily enough, I was just watching that movie in my trailer".'

Shooting *The Dark Knight* was a logistical nightmare. Nolan wanted to film as much as possible in real places rather than on sets, and Chicago once again became Gotham City, as it had in *Batman Begins*. Although the crew filmed under the movie's bogus title of *Rory's First Kiss*, it was impossible to hide what the movie really was when some guy turned up in a Batman suit. Local radio was broadcasting daily details of casting calls and road closures, and the paparazzi invaded town to get shots of the cast including Maggie Gyllenhaal, Jake's older sister, who played Assistant District Attorney Rachel Dawes.

Heath was finding being a part-time dad very tough. Friends said his whole life revolved around Matilda, and Heath appeared lost without his daughter. He said that being without her was 'kind of like your whole body has a lump in its throat'. After he separated from Michelle, he had his neighbourhood tattoo artist in Brooklyn, Joseph Ari Aloi, tattoo 'Matilda' on his chest, close to his heart.

'Heath, in between takes, would laugh and joke and sit down on the kerb and have a cigarette and talk about Matilda,' said Oldman.

Aaron Eckhart, who played District Attorney Harvey Dent, felt a bit left out because he had no kids of his own.

'Everybody was talking about kids. Everybody was showing pictures of their kids. I was the only one in the trailer that didn't have kids. Heath showed me pictures and talked about it, and would come in and say, "She [Matilda] did this and she did that",' he told *Cinema Confidential*.

Eckhart said that film crews are usually blasé, but Heath really grabbed their attention.

'The Joker's mind really didn't fly on any straight line, it was always going everywhere. Heath really kept that alive by talking to himself and by doing the things that an actor does to keep a character alive,' said Eckhart.

'It's interesting, because whenever I've done that, the crew thought I was crazy, but the crew here was so with Heath. For that matter, everybody was. Everybody was watching him as a fan. He was electrifying the room all the time.'

Much of the filming was done at night, but because it was summer the nights were short—they couldn't start until almost 9 p.m. and had to wind up when it got light at 4 a.m. This disrupted Heath's already bad sleep patterns and even the sleeping pills he had been prescribed, Ambien (marketed as Stilnox in Australia), weren't working.

He gave a journalist from the *New York Times* some idea of his problem towards the end of filming *The Dark Knight*.

'Last week I probably slept an average of two hours a night,' he said. 'I couldn't stop thinking. My body was exhausted, and my mind was still going.'

When one Ambien didn't work, he took a second one and 'fell into a stupor, only to wake up an hour later, his mind still racing'.

The city of Chicago closed down the whole financial district at night to allow filming. As Nolan wanted to make everything as real as possible, with few computer-generated images, the stunts needed careful planning—for example, the one where the semi-trailer flips over with the Joker at the wheel.

Split-second timing was needed when shooting the scene where the Joker blows up Gotham City General Hospital. An old candy factory in Chicago which was about to be demolished was given all the signage to look like the hospital, and Heath, in one of his most memorable scenes as the demented Joker dressed in drag as a nurse, walks away with the place blowing up behind him.

Twice during filming, production moved to England where Heath was able to see Matilda, who was staying with her mum while Michelle filmed *Incendiary*. While Michelle worked, Heath took their daughter for walks around the city in her stroller. While regretting that he couldn't spend more time with her, he appreciated the changes she had made to his life.

'You're forced into kind of respecting yourself more,' he said in a strangely personal interview with WJW-TV during *The Dark Knight* shoot.

'You learn more about yourself through your child, I guess. I think you also look at death differently.

'It's like a catch 22: I feel good about dying now, because I feel like I'm alive in her, you know; but at the same hand, you don't want to die because you want to be around for the rest of her life.'

In London, the old Battersea Power Station was used for the scene where Rachel Dawes is blown up. The ward inside Gotham Hospital was built on set, and an old airship hangar which the British government used to test concrete and steel was used in one of the spectacular high-rise sequences with Batman and the Joker.

In London, Heath was put up in an ultra-modern house with a courtyard and roof garden hidden behind an industrial frontage. It was here he was interviewed by the *New York Times*. The reporter, Sarah Lyall, was struck by how he was unable to stay still.

'He got up and poured more coffee. He stepped outside into the courtyard and smoked a cigarette,' she wrote.

'He shook his hair out from under its hood, put a rubber band around it, took out the rubber band, put on a hat, took off the hat, put the hood back up. He went outside and had another cigarette.'

Although Heath was renting the house for some time, he appeared not to have unpacked: an open bag with clothes falling out lay on the bedroom floor. The kitchen table was strewn with items, including one of his ever-present companions, a chess set.

The logistics of filming meant he had quite a bit of time off between scenes.

'But it was required, because whenever I was working, it exhausted me to the bone,' he said.

'At the end of the day, I couldn't move. I couldn't talk. I was absolutely wrecked. If I had to do that every day, I couldn't have done what I did. The schedule really permitted me to exhaust myself.'

Always totally focused on his characters, he had to dig deep to inhabit the Joker, who, unlike Ennis Del Mar, had no parallels in his own life.

'It's pretty amazing,' said Nolan, 'the disparity between the person he was and the monster that he created for us for the film. To see that on a daily basis, to see that being created from this very gentle person, is a real testament to his skill as an actor, and it was very exciting to watch.'

But Heath found it increasingly difficult to switch off.

'I need to do something with this head, because sometimes I just don't sleep, it just keeps ticking,' he said.

Sir Michael Caine, who reprised his role as Bruce Wayne's faithful butler Alfred, said he had been wrong to doubt Heath could match Jack Nicholson's Joker.

'I have worked with Jack and I know him really well. You do not really want to follow Jack into anything. Unless it's a nightclub. Heath Ledger stunned me,' said Caine.

'Jack played the Joker as sort of a benign nasty clown—like a wicked uncle. Heath plays him like an absolutely maniacal, murderous psychopath. You have never seen anything like it in your life.'

Caine saw what Heath put into the Joker.

'He's terrifying. The first time I saw him, we were rehearsing.

He comes up in the elevator to me in Batman's flat and raids the place,' he said.

'And I hadn't seen him, I'd never met him and he comes out screaming and it's like "Wow". I completely forgot my lines. Scary. It will frighten the life out of people.'

But he also saw what the role took out of Heath.

'He was exhausted; I mean, he was really tired,' said Caine.

'I remember saying to him, "I'm too old to have the bloody energy to play that part". And I thought to myself, I didn't have the energy when I was his age.'

Heath's energy, which had always been so infectious, now seemed to observers to be more frenetic—and draining.

Experienced cinematographer Wally Pfister, who had worked on *Batman Begins*, said Heath was so intense as the Joker that it seemed 'like he was busting blood vessels in his head. It was like a séance where the medium takes on another person and then is so completely drained.'

At the Chicago wrap party for *The Dark Knight* at the Carnivale nightclub, before filming wound up in England, Heath spent the evening playing poker.

Something else which may have been on Heath's mind at this time related to that embarrassing moment when he was still at school and his uncle, Mike Ledger, sprung him at home with an older woman. The woman, who had been living with another man at the time, later had a child, a daughter, who was brought up by the man as his own. The conception would have corresponded to the time the woman was friendly with Heath. Out of the blue, sometime in early 2007, Heath wrote to the man and admitted to having had an affair with the woman, according to sources in Heath's home town of Perth. The letter allegedly even suggested a DNA test. Perhaps it was triggered by Matilda's birth, and Heath wanted to put the record straight. The man confronted his former partner, who was said to be 'extremely distressed'.

When Gemma Jones, a reporter for Sydney's *Daily Telegraph*, heard about this claim a couple of months after Heath's death while she was seconded to the *New York Post*, the *Daily Telegraph* set about trying to ascertain the truth of it. In Perth, the newspaper spoke to the woman involved a number of times, and asked if Heath could be the father of her daughter. The woman, who was always polite, would not deny the claim, but refused to say anything on the record. 'I have my children to think about,' she said. 'I really can't comment.'

One member of Heath's family said, 'She had the baby. Everyone lived under the assumption that [she] was the daughter of the mother's boyfriend, and that is how she has been brought up.'

Heath's uncle, Haydn Ledger, said he knew more about the background to events, and went on the record to say, 'There is a very real possibility that Heath was the father.'

The woman and her family were besieged by the media when the story broke, but their identities were never revealed, to protect the daughter. The woman had since married, and her husband confirmed the letter, apparently from Heath. He said he had not seen the actual letter, but said it had been mentioned by the man who had brought the girl up as his own daughter.

'There's a whole minefield with this guy,' he said, 'but … the fact is [the girl] is not [Heath's] daughter. End of story.'

Heath's parents refused to comment, responding as they consistently have to all media requests since their son's death. They have protected Heath's memory with the same privacy that he sought while he was alive. But perhaps the woman's pregnancy was one of the reasons behind Heath's decision to quit school early, leave Perth and head over east.

During one of the breaks in filming *The Dark Knight*, Heath returned to the canals of Venice for the 2007 International Film Festival where *I'm Not There* was a joint winner of the prestigious Special Jury Prize, along with French entry *The Secret of the Grain*. A last-minute change of rules allowed two winners—the judges had been almost at blows, unable to decide between the movies.

It seemed a much more sombre Heath than the one who had promoted *Brokeback* the year before, and who had dashed across the city's canals as Casanova. He had given up alcohol and was sticking to Diet Coke, but had not given up smoking, the ever-present Camel cigarette in his mouth. News had just broken about his split with Michelle, although it had happened a few months earlier, and he was very wary of media questions about it. He never looked anything but awkward in front of the banks of photographers. He was hiding not only behind his dark glasses, but had his hat tipped down just that bit lower over his eyes. Reporters noted that he seemed to be in his own world at times, staring off into space. The strangest thing was his dress.

He and co-star Richard Gere had been invited to a party thrown by Italian designer Alberta Ferretti on a yacht moored off the main city. Heath was said to have arrived alone, dressed like a homeless man, and drifted around not talking to anyone for half an hour before leaving 'like a lost soul'.

While he had always had a touch of grunge, the outfit that he turned up in for the festival's closing ceremony was even weirder: baggy shorts, a pork-pie hat, his mate Shem Watson's yellow anti-war T-shirt with red Shell logo in the shape of a skull, grey waistcoat, black jacket—and red and white striped ankle socks with black dress shoes. Scuffed, of course. Oh, and a backpack over his shoulders.

It was at a press conference for *I'm Not There* that Heath

volunteered the information that he was infatuated with Nick Drake. Sitting up on the stage Heath told the assembled media how Drake 'died in 1975 at twenty-five'. He paused and took a breath before continuing, 'Suicide'.

'I was obsessed with his story and his music, and I pursued it for a while, and still have hopes to kind of tell his story one day,' said Heath.

Afraid of taking liberties with Drake's memory, he had been working on an idea along the lines of the Bob Dylan biopic.

'He was starting to approach it through a more allegorical method,' said *I'm Not There* director Todd Haynes, 'where it was going to be about a woman travelling on a train ride through Europe—which Nick Drake, I think, did do—and he was going to have Michelle playing that role.'

Heath had completed a video set to Drake's song 'Black Eyed Dog', from one of his last recording sessions in February 1974. The title came from Winston Churchill's description of depression as a black dog. In the black-and-white video, Heath turns the hand-held video camera on himself, and the video ends when he drowns in the bath. He showed it to Haynes.

'He did it in one day in London,' said Haynes. 'He went out and shot it in black and white—it's the only video that he himself appears in. It is just a stunning piece of work. He had an instinct.'

About a month after the Venice festival, Kim Ledger spent some time with his son and told close acquaintances when he got home that he was worried about Heath's welfare. By this time, Heath was taking a variety of medications, including sleeping tablets and the anti-depressant Zoloft. His constant travelling meant he didn't have just one regular doctor, and he had been given various prescriptions. Whether it was the prescription drugs or something else, but Kim said he was worried that Heath seemed forgetful.

With hindsight, it appeared that he was slipping deep into depression.

But whatever was going on personally for Heath, his fellow cast members on *The Dark Knight* saw no evidence that his role as the Joker had messed with his mind.

'I know there are these rumours out there that playing the Joker drove him to his grave,' said Gary Oldman, 'but I never saw any of that. He was always on time. He knew his part backwards and forwards.'

Heath and Christian Bale had become particularly close on set, and socialised off set. Bale described Heath as 'incredibly intense in his performance, but incredibly mellow and laid-back'.

'Heath got the same kick out of acting that I do,' he said. 'He enjoyed the sort of crazy immersion of acting. He took it incredibly seriously, but simultaneously recognised how ridiculous it all is.'

Heath himself said that playing the Joker was 'the most fun I've ever had playing a role'.

'I'm really surprised Chris knew I could do it or thought I had something in me like this,' he told *Empire* magazine. 'But, yeah, it's the bomb. Definitely the most fun I've had, and the most freedom.'

The bleak streets of London in winter were the backdrop for Heath's next—and final—movie. He went from *The Dark Knight*, with a budget of at least $185 million, to the relatively low-budget $30 million film, *The Imaginarium of Dr Parnassus*.

'If big-name actors didn't want to work with me for bad money, I wouldn't be able to do it,' said director Terry Gilliam, of the problem of getting funding for his left-of-centre movies.

In this one, Christopher Plummer played Dr Parnassus, a thousand-year-old storyteller with a horse-drawn travelling theatre show called an Imaginarium, which gave people the opportunity to transcend reality through a magic mirror. Heath's character, Tony, is a member of Dr Parnassus's theatre troupe, which has to save the doctor's daughter, played by willowy Lily Cole, from the devil, played by Tom Waits.

Gilliam wrote the script with Charles McKeown, who had worked with him on *The Adventures of Baron Munchausen*, and said it was autobiographical.

'I'm trying to bring a bit of fantasticality to London, an antidote to modern lives,' Gilliam told *Variety* magazine.

'I loved this idea of an ancient travelling show offering the kind of storytelling and wonder that we used to get, to people who are just into shoot-'em-up action films. Parnassus is trying to bring amazement to people ... If they will enter his mirror, and allow their imagination to mix with his, they enter these extraordinary worlds, and they come back transcendent—or they strangely disappear.'

Heath had hardly any time back in his bare box of a bachelor apartment in New York after *The Dark Knight* wound up before he moved back to London—which was just as well, because of his fear of being alone.

Shooting on *Imaginarium* began on 9 December 2007, and the sets were beseiged by London's paparazzi as well as hoards of screaming girls wanting to get a glimpse of Heath, who was looking far from glamorous as always in skinny jeans and a hoodie most days. Inevitably, photographs leaked out. In one chilling shot secretly taken on the set, Heath, as Tony, is seen hanging by the neck from Lambeth Bridge while dressed in a white suit and white shoes.

According to a leaked copy of the script which ended up on the Internet, Tony appears to have lost his memory, and has no idea why he was hanging from the bridge. He has strange symbols on his forehead, odd weights in his pockets, and a little metal tube in his mouth.

He is apparently saved by the character Anton, a sleight-of-hand expert played by Andrew Garfield. Garfield later summed up Heath by saying, 'it just seemed like he had the secrets of the world within him'.

'He was the driving force, and he was steering the ship. He had all the fuel and was putting the fuel in the engine,' he said of Heath's frenetic input as he immersed himself in the filming.

Heath put a lot into the shoot, throwing himself around as he did his own stunts despite a back injury. As he had when filming *The Brothers Grimm* with Gilliam, he raced over to the monitor after each take to see how it looked. He had long discussions about directing with Gilliam, and the former Python was as intrigued as ever by his ideas and intelligence.

'I think that Terry Gilliam really unleashed that talent that was always in Heath, but which perhaps he was afraid to tap into,' said Naomi Watts.

'Terry just tapped right into Heath's interior life, and could see that he was this deep-thinking person, and had all kinds of things in there.'

On set, while Heath seemed happy and content to share a laugh and a cigarette with the cast and crew, he also appeared tired and drawn, and was spending more time than usual on his own. Most believed Heath to be simply focusing on his character, but some saw his privacy on set as his becoming 'unhinged'.

One of the troupe members was a dwarf, played by Verne Troyer, 'Mini Me' from the Austin Powers movies. Troyer said it was obvious to everyone that Heath was having trouble sleeping.

'Everyone knew that he had a hard time sleeping, and from working in the cold weather in London—we were out in the rain and things like that—so everybody got sick,' said Troyer.

One of Australia's most prestigious art competitions is the Archibald Prize for portraiture, awarded by the Art Gallery of New South Wales. The prize goes to 'the best portrait, preferentially of some man or woman distinguished in Art, Letters, Science or Politics', as judged by the trustees of the Gallery. A condition of entry is that each portrait must be painted from life, rather than being copied from a photograph. That Christmas, Heath swapped the cold and damp of London for the sweltering heat of a Perth summer, and sat for an artist friend of his, Vincent Fantauzzo.

Fantauzzo and Heath had been talking for three years about him sitting for an Archibald portrait, but there had been no time due to Heath's whirlwind of work commitments. There was also his need for privacy.

'He never let anyone paint him for that reason, because he felt it was quite a personal thing, to be painted. I think Heath was really feeling quite comfortable with himself recently, so it was easy to do it this time around,' said Fantauzzo, who lives in Melbourne and knew Heath through their mutual friend N'fa.

When he received a call from Heath in December saying he was excited and ready to do it, Fantauzzo jumped on a plane to Perth. At Heath's mum's immaculate modern home in Applecross, the two men talked for many hours about what the painting would be like, fuelled by Sally Bell's coffee and pikelets, which Fantauzzo said created a homely atmosphere.

'The night before, we talked about the painting and about art, and about all sorts of things,' said Fantauzzo.

'I wanted it to be dealing with self, your own consciousness and your thoughts.

'An artist is their own biggest critic. I had seen his eyes wander off or stare into the camera while doing interviews, and wondered what he may have been thinking. I felt that being a celebrity, you are always under constant scrutiny with so many demands made of you that you have to hold part of yourself back, and not give too much away.'

He said he had been nervous about entering the work for the Archibald Prize, but that Heath was encouraging.

'My confidence was a bit low, so he kept trying to boost me a bit. He kept saying, "It's going to be great, it'll win", said Fantauzzo.

He said that once the session started, Heath became very focused and serious, almost as if he was meditating.

The result was a dark painting showing a bare-chested Heath apparently haunted by two mischievous images of himself. The central figure of Heath is staring straight ahead and looks troubled and tired, while the Heaths on either side whisper to him from behind their hands.

As events unfolded, the painting was interpreted as Heath being troubled and depressed, but Fantauzzo said that was not the case. He and Heath had discussed the theme.

'It was about how we all have different consciences and voices in our head that tell us what to do and how to react. They're not good or bad, they're just voices that we hear, telling us how to behave. That's what the other figures are, in the painting,' he said.

He said he found Heath relaxed and happy, and dismissed as rubbish any suggestion that he was using illegal drugs.

'I was drinking, and he was drinking soda water, and he was talking about how clear-headed he was feeling; he was really adamant about not drinking, and was encouraging his friends to do the same,' said Fantauzzo.

Fantauzzo's portrait, titled simply *Heath*, was hung in the Art Gallery of New South Wales along with the other Archibald Prize finalists. While it didn't win the main prize, it was voted the winner of the People's Choice award, given to the portrait that is most popular with gallery visitors.

Another local star who was back on home turf with her family in Perth for Christmas was the model Gemma Ward—who Heath had been secretly dating in New York. He had also been out with actor Kate Hudson, who he had met on *The Four Feathers* set, and model Helena Christensen.

Ward and Heath were spotted together almost every day over Heath's ten-day holiday break. They spent an evening under the stars in the reclining deckchairs in the front row of Perth's picturesque Camelot Outdoor Cinema, where they saw the offbeat movie *Two Days in Paris*. On Boxing Day, they watched the sun set over the Indian ocean, dining with friends in the leather booths at Fremantle's trendy Little Creatures Brewery.

But even on a peaceful hiatus from work, Heath couldn't relax for long. Gemma's sister, Sophie Ward, who is also a model, said he was distressed about splitting with Michelle and being away from Matilda, who was with her mother in Sweden while Michelle filmed the movie *Mammoth*.

'We went to the movies and just did normal stuff ... but he was a bit edgy. He couldn't really relax,' said Sophie.

'He smoked cigarettes, but that's about it. He said he was very committed to not drinking alcohol.'

Before he said goodbye to his family and flew out of Perth back to London, Heath left a rambling message on the answering machine of the *West Australian* newspaper's film editor, Mark Naglazas, on Sunday 30 December.

'It's Heath again ... Listen if I don't catch you 'cause I leave soon, basically I don't have anyone else to call, and I thought as I've spoken to you before ... I'd ring up and just send some thanks out there to the peeps at the *West Australian* and the *Sunday*

Times and everyone in Perth in general,' said Heath's message.

He said he wanted to thank the people of Perth and its media for letting him holiday in peace. 'I don't know whether it's a conscious thing or an unconscious thing, giving me space and respecting my privacy,' he said.

'It's just been awesome, and I've had the most beautiful time back here, and being able to see all my friends and family … it's been so lovely. It's really enabled me to be a boy again from home, and feel like I'd never left.'

Heath described his holiday as 'incredibly therapeutic', and said that being left in peace had 'made it all that more special'.

'I hope you had a wonderful Christmas and certainly a Happy New Year, if I don't speak to you before I leave,' he said.

'I will no doubt be talking to you, probably next year when the Batman comes out.'

He thanked Naglazas for listening to his 'long-winded' message, and ended, 'Thanks again, okay, bye-bye!'

Back in the grey chill of a London January, Heath threw himself into a hectic twenty-day schedule, rushing about the city and putting in long hours. Photographs show him looking far from a relaxed Perth boy. He's tired and drawn.

As with *The Dark Knight*, a lot of the filming was done at night, and fellow actor Christopher Plummer believes the cold, damp night air contributed to Heath's ill-health.

'Heath did have a terrible, lingering bug in London, and he couldn't sleep at all,' said Plummer. 'I thought he'd probably got walking pneumonia, which they seem to think he had … We were working in such dire conditions in London, outside every night in the cold. Which may have contributed somewhat to his health.'

Verne Troyer said Heath had confided in him about some of his problems: 'There were things in his life going on … I don't want to say anything about it, because it was personal and he trusted me ... Anybody would have been a little bit depressed [in Heath's situation].'

Heath appears to have been a mass of contradictions during those final days filming in London, swinging between playful enthusiasm and a manic energy which left him slumped, exhausted. His playfulness can be seen in stunts like the one he pulled on the final night's filming in London before the shoot moved on to Vancouver.

They had been filming in and around what has been described as a 'tatty' pub, the Ring o'Bells in the London borough of Clerkenwell. Outside, the ubiquitous paparazzi had gathered. Heath wandered through them, unrecognised.

'[He] snuck his way out into the crowd without anyone noticing, and came right up next to one of the photographers and asked him, "Who are you trying to shoot? Who are you trying to get?"' said Troyer.

When the photographer told him he was there for Heath Ledger, Heath said, 'Oh, really, that's cool.'

'I thought that was classic, just classic and hilarious,' said Troyer.

But one of the extras, Sean Porter, said that on set it was a different story. On that last day of filming, 'there were arguments, and a bad vibe descended on the pub,' Porter wrote in the *Independent on Sunday*.

Heath was dressed for his role in a baggy Poirot clown outfit, but according to Porter: 'Heath himself no longer looked like a clown. He was dirty, wired and manic: he hadn't stopped for three days.'

Then one minute after midnight on that final night, with Gilliam and Heath wanting to do at least one more take, the crew started to pack up, the permit to film having run out.

Porter said Heath was furious, ripping off his frilly hat and throwing it to the floor.

'C'mon, guys … Please! Just one more take … I mean, c'mon, what difference is another ten minutes going to make,' Heath cajoled, to no avail.

Porter said that once everyone had calmed down and people were leaving, Heath walked around hugging and thanking people. He even took time to thank the few extras who were still hanging around.

It was way after midnight when Heath got back to his hotel room, but early that morning, Sunday 20 January, he was on a plane from London back to New York, jumping across more time zones. With New York five hours behind London, Heath got there with most of the day to spare—alone in his Broome Street apartment with only his iPod and mobile phone for company. His beloved Matilda was still in Sweden with her mum.

He popped out for a coffee at one of his regular spots, the Miro Cafe on Broadway, where he was always so low-key that staff had no idea he was a famous actor. This time, he cut down on the chat and had his iPod earphones in.

It seemed that, once again, he could not bear to be home by himself. One of his usual haunts when he was on the party scene was the Beatrice Inn, a quasi-private club in the West Village where guests were the celebrity elite and regularly included Kate Moss, Owen Wilson and Kirsten Dunst. This Sunday night, guests were disturbed to see Heath wearing a ski mask, with holes cut out at the eyes and mouth, and a hoodie, with the hood pulled up over his head. The outfit points more to a seriously deteriorating mental problem than a bid for anonymity, because the Beatrice Inn was one of those places where people like Heath would usually be left alone. He was obviously not wrapped up for the cold, because reports said he didn't remove the mask once inside. Was he trying to shut the world out?

On Monday morning, he had breakfast at Le Pain Quotidien, near his apartment. He ate a bowl of granola, again with his iPod switched on loud, according to *People* magazine.

That evening, around 6 p.m., he stocked up on groceries at the Gourmet Garage.

'He had three bags of groceries, mainly produce like fruits and vegetables. I remember he had organic chicken sausages,' said catering sales manager Liz Bullis. 'He packed his own groceries. About half of our customers help out like that. He was always friendly and pretty quiet.'

Heath may have dined with two women that evening at Angelica Kitchen, a vegetarian restaurant in the East Village, and he spoke to new age guru Deepak Chopra on the phone. Chopra told *People* magazine that he knew Heath as a doting dad with a spiritual side.

'He was always questioning about the meaning of existence. He'd always bring up existential dilemmas and conundrums ... Is there a higher consciousness? What's the meaning of existence?' said Chopra.

They had a mutual friend in Shekhar Kapur, who had directed Heath in *The Four Feathers* and was arriving in New York that night.

'He was a little depressed about not having seen his daughter,' said Chopra.

'It was like, "I'm missing my girl". He hadn't seen her over the holidays, he mentioned that.'

Heath had told Chopra he was having trouble sleeping: 'He's a very, very ambitious actor and hard-working guy. He was still high from the experience [of filming in London] and he hadn't come down ... He was exhausted.'

Kapur had another project for Heath. They had been discussing a satire called *The Nine O'Clock War* in which the lead role was a TV war reporter whose coverage gets such high ratings that he starts turning the war into a reality show for a Western audience. Kapur had envisaged Heath in the role.

When Kapur got to New York that evening, he rang Heath, who he called 'brother'.

'He said he could not see me that night, but really wanted to meet me the next day,' said Kapur.

Kapur and Chopra had arranged a massage for Heath at New York's Chopra Centre to help him relax.

'We were talking about meeting up, and laughing about synchronicity, because I had booked a massage for him at 3 o'clock, and he'd booked one for himself at the same time. He told me to call him in the morning. I said, "I won't disturb you if you're tired",' said Kapur.

But Heath said, 'No, call me. Wake me up, and we'll meet.'

A few months earlier, Heath and Michelle had looked like the perfect couple living an idyllic life: wealthy, with a comfortable home, in love, dreaming of a big family, happy just walking their beloved daughter down to the shops through the streets of Brooklyn, at the top of their careers.

'I only do this because I'm having fun,' Heath had said of making movies.

'The day I stop having fun, I'll just walk away.'

On the night of 21 January, he was jet-lagged, worn out from pneumonia, tired to the bone, but unable to sleep. Alone, without his beloved Matilda. He tossed and turned, his mind racing while his body longed for sleep, before he took another tablet.

13
HOME
AT LAST

TWO TINY FOOTPRINTS CAST IN CEMENT OUTSIDE A NEW YORK BROWNSTONE ARE PART OF MATILDA ROSE LEDGER'S MEMORY OF HER DOTING FATHER. NEXT TO THE FOOTPRINTS, HEATH WROTE MATILDA'S NAME IN NEAT CAPITAL LETTERS IN THE WET CEMENT. INSIDE THE HOUSE, MATILDA WAS SURROUNDED BY THE WOMEN IN HER LIFE: HER MUM MICHELLE, HER GRANDMOTHER CARLA WILLIAMS AND HER GODMOTHER, BUSY PHILIPPS. MICHELLE ARRIVED BACK IN NEW YORK ON WEDNESDAY EVENING, THE DAY AFTER HEATH'S DEATH, MATILDA CLUTCHED TO HER CHEST AS SHE RUSHED THROUGH THE AIRPORT, CLEARLY DEVASTATED. SHE HAD HEARD THE SHOCKING NEWS LATE AT NIGHT IN HER HOTEL IN TROLLHÄTTAN, SWEDEN, AND MADE THE EMERGENCY TRIP ON THE FIRST FLIGHT HOME.

A day earlier in Perth, on the lawn outside Sally Ledger Bell's house in Applecross, Kim, Sally and Kate faced the reporters and cameras, their arms around each other, dark glasses unable to conceal their grief. It was 11 a.m. and mere hours after they had learned of Heath's death through the media—such was the speed with which the news raced around the world.

'We, Heath's family, confirm the very tragic, untimely and accidental passing of our dearly loved son, brother and doting father of Matilda,' Kim said.

'He was found peacefully asleep in his New York apartment by his housekeeper at 3:30 p.m., US time. We would like to thank our friends and everyone around the world for their well wishes and kind thoughts at this time.

'Heath has touched so many people on so many different levels during his short life, but few had the pleasure of truly knowing him. He was a down-to-earth, generous, kind-hearted, life-loving and selfless individual who was extremely inspirational to many. Please now respect our family's need to grieve and come to terms with our loss privately.'

Kim was understated and dignified in public. In private, his grief was so great he could barely speak. Although they had not willingly spoken to each other for years, Kim's brothers called him as soon as they heard the news. It was his wife Ines who answered the phone, and in the background Kim could be heard howling and screaming and sobbing.

Heath's death left the whole family feeling as if they had fallen off the edge of a cliff.

Haydn Ledger drove to his ex-wife's house in Perth, where she and their four children were sitting on the front verandah with their heads down. His youngest son, Luke, who has aspirations to be an actor like his big cousin, couldn't go to school for four days.

Heath's extended family, which had so far remained out of the public eye, suddenly found out how intrusive the media could be. His godfather, Mike Ledger, couldn't work out how they discovered his home number, but there was a barrage of calls from the press worldwide, all wanting to talk to a Ledger—any Ledger. When Haydn got to work, he found his business surrounded by media cars.

Flowers and tributes from Italy, Canada, America and the UK poured into Mike and Di's home in the Perth hills and Heath's old school, Guildford Grammar, from people who never knew Heath but who wanted to let the family know that they were sorry for the loss. Mike and Di tried to pass the tributes on to Kim, but he never returned their calls. Under seige from the media, the uncles decided to do one TV interview, to try to put a stop to speculation that Heath's death was anything but accidental.

'After much thought we decided to go ahead, because we felt there were people who wanted to hear from Heath's family, and we had our memories of him as a young boy growing up. We thought long and hard about it,' said Mike.

Bouquets, candles, notes and photographs were laid outside Heath's Broome Street apartment, the Brooklyn house and the Treehouse in LA where he had lived with Michelle.

The outpouring of grief around the world was universal and immediate. Heath had been such a private person that only those closest to him were aware of his problems, which made his death even more surprising and shocking. Even those who knew he had been battling some inner demons thought he was going to get through the personal crisis.

Because he had eschewed Hollywood airs and graces, Heath was seen as someone people could relate to: he was down-to-earth, and cooler than a young Steve McQueen. In his work, as in his life, he had humility and integrity, and showed promise of greater things to come—promise that would now remain unfulfilled. People who hadn't even been particular fans were surprised that they were so upset at his death.

Heath's closest friends shut down. The boys he had known from school have still been unable to speak publicly about their best mate, feeling it is too soon to dive deep into memories that are happy, but at the same time so sad. They also remain very protective of him.

Naomi Watts, who was at the Sundance Film Festival to promote her movie *Funny Games*, broke down in tears and cancelled all public appearances, including the premiere of the film. Nicole Kidman released a statement through her publicist saying her heart went out to Heath's family over the 'terrible tragedy' as tributes poured in from everyone from Australian Prime Minister Kevin Rudd to Heath's old headmaster Robert Zordan and celebrities worldwide.

As his heartbroken family prepared to travel to New York and bring Heath's body home to Perth, the NYPD investigation into his death was already in full swing. In his bare apartment, detectives found nearly-full bottles of an array of drugs including anti-anxiety medications, sleeping pills and powerful pain-killers. They also found a rolled-up $20 bill, leading to speculation that Heath had used it to snort cocaine. This was later discounted, when tests showed no traces of drugs on the note.

Attention also turned to why the ambulance and police weren't called immediately once housekeeper Teresa Carino Solomon and masseuse Diana Lee Wolozin realised something was seriously wrong. It would seem that Wolozin thought it was only a minor emergency which could somehow be solved without calling in the authorities. Despite an autopsy finding that Heath was probably already dead when she went into his room, which cleared her of any blame for his death, the masseuse has become famous as the person who called child star Mary-Kate Olsen on the other side of the country before she called for an ambulance for Heath Ledger.

The awkward, reluctant star who was Heath Ledger would seem to have little in common with Olsen, who had grown up a product of the Hollywood system, yet it emerged that the two of them had been seeing each other for a few months. Olsen released a statement saying, 'Heath was a friend. His death is a tragic loss. My thoughts are with his family during this very difficult time.' Her involvement would become a key part of the investigation.

Police immediately said they believed Heath died of an overdose. An initial ninety-minute autopsy on his body proved inconclusive, and the New York City Medical Examiner's Office announced that additional toxicology and tissue testing were needed. They released Heath's body, and it lay in the Frank E Campbell funeral chapel at 1076 Madison Avenue, New York while arrangements were made to transport it home. As one of New York's oldest funeral homes, the chapel had been a temporary resting place for many famous people, including Jacqueline Kennedy Onassis, John Lennon, Judy Garland and James Cagney. In Heath's case the bill for its services was US$39,030, including a $25,000 casket. The cost included forty certified copies of Heath's death certificate, which lists his place of death as 421 Broome Street, at 3.35 p.m., and the Treehouse at Woodrow Wilson Drive, LA, as his usual residence.

It was in two columns of death notices in Perth's daily newspaper, the *West Australian*, that Heath's family opened up about the depth of their heartbreak. In messages full of warmth and love, and devoid of any of the family infighting, Heath's dad, grandparents, sisters and uncles showed that Heath might have been an Oscar-nominated star, but he was not too big to be called by his pet names—Heatho, Beef and Roast.

'My body aches for the sound of your voice, our chats, our laughs and our life and times together,' wrote Kim.

'Heatho, Beef ... my beautiful boy, so loving, so talented, so independent. No more chess games, mate—this is it, couldn't beat you anyway. We were one in soul and commitment, just father and son.'

Kate Ledger wrote, 'I can hardly breathe when I write this. We were the ultimate in soul mates. I feel both my heart and life have been torn apart. I loved our special talks, our daily chats from wherever you were in the world.

'You were so many things to so many people, but to me you were just my little brother. You will never leave my thoughts, "Roast", ever.'

His little sister Olivia, whose portrait Heath had painted and taken with him to LA where it was hung in his home, wrote, 'You're my idol, my hero, but most importantly my loving big brother. I'll treasure every moment we spent together.'

A joint notice by his immediate family read, 'You so loved us, as we dearly loved you. As a close-knit and very private family unit, we have observed you so determined yet quietly travelling in your self-styled path in life, nothing would get in your way ... no mountain too tall, no river too wide ... Your true legacy lives on in beautiful little Matilda, who will always remain in the greatest of care.'

It was obvious that Heath's parents and sister were in no state to deal with the public's show of grief or the media, and when they left Perth their trip was shrouded in secrecy. They were shocked and in mourning, and Heath had been so intensely private in his life that they decided they were not going to help the media after his death. They had been appalled at the huge, jostling mob with cameras which had surrounded Heath's body, strapped to the gurney as it was wheeled by paramedics out of his apartment and loaded into the white New York City Medical Examiner's van. And they had already been let down by the Australian TV and newspaper reporters in Perth, who had persuaded the family to make that statement on the lawn with the promise that the cameras would then leave them alone. They didn't.

The family flew not by private jet but by scheduled flights from Perth Airport through Sydney to LA. Australian fashion designer Jayson Brunsdon gave an insight into how Heath's death affected everyone, describing the scene in the Qantas lounge at Sydney airport when the family arrived en route.

'It was just horrible. They were in tears, and the whole place started crying. It was very sad,' said Brunsdon.

In New York, what had become an annual tourism and trade fair called G'day USA was totally overshadowed by Heath's death. The day after he died, it was an emotional group of high-profile ex-pats and visiting celebrities who gathered at Manhattan's Lincoln Centre for one of the fair's first events, a benefit for Terri Irwin's Wildlife Warriors foundation.

Terri Irwin, who lost her 'Crocodile Hunter' husband Steve in a fatal accident in September 2006, said life was something 'we all take for granted'.

'Life is precious, and we have to remember that none of us are immune to tragedy,' she said.

Among the group were Jamie Durie, Shannon Noll, rock band Eskimo Joe and Hollywood star John Travolta, in his role as an ambassador for Qantas.

'It's hard to be here celebrating Australia under these circumstances,' said Travolta.

Eskimo Joe, Perth boys like Heath, said they were totally shocked.

'We grew up just down the road from him in Perth, so it's pretty close to home,' said frontman Kav Temperley.

The usually glamorous G'day USA black tie ball—held in the grand ballroom at the famed Waldorf-Astoria to mark Australia Day, 26 January—became an impromptu wake. The 1,200 guests rose to their feet and bowed their heads to begin the evening with a minute's silence as a picture of Heath's Ennis Del Mar filled two huge TV screens. The Australian Consul-General in New York, John Olsen, read out a brief note from Kim Ledger.

'Heath is and always will be an Australian. He adored his home. His last two weeks with us over Christmas were just bliss,' Kim Ledger wrote.

'Heath did not become an actor for the fame or fortune. He just loved his craft and he loved helping his friends. He loved chess and skateboarding too.

'My image of Heath in New York is him with his skateboard, a canvas bag and beanie. That was Heath.'

On the other side of the country, a much more private memorial gathering was taking place. Heavy security surrounded the Pierce Brothers Westwood Village Memorial Park Cemetery, the resting place of Marilyn Monroe and many other celebrities. The service was held in private, to keep away both the paparazzi and the radical US religious groups who had vowed to picket any commemorative events in protest at Heath's gay *Brokeback Mountain* role. The privacy also gave Heath's family much-needed breathing space. Heath's coffin had been transferred from Manhattan and lay in the chapel, where Kim, Sally, Kate, Michelle Williams and little Matilda were joined by Watts and only about another ten close friends for an intimate thirty-minute service.

The group then moved on to a private dining room at the Beverly Hills Hotel for a quiet dinner.

'Even though it was a sad occasion, everyone was smiling, hugging each other and holding hands,' someone else at the hotel that night told *US Weekly* magazine. 'It was a really positive group.'

There was one thing that had to be done that Heath's mum and sister could not face—cleaning out the rented loft that Heath had called home for the last few months of his life. It was down to Kim, who made the brief trip from LA to New York. A week after Heath's death, his dad arrived in a black SUV at the back entrance of the Broome Street building, and was ushered in by security guards. For about an hour, Kim was alone with his thoughts inside the apartment.

When Michelle Williams broke her silence on 1 February, after days of being with her mother and close friends, it was with a touching statement.

'My heart is broken. Please respect our need to grieve privately,' she said.

'I am the mother of the most tender-hearted, high-spirited, beautiful little girl who is the spitting image of her father. All that I can cling to is his presence inside her that reveals itself every day.

'His family and I watch Matilda as she whispers to trees, hugs animals, and takes steps two at a time, and we know that he is with us still. She will be brought up in the best memories of him.'

Though Heath was a star who shunned the celebrity of Hollywood, his death devastated many who made their living in the movie capital. So many throughout the industry wanted to pay their respects—people who had worked with Heath, had met him or who simply admired his understated work—that his management agency, Creative Artists Agency, helped organise a farewell service in LA before his family took Heath's body home to

Australia. On 2 February, the family was joined by a Hollywood A-list behind the security of closed gates at Sony Pictures Studios, Culver City. It was the same studio lot where Judy Garland sang 'Over the Rainbow' and where *The Wizard of Oz* was filmed.

There were five eulogies during the hour-long service, including those from Kim, Kate and Todd Haynes, who directed Heath in *I'm Not There*. Heath's friend Ben Harper sang a moving tribute, performing 'Morning Yearning', the song for which Heath had directed a video. A ten-minute memorial video of Heath, edited by Matt Amato, was shown to the track 'Old Man' by Neil Young.

Tom Cruise and his wife Katie Holmes were among the mourners, along with Ellen DeGeneres, Sienna Miller, Heath's co-star in *Casanova*, Shannyn Sossamon, who starred alongside him in *A Knight's Tale* and *The Sin Eater*, Lily Cole from *The Imaginarium of Dr Parnassus*, Orlando Bloom, who had worked with Heath on *Ned Kelly*, Gemma Ward, Lindsey Lohan, Sean Penn, Josh Hartnett, director Gregor Jordan, who had guided Heath through *Two Hands* and *Ned Kelly*, and a clearly distressed Naomi Watts.

Before the family headed back to Australia the following evening, Kim reportedly invited some of Heath's closest friends to each choose a piece from Heath's personal chess set. It was a fitting move.

Just five weeks after he left Perth telling Mark Naglazas that he felt just like a boy from home again who had 'never left', Heath Ledger was back for the last time. It was with a mixture of sadness and confusion that he was finally farewelled as family, friends and the public struggled to comprehend how someone so genuinely decent and talented, who seemed as laid-back as his home town of Perth and who had such a loving family to fall back on, could have died such a lonely death, relying on pills to get him through another night alone.

Heath's art teacher Barry Gardner from Guildford Grammar was among the 500 mourners who gathered at Perth's exclusive Penrhos College on Saturday 9 February for a celebration of Heath's life. It was the same school where Heath had happily been his sister Olivia's 'show and tell'.

Gardner reflected on the advice he had given Heath at school, to follow his dream.

'I saw that dream had become a nightmare ... but then, nobody knows what's in front of them,' said Gardner.

'Heath was always a clean-cut, physically strong boy, and when I heard the news, I thought "Heath, Heath, Heath, I hope it was accidental". It haunts me that there was nobody there with him.

'People say, "Oh, he knew what he was getting into", but he didn't. It is the kind of industry that can chew you up and spit you out.'

The publicity that Heath shunned in life was going to follow him right to the end, despite Kim Ledger's plea to the worldwide media to respect the guests' privacy.

Before the service, Kim fronted the cameras again on the lawn outside his ex-wife's house in Applecross.

'I know that a lot of you have travelled from all around the world to take footage of as much as you can of our ceremony for Heath,' he said.

Kim said that after the ceremony at Penrhos, there would be a private service.

'I just ask you if you wouldn't mind to respect our privacy. The funeral will be very, very private. There will only be ten people there, immediate family and nobody else,' he said.

'It's a pretty sad time, and we're finding it difficult to cope by ourselves, let alone cope with everybody around the world.

Having said that, we do really appreciate the outpouring and emotional support from all over the world which, suffice to say, we're luckier than most families. Most families that are in our position, our grieving position, don't have that kind of support. So thank you all very much.'

At Penrhos, celebrities like Geoffrey Rush, Cate Blanchett, who was pregnant with her third child, Gemma Ward, Bryan Brown and Joel and Nash Edgerton rubbed shoulders with a lot of old boys from Guildford Grammar, including Trevor Di Carlo and Ben and Tom Rogers.

'They were all broken up,' said Barry Gardner. 'He was very loyal to those guys, and they to him.'

As the mourners arrived for the ceremony, they were handed a program featuring a photograph of Heath sitting on a New York park bench, grinning.

'This room is filled with the love we all felt for a great friend who will be missed by all of us,' read the program.

'We want to thank those of you who took care of him and participated in his beautiful life.'

Michelle Williams, who was accompanied by a police escort, had left Matilda with friends. Her devastation was clear as she broke down during the service when Matilda's montage played on the big screen. It featured pictures of Heath and his daughter to the soundtrack of Ben Harper's 'Happy Everafter in Your Eyes'.

Family video tributes and montages of Heath's on-screen performances and off-screen moments played throughout the ceremony, accompanied by The Beatles' 'Here Comes the Sun', Neil Young's 'Old Man' and The Smashing Pumpkins' '1979'—the year Heath was born.

The service included other songs which had been the soundtrack to Heath's life, including Powderfinger's 'These Days' from *Two Hands*, Bob Dylan's 'The Times They Are a-Changin', marking his role in *I'm Not There*, Pink Floyd's 'Wish You Were Here', 'Superstition' by Stevie Wonder, 'Seven Nation Army' by the White Stripes and 'The Past and Pending' by indie rock group The Shins.

During a service that managed to be both sombre and humorous, Kim Ledger, Sally Ledger Bell, Kate Ledger, Cate Blanchett and Neil Armfield, who directed Heath in *Candy*, gave moving and funny tributes to Heath.

After the ceremony, the immediate family moved off to Fremantle Cemetery Crematorium for their final farewell. The windows of the chapel were blacked out to stop the media filming the intimate service. Michelle Williams read Shakepeare's Sonnet 18, which begins 'Shall I compare thee to a summer's day?':

But thy eternal summer shall not fade,

Nor lose possession of that fair thou owest;

Nor shall Death brag thou wander'st in his shade.

Heath Andrew Ledger, address Los Angeles, became crematorium record number FC00052109 as in his death he found peace in Australia, the country where he had no peace while alive.

With Trevor Di Carlo's arm slung protectively over her shoulder, Michelle and Heath's family joined the other mourners for the wake at oceanside restaurant Indiana Tea Rooms. The restaurant stands above the white sand at Heath's favourite Cottesloe Beach, and what had been a hot and dry Perth day ended with around 200 of the group throwing off their funereal suits and dresses and leaping laughing and cheering into the water in their underwear. Michelle looked visibly relaxed as Kate held her hands and spun her around on the beach.

'It's what Heath would have wanted,' said one mourner, as Kim watched the hugging and celebrating from the balcony.

As the sun slipped down to the horizon, turning the ocean red, the mourners sat on the sand in silence. 'The sun goes down on our love, but it will never go down on our Heathy,' said one.

Michelle left the next day to return to New York accompanied by Joel Edgerton as Heath's family began to deal with the quiet and reality that comes after any funeral and wake.

But while the ceremony at Penrhos was attended by the who's who of Perth, with such diverse guests as West Coast Eagles footballer Ben Cousins, and the West Australian Opposition Leader, Troy Buswell, who did not know Heath, one group of people was noticeably absent. Kim had not invited any of his brothers or cousins from his side of the family. Heath's godparents Mike and Di Ledger were not invited, nor Heath's twelve first cousins, nor indeed Heath's great-aunt Margaret, Kim's mother's sister, the sole surviving relative of Grandma Esma Ledger. The family row had gone much deeper than sibling rivalry, and there was no sign of forgiveness on Kim's part as he seemingly snubbed his family over the court case twenty years earlier.

Like all of them, Di Ledger was disbelieving.

'As soon as Heath died, everything that had gone on between those guys, it was all forgotten. So many times Mike and Haydn wanted to go and see Kim, but he wouldn't reach out to them. He didn't want them,' she said.

So while Heath was being farewelled by the acting, sporting and political elite, his cousins, uncles, aunts and other extended family gathered at Mike and Di's Gidgegannup farm in the hills behind Perth for their own gathering, which involved prayers, moments of silence, and tears as well as laughter.

Despite the bitterness, Kim's younger brothers just wanted him to open that door a little and let them back in. Being ignored at this time really stung, and the adults were particularly sad for

Heath's cousins, who had been totally remote from any of the issues that had split the older part of the family.

'Nothing in the world could ever take precedence over the loss of a son or daughter, regardless of fame or fortune,' said Mike.

'We were also grieving, and yet as the days went by it seemed to us that Kim was going to do the most unthinkable [thing] that anyone could ever do, and that was to exclude family members from paying their final respects to their cousin, nephew and godson.'

During the afternoon of drinks and memories at the farm, Heath's young cousin Tim said something that resounded with them all: 'Hey, dad, we started to get to know Heath as the famous Heath, and now he is our cousin again.'

While preparations had been going on for the funeral, the New York City Medical Examiner's Office announced the final results of the autopsy—Heath had died of acute intoxication, a fatal cocktail of six drugs which had suppressed his breathing.

On 6 February, Ellen Borakove, a spokesperson for the New York City Medical Examiner's Office, released a brief formal statement: 'Mr Heath Ledger died as a result of acute intoxication by the combined effects of oxycodone, hydrocodone, diazepam, temazepam, alprazolam and doxylamine.

'We have concluded that the manner of death is accidental, resulting from the abuse of prescription medications.'

Heath's death had coincided with the launch of a US federal advertising campaign aimed at preventing prescription-drug abuse. The White House postponed the event to avoid appearing opportunistic or tasteless in riding on the back of such a tragedy. But the outcome of the autopsy brought home the dangers of mixing prescription drugs.

For Heath's family, at least it put an end to speculation that he had committed suicide.

'Few can understand the hollow, wrenching and enduring agony parents silently suffer when a child predeceases them. Today's results put an end to speculation, but our son's beautiful spirit and enduring memory will forever remain in our hearts,' Kim Ledger said in a statement.

'While no medications were taken in excess, we learned today the combination of doctor-prescribed drugs proved lethal for our boy. Heath's accidental death serves as a caution to the hidden dangers of combining prescription medication, even at low dosage.'

While the Medical Examiner's Office used the generic names for the drugs, diazepam is marketed as the anti-anxiety drug, Valium; temazepam as the sleeping tablet Normison; alprazolam as Xanax, used to treat anxiety disorders sometimes linked to severe depression; and doxylamine is a sedating anti-histamine used in some over-the-counter cold and allergy tablets. Of more concern was oxycodone, a habit-forming pain reliever as strong as morphine, and hydrocodone, another powerful narcotic pain reliever.

Known as 'hillbilly heroin', oxycodone is mostly sold under the brand name OxyContin. Highly addictive, it is regularly abused because it produces a longer-lasting effect than heroin, is cheaper on the black market, and can be obtained on prescription. It earned its nickname because of its widespread abuse in the states of Kentucky and Virginia.

OxyContin and hydrocodone, one of the main ingredients of Vicodin, are among the most commonly abused prescription drugs in the US.

The US federal Drug Enforcement Administration took over the investigation of Heath's death because of the possibility that some of the drugs may have been obtained illegally. A spokesman said it was common for the DEA to investigate an overdose death when there were so many different drugs involved; however, the DEA has been accused of seeking to raise their profile using what was an accidental overdose.

The wide-ranging investigation involved interviewing all potential witnesses, including Michelle Williams, anyone who was in Heath's apartment around the time of his death, his business associates and his doctors. They have all willingly spoken to investigators—except for Mary-Kate Olsen.

Investigators have discovered that doctors in California and Texas had legitimately prescribed the anti-anxiety medication and sleeping tablets for Heath—but not the oxycodone and hydrocodone. The evidence is that the pain-killers were obtained using phony prescriptions or other illegal means.

One of the enduring mysteries of Heath's death is why Mary-Kate Olsen didn't alert the authorities when called by Diana Lee Wolozin, but instead sent around her personal bodyguards. The respected news agency Reuters quoted DEA sources in August 2008 as stating that Olsen had refused to co-operate with the investigation unless she was given immunity from any prosecution that might result. Prosecutors had obtained a subpoena which would have forced her to appear before a grand jury for questioning. It all led to speculation that the young actress had something to hide.

But her lawyer, Michael C Miller, said she had 'nothing whatsoever to do with the drugs found in Ledger's home or his body', and did not know where he had obtained them from.

'Regarding the government's investigation, at Ms Olsen's request we have provided the government with relevant information including facts in the chronology of events surrounding Mr Ledger's death and the fact that Ms Olsen does not know the source of the drugs Mr Ledger consumed,' said Mr Miller in a statement.

Prosecutors in the US Attorney's office in Manhattan decided not to take the case any further 'because they don't believe there is a viable target'. Case closed.

╫

It was when Michelle Williams' father Larry and Mike and Haydn Ledger got in touch with each other concerning Heath's will that the Ledger family's dirty laundry was finally aired in public.

Heath was obviously a multi-millionaire, with a fortune estimated at at least $20 million, but documents by lawyers for the executors of his estate filed with the New York City Surrogate's Court on 29 February, a month after his death, listed assets worth only $145,000, specifically furniture and fixtures said to be worth $20,000, a Toyota Prius worth $25,000, and $100,000 in miscellaneous bank accounts. According to the statement, he owed $25,000 in rent and an estimated $15,000 had been put aside for expenses, including legal fees, for which his estate was liable. Heath's will had not been updated since 12 April 2003, and in the court documents, Matilda Rose was listed as an 'interested party'.

Larry Williams was surprised that Heath had not left a more recent will and was said to have only $145,000 in assets.

'It doesn't make any sense, because Heath professed many times his love for Matilda—it makes no sense that he would not leave anything for his daughter,' Larry told Sydney's *Daily Telegraph*.

'He just wasn't that type of person.'

If there is anything Williams knows a lot about, it is money. The wealthy futures and commodities trader with a home in the US Virgin Islands is a former board member of the US National Futures Association. In 1987 he won the World Cup Championship of Futures Trading by increasing US$10,000 to $1,147,000 in twelve months. Ten years later, Michelle, then aged 16, won the same competition with a 1000 per cent return on her money. Other winners have taken the top award with as little as a 53 per cent return.

Larry, who had run for the US Senate in his home state of Montana, originally travelled to Australia in May 2006 for a series of finance seminars and to promote his stock market trading books, but was arrested at Sydney airport and charged with evading US$1.5 million in US income tax. In 2008, he remained in Sydney on $1 million bail put up by his fiancée Louise Stapleton.

While estranged from his famous daughter, Larry Williams maintains some contact with his ex-wife Carla and other family members.

He had never previously met any of Heath's family, but he was concerned that his daughter, and granddaughter in particular, get their share of Heath's fortune. It was out of the blue in March 2008 that Mike and Haydn had a conversation with him as to whether Kim was capable of handling Heath's estate.

The uncles advised Larry that, based on Kim's handling of their grandfather's estate, Michelle should get legal advice. It was the first time any of the family had spoken publicly about the row over Sir Frank's Ledger's will.

Haydn said the brothers just wanted Larry to be on his guard. They were told that their concerns had been passed on to Michelle and her mother, Carla Williams.

'I had to say this about my brother. I don't care any more. If Heath was alive, we would never, ever do it, [but] when Heath died, we could see what could happen,' Haydn said.

The sensational news of Heath's uncles turning on their brother and casting doubt on the disposal of Heath's assets went around the world—and Kim was furious.

Speaking in LA on business, Kim said, 'Matilda is our absolute priority and Michelle is an integral part of our family. They will be taken care of, and that's how Heath would want it to be.'

He said that he hoped 'for Matilda's sake' that his brothers would remain dignified.

'It is sad at this extremely difficult time in our lives, while we are grieving the loss of our beloved son, that estranged family members publicly discuss matters they have not been privy to in the past or now,' he said.

But with the full value of Heath's assets not listed in the court documents, Larry Williams said Kim Ledger should just come clean about where Heath's wealth lay.

'It's so easy to resolve this. He just has to say where the income went, and where the assets are,' said Larry.

'I'm certain there is grieving in the Ledger family but [lawyers for] Kim have already filed papers in New York, so it seems like it's time to be transparent about it.

'I have no idea what Heath Ledger was worth, [but] they certainly haven't stated all the assets to the court.'

Larry Williams said he was sure Michelle would do what was right in dealing with Heath's family over the will.

'She is a smart kid and her heart is in the right place, and whatever she's going to do is fine,' he said.

'Michelle was raised well, she has good values and is very, very intelligent, and she makes good decisions. I deeply respect her doing what's right.'

But the genie, so to speak, was out of the bottle.

The lack of an updated will by Heath caused friction between Michelle Williams and Kim Ledger. After heated discussions, Michelle has hired top probate lawyers to protect her daughter's interests as the divvying up of Heath's assets winds its way through the courts in both New York and Perth.

'Michelle is wary of people around the estate, and has hired lawyers to take charge,' said a close source.

The executors of the will, Robert Collins and Mark Dyson, had to file in New York for temporary administration of Heath's estate, to pay expenses and get access to his properties and goods in the United States, before they could apply for probate in Western Australia. Despite officially listing Heath's residence as LA on both his death certificate and his cremation certificate, the executors argued through lawyers that he was domiciled in Australia, and that that is where his will should be administered.

'Although the decedent had temporary homes in both New York, where his daughter lives, and in Los Angeles, where he worked in the film industry, he considered Australia his home. The decedent did not have a green card and could not establish a permanent residence in the United States,' their lawyer told the court in a statement.

'Therefore, although Heath Ledger died in the United States, his domicile is in Australia.'

The argument prompted much speculation in legal circles about where the probate should be granted. Under the intestacy laws of New York and California, where Heath's homes were, Matilda 'could not be accidentally disinherited', according to lawyers Joanna Grossman and Mitchell Gans, both professors who lecture in family law, wills and trusts in the US.

'In this case, New York intestacy laws lead us to a somewhat striking result,' they wrote for the respected website FindLaw.

'Matilda, who was omitted from her father's will entirely, would be entitled to everything.'

The executors have applied for probate in the Supreme Court of Western Australia. This process takes around six months, and was expected to be finalised by the end of 2008. The executors have not spoken publicly about their role, but sources close to them said that while Heath left everything to his parents and sisters, they had been given legal advice that Matilda 'gets the whole estate'.

However, Michelle has been advised to legally lodge a claim on Matilda's behalf, supported by an affidavit, so that her daughter's inheritance can be ratified by the court. Details of the affidavit may become public under WA law once the case is completed, something which these very private families will hope to avoid.

In a further twist, Michelle Williams is fighting on another front—with the insurance company with which Heath had a $10 million policy in favour of Matilda. The company has refused to pay up, invoking a get-out clause in the policy and claiming that Heath failed to make full disclosure when taking out the insurance. Heath's only criminal conviction is a previously undisclosed Californian speeding fine from 2001 for exceeding a 70 m.p.h. speed limit. Another charge of not having his licence in his possession at the time was dismissed.

However, in a dispute that relates directly to the final months of Heath's life, the insurance company claims that he did not inform them of what they have called his 'recreational drug use'.

Michelle has hired top lawyers in LA to take on the insurance company.

'While neither side wants it to end up in an open courtroom, the disagreement has been heading towards litigation,' said a source close to the case.

'Insurance companies work on three rules: deny, delay, don't pay.'

Stories about Heath's use of recreational drugs emerged immediately after his death, many of them contradictory, and some from more reliable sources than others. They ran the gamut, from Heath being a party animal, knee-deep in heroin and cocaine while taking six ecstasy tablets at a time and swigging them down with champagne from the bottle, to his being squeaky clean. The truth is probably somewhere in the middle. He was twenty-eight, single, wealthy, handsome and hanging out in circles where drugs were freely available. On top of smoking dope, there are allegations that he also dabbled in cocaine. There is no evidence, only wildly conflicting claims, that he ever injected heroin, and it does seem highly unlikely.

Among the less sensationalist claims, *People* magazine senior editor J D Heyman said Heath liked to party.

'He liked to go out, he was a known user of drugs, he used cocaine,' Heyman told the TV entertainment news program 'Access Hollywood'.

'He had a lifestyle that really wasn't—at least in Michelle Williams's eyes—compatible with raising a child and continuing in that relationship.'

On the other hand, *New York* magazine spoke to someone with a different story on Heath's drug use. The woman, who was not named, said she had a three-month affair with Heath before and after Christmas 2007. At his SoHo apartment they played backgammon, and he was friendly, if quiet and introverted, she said.

'Heath was obviously in a vulnerable state. He didn't like being this star,' she was quoted as saying.

'He was kind of quiet unless he was comfortable, and it really seemed like he was just trying to have fun.'

She said she was at a party in his loft once.

'And it was really crazy. There were drugs there, but he didn't touch them. I saw [drugs] offered to him multiple times. Ecstasy, cocaine, even prescription stuff—but he never touched it. I was with him at least a dozen times, and he was always sober. Just cigarettes.'

More information about the video of Heath in that room at the Chateau Marmont—the video in which he admitted the extent of his marijuana use—emerged in documents filed with the Los Angeles Superior Court as part of a lawsuit launched by a freelance reporter who was covering the Screen Actors Guild Awards after-parties for *People* magazine. The woman, known only as Jane Doe in the court papers to protect her career, has sued Splash News and two of its employees, one of whom was her boyfriend at the time, claiming damages to her professional reputation and emotional distress because she has a privacy interest in her 'conversations, in her voice and likeness'. The case is being defended by Splash News.

The woman claimed the two male employees, one of them a videographer, befriended Heath in the lobby of the Chateau Marmont and invited him to her bedroom. They had a secret camera set up on the balcony outside the room and, according to the woman, set Heath up in order to make money by plying him with drugs, including cocaine.

The documents claim that Heath was not only distraught when he discovered he had been filmed, but became emotional, even hysterical, throughout the early morning when he realised the potentially devastating effects of the film on his family and his film career.

The woman claimed the two men calmed Heath down by claiming they would destroy the tape, but 'at least once an hour for nearly seven hours, Mr Ledger would remember he had been videotaped and get upset all over again'.

The filing claimed the agency chose not to release the tape on legal advice that Heath would have a strong case to sue for millions on the grounds of entrapment and defamation, as the two men had invited him to the hotel room and provided the drugs. But after he died, it was eventually sold to the highest bidder for an estimated US$200,000. Heath was right to be wary of the paparazzi—the first time he let his guard down, he was caught.

Heath's true friends have remained publicly silent on what he did behind closed doors and whether he used illegal drugs over and above cannabis. But at the end of the day, it was prescription drugs that killed Heath in what was simply a terrible mistake. There were obvious reasons why he had turned to these drugs: the breakdown of his relationship with Michelle; the strain of missing his daughter; his perfectionism at work, coupled with never feeling satisfied with his performance. The intensity of his portrayal of the Joker may also have taken its toll, but Heath was having problems long before *The Dark Knight*. His wildly fluctuating emotions, which ranged from euphoria to despair, and his anxiety and inability to switch off are out of the ordinary, and some believe that they were linked to something deeper.

Perhaps a piece of the puzzle could be the fact that the Ledgers have a history of depression and bipolar disorder. The family saw clues in the behaviour of Heath's beloved Papa, Colin Ledger. He presented as a sensitive, easily hurt man, and in private would sit down and cry inconsolably, for no apparent reason. He found it difficult to cope with even minor disappointments—displaying another symptom of depression—but these were not things men in those days would seek professional help for.

Taking it one step further, Heath's uncle Haydn has been diagnosed as a sufferer of bipolar disorder, a condition that psychiatrists say is more common than generally thought, occurring in between 1 and 4 per cent of the population. It typically manifests in late adolescence or early adulthood, but can go undiagnosed for many years as the symptoms are not always recognised by the sufferers, or by mental health professionals.

A major cause of the illness, which used to be called manic depression, seems to be genetic—it runs in families. It is also affected by traumas such as relationship breakdowns. It may go some way to explaining Heath's developing problems, although it remains a supposition that he may have suffered from the condition, which is caused by a chemical imbalance in the brain, and could easily have been controlled with medication.

⊩⊩

14

BETWEEN ACTION— AND CUT

'BE CAREFUL WHAT YOU DO ON FILM, BECAUSE FILM IS FOREVER.' IT WAS A PIECE OF ADVICE GIVEN TO HEATH BY A DIRECTOR WHEN HE WAS STARTING OUT, AND ONE WHICH HE ALWAYS REMEMBERED. WHEN HE DIED, HE HAD ONE FILM IN THE CAN AND AWAITING RELEASE—*THE DARK KNIGHT*—AND A SECOND, *THE IMAGINARIUM OF DR PARNASSUS*, UNCOMPLETED. THE *IMAGINARIUM* CAST WAS LEFT IN LIMBO AS FILMING WAS SHUT DOWN AND DIRECTOR TERRY GILLIAM CONSIDERED WHETHER HE SHOULD JUST SHELVE THE MOVIE. HIS SOLUTION WAS NOT ONLY INSPIRED, BUT IT ALLOWED THREE OF HEATH'S CONTEMPORARIES TO PAY THEIR RESPECTS TO HIM BY TAKING OVER HIS ROLE.

Gilliam chose to use the part of the fantasy movie where Heath's character falls through the magic mirror to bring him back in the guise of Johnny Depp, Colin Farrell and Jude Law.

Touchingly, all three actors have donated their earnings from the movie to Matilda Ledger, with reports stating they were concerned for her financial future because Heath had not updated his will to include his little girl. The move has put fresh pressure on the executors of Heath's estate to make sure Matilda is taken care of.

Gilliam described their decision as heroic.

'They came, they allowed the movie to be finished, and they didn't take the money—it goes to Heath's daughter,' said Gilliam.

'That's extraordinary and wonderful … and we've got a movie full of wonderful people who did extraordinary things to help.'

The Dark Knight was another matter altogether. Heath's death propelled it to an unparalleled sense of expectation, and his performance was greeted with a buzz that earned him an almost mythological status. He would have been totally bemused and embarrassed by the whole thing had he still been alive.

The production was only halfway through the editing process when Heath died.

'I was obviously never able to show him the finished performance. That's very sad,' said director Chris Nolan.

However, he said Heath was happy with what he did get to see, which was an introduction to his character put together as a short film by Christmas 2007.

'We screened that for him, and he enjoyed it very much. I'm very pleased that it gave him a taste of how it was going to come across.'

He said it was very important to him that Heath's Joker was edited the way Heath had intended it to be seen.

Amid all the hype, the Joker dolls depicting Heath sold out even before the movie came out. When it hit the cinema screens in Australia, before the rest of the world, its release was cloaked in unprecedented security. With 90 per cent of pirated movies being secretly filmed by camcorders or even mobile phones in the cinema, bags were searched and all phones confiscated from those attending what was a low-key Australian premiere at Sydney's Fox Studios. The distributor, Village Roadshow, issued night-vision goggles to staff in its other cinemas so they could spot anyone filming the movie, which would not be seen around the world for another two days. The result was that not one pirated scene from the two and a half hour movie found its way onto the Internet out of Australia. The rest of the world was kept waiting.

Heath's dad Kim and his wife Ines, his mum Sally and her husband Roger Bell, and his sister Kate all slipped quietly into the New York premiere of *The Dark Knight* on 14 July 2008, where there was a black carpet, rather than a red carpet, in honour of Heath. The other stars of the movie were overshadowed not only by his death, but by his show-stealing portrayal of the maniacal Joker.

As tough as it must have been for Kim to watch his son's final performance, he was asked by reporters as he left the cinema what his thoughts were. He gave them a thumb's up signal.

'*The Dark Knight* is everything we hoped it would be, and more,' said Kim.

'Heath loved the experience of creating this character and working on the film. We are so proud of our boy.'

While Heath's former girlfriend Naomi Watts arrived with her husband Liev Shreiber, it was all too much for Michelle, who chose not to attend the premiere. There were reports that she was staying away as a snub to Kim over his handling of Heath's estate, but these were denied on her behalf by her publicist.

In the months following Heath's death, Michelle and Heath's best mate Trevor Di Carlo leaned on each other for support, with Trevor spending several weeks with her in the Brooklyn home she had shared with Heath. He spent as much time as he could with Matilda, whom he thinks the world of and who is his link to Heath. He was often seen out in Brooklyn carrying her on his shoulders in exactly the way Heath had, which a friend said was a coincidence and nothing deliberate on Trevor's part. His closeness and ease with Michelle led to speculation of a romance, which was quashed by his mum, Dianne Di Carlo.

'Michelle and he are the best of friends. It is a very special time for him to be with Matilda,' she said.

Michelle has since found love again with director Spike Jonze, their relationship obviously special because he has been introduced to Matilda. Jonze is divorced from Sofia Coppola, and he and Williams met when she auditioned for his film adaptation of the children's book *Where the Wild Things Are* in 2006. She did not take a part in the movie, but the couple worked together in New York in the summer of 2007 on *Synecdoche, New York*, for which Jonze was a producer.

One quiet casualty of Heath's death has been Gemma Ward, Heath's frequent companion during his last Christmas break in Perth. She had fallen in love with him, and believed he was in love with her—which he may well have been, despite seeing other women. Ward took time out from her lucrative modelling career to try and find peace trekking in the foothills of the Himalayas, before spending time in an ashram in Rishikesh, India.

'She took it really hard,' said a source.

Only one actor has ever been awarded a posthumous Oscar, and that was Australian Peter Finch for *Network*, which was released in 1976. Other actors have received posthumous nominations, including James Dean for *Giant* and *East of Eden*, Spencer Tracy for *Guess Who's Coming to Dinner* and Ralph Richardson for *Greystoke: The Legend of Tarzan, Lord of the Apes*.

The announcement of the nominations for the 2009 Oscars are expected to be made on 22 January—the anniversary of Heath's death—and there is growing momentum for his name to be among them.

His co-star Michael Caine is among those predicting Heath will get an Academy Award, saying his performance is up there with Anthony Hopkins' Hannibal Lecter.

'He was a young actor, and this is his moment. He's going to get the Oscar for this,' said Caine, a veteran of six nominations and two wins himself.

Most movie reviewers agreed, with none of them holding back praise for Heath's chilling Joker.

'If there's a movement to get him the first posthumous Oscar since Peter Finch won for 1976's *Network*, sign me up,' said *Rolling Stone*'s respected film critic, Peter Travers.

'I can only speak superlatives of Ledger, who is mad-crazy-blazing brilliant as the Joker. Miles from Jack Nicholson's broadly funny take on the role in Tim Burton's 1989 *Batman*, Ledger takes the role to the shadows where even what's comic is hardly a relief.'

The *New York Times* described Heath's Joker as 'some kind of a masterpiece'.

'Mr Nolan has turned Batman into a villain's sidekick. That would be the Joker, of course, a demonic creation and three-ring circus of one, wholly inhabited by Heath Ledger,' said the *New York Times* reviewer.

Britain's *Sun* newspaper said Heath stole the show.

'His electrifying performance as the Joker serves up the most menacing, villainous appearance on screen,' said its reviewer.

An Associated Press review described the Joker as possibly Heath's finest performance, surpassing even his Oscar-nominated Ennis Del Mar.

Director Nolan, however, has avoided directly answering questions about the possibility of a posthumous Oscar for Heath, perhaps not wanting to jinx it. His caution may also come from the knowledge that action movies, especially ones involving comic-book characters, are usually not rewarded with Academy Awards.

Heath's death was not the only one to hit the movie. New Zealand special effects technician Conway Wickliffe, forty-one, a father of two, died in an accident on the English set of the film when a camera truck from which he was filming struck a tree. Both men are remembered in a special dedication at the close of *The Dark Knight*. Meanwhile, the media whipped itself up into a frenzy about whether the movie was 'cursed', as unpleasant incidents continued to haunt its cast. First, Christian Bale was arrested in London over allegations he had assaulted his mother Jenny, sixty-one, and sister Sharon, forty, in a plush suite at the city's Dorchester Hotel before the UK premiere of the movie. Then Morgan Freeman, who played Lucius Fox, the man who runs Bruce Wayne's business enterprise, had to be cut free from his car after it flipped off a highway near his South Carolina ranch. It was also confirmed that Freeman was getting a divorce from his wife Myrna Colley-Lee.

There was certainly no box office curse as *The Dark Knight* continued to break records—in its opening weekend it raked in $155.34 million, topping *Spider-Man* with the best opening weekend ever. It became the fastest movie to take $400 million, according to Box Office Mojo. The website also estimated that by mid-August 2008, the movie had zoomed past the $720 million mark worldwide.

The money will further swell Heath's estate, as he is believed to have taken a share of the profits of the movie as well as the merchandising. While not officially the executor of his son's estate, Kim Ledger has had a major say in how it has so far been managed. The estate pulled out of financing Heath's pet project, the Masses, but Kim said it would go ahead with Heath's investment in another business venture, a Brooklyn bar called Five Leaves. Heath was a silent partner in the nautically-themed bar on the corner of Lorimer and Bedford, which may well have been named after Nick Drake's album 'Five Leaves Left'. The album was in turn named after the message found as a pack of cigarette papers was running out. Kim has been quoted as saying that he knew how much the project meant to Heath, which was why he released the funds to complete its construction.

Back home in Perth, the West Australian government is building a $91 million performing arts centre in the trendy central suburb of Northbridge, which it will name the Heath Ledger Theatre. Heath's family has offered memorabilia to be displayed in the theatre, which is due for completion at the end of 2010.

'I think if he was here today, because he was such a giver to the arts right across the board, there's not a lot of things he'd put his name to, but I'm absolutely positive he would put his name to that,' said Kim.

Heath will be remembered for his daughter Matilda, his quiet support for the arts, his loyalty and generosity to his family and friends, his offbeat sense of humour — and he could be so funny — and the energy he put into everything he did, his unassuming but incandescent character, and his incredible talent.

But Heath's real legacy has been captured on celluloid, and he will be best remembered for his brilliant acting. He said that once the film was over, he walked away: 'I kind of save the living for the time between action and cut.'

⊬⊢

PHOTOGRAPH CAPTIONS

COVER

FRONT: Heath Ledger poses for a Polaroid portrait while promoting *Brokeback Mountain* at the Toronto International Film Festival, 10 September 2005. (Photo Carlo Allegri/Getty Images)

BACK: In Melbourne for the premiere of *Ned Kelly*, 17 March 2003. (Photo Sandy Scheltema, *The Age*)

CENTRE

First spread

LEFT: At the Victoria State Library for the launch of *Ned Kelly*, 17 March 2003. (Photo Paul Harris, *The Age*)

RIGHT: Heath Ledger, left, and Jake Gyllenhaal in a scene from Ang Lee's *Brokeback Mountain*. (Associated Press)

Centre spread

TOP ROW (FROM LEFT TO RIGHT)

Ledger ancestors. Heath's great-grandfather, Sir Frank Ledger, is in the back row, second from the left, and his wife, Gladys (née Lyons) sits in front of him. Their son and Heath's grandfather, Colin Ledger, is the baby on the far left. (Courtesy Mike Ledger)

With Kate Ritchie in TV series *Home and Away*. (Newspix)

Posing for a portrait at the time of *Roar*, 1997. (Photo Fox/Getty Images)

With Tai Nguyen (centre) and Martin Henderson (right) in *Sweat.* (Newspix)

Heath's sunglasses, during photocall for *I'm Not There* at the 64th Venice International Film Festival, 4 September 2007. (Alberto Pizzoli/ AFP/Getty Images)

As Skip Engblom in *Lords of Dogtown.* (Associated Press)

At the premiere of *Candy* at the 56th Berlinale International Film Festival. (Photo Kurt Vinion/WireImage)

Family and friends watch the sunset in memory of Heath on Cottesloe Beach, Perth, on 9 February 2008. (Photo Matt Jelonek/Getty Images)

CENTRE ROW (FROM LEFT TO RIGHT)
Heath, in the foreground with a cheeky smirk on his face, playing dominoes with his younger cousins Verity and Adam, 1989. (Courtesy Mike Ledger)

'At the farm' in Gidgegannup, Western Australia. Heath, aged 10, is standing alongside his godparents, Uncle Mike and Aunt Di, with his cousins Verity, Adam and Tim in the foreground. (Courtesy Mike Ledger)

Photo from an original casting folder, 14 July 1995. (Newspix)

In Sydney, 13 May 1996. (Photo Matthew Munro/Newspix)

Playing Jimmy in Gregor Jordan's *Two Hands.* (AAP Image)

With Michelle Williams when she was nominated for Best Female Lead for *Land of Plenty* at the 2007 Film Independent Spirit Awards. (Photo by Jeremy Kost/WireImage)

With mother Sally Ledger Bell and sister Ashleigh Bell at the VIP pre-party for the world premiere of *Ned Kelly* at the Old Melbourne Jail, 22 March 2003. (Newspix)

With Rachel Griffiths and Naomi Watts at the closing night of the play *Proof* on 21 June 2002 in Melbourne. (Photo Serge Thomann/WireImage)

With Naomi Watts and Joel Edgerton in Melbourne to protest against the US-led military strike on Iraq, 20 March 2003. (Photo Paul Trezise/Newspix)

With director Todd Haynes at the after-party for the *I'm Not There* New York Premiere at the Bowery Hotel, New York City, on 13 November 2007. (Photo Dimitrios Kambouris/WireImage)

A small floral tribute is pictured at the front of the Indiana Tea House as family and friends attend the private wake for Heath on 9 February 2008 in Cottesloe, Perth. (Photo by Paul Kane/Getty Images)

Sydney commuters reach for copies of the *MX* newspaper reporting the news of Heath's death, Wednesday, 23 January 2008. (Associated Press)

Artist Vincent Fantauzzo at the Art Gallery of New South Wales in Sydney submitting his Archibald Prize entry portrait of his good friend Heath Ledger, 23 February 2008. (Photo Katrina Tepper, *Daily Telegraph*)

BOTTOM ROW (FROM LEFT TO RIGHT)
Heath's family in the late 1980s. *Back row (l to r):* uncle Wayne (holding cousin Esma), uncle Mike, aunt Dianne (with cousin Tim), aunt April, uncle Haydn, mother Sally, father Kim. *Middle row (l to r)*: grandmother Esma, sister Kate, cousin Jessica,   Nanna McFarlane (grandmother Esma's mother), great-grandfather Sir Frank, cousin Verity on grandfather Colin's

knee. *Front row (l to r):* cousins Natalie, Bruce, Peggy, Adam, and Mitchell sitting on Heath's knee. (Courtesy Mike Ledger)

Heath, by now a famous actor, returns to his old school, Guilford Grammar, to speak with students, 1999.

Rehearsing a scene for *Ned Kelly*, 29 May 2002. (Photo Mark Smith/ Newspix)

Attending the 64th Venice Film Festival on 8 September 2007. (Photo Joe Cole/WireImage)

'Retrospective in Black & White', Heath Ledger and Michelle Williams, 21st Annual Santa Barbara International Film Festival. (Photo Chris Weeks/WireImage)

Best supporting actor nominee Jake Gyllenhaal (left), and best actor nominees George Clooney (second left), Philip Seymour Hoffman (centre) and Heath Ledger (right) before the start of the 78th Academy Awards, 5 March 2006. (AFP PHOTO/Timothy A. Clary)

Grieving parents Kim (left) and Sally (centre) with sister Kate outside their home in Perth, 23 January 2008. (Photo by Tony Ashby/AFP/Getty Images)

Back page
As The Joker in *The Dark Knight*. (Associated Press)

ACKNOWLEDGEMENTS

My sincere thanks go to everyone who shared their memories of Heath. I have been respectful of those who asked for their names not to be used, including many people in Perth and Sydney who wanted to help set the record straight and have helped me piece together what went on behind the headlines in the interests of accuracy but were mindful of how Heath protected his own privacy. They know who they are and deserve my gratitude.

I am grateful to Haydn Ledger, Mike Ledger and Ric Syme, who were generous with their time and their unique brand of Ledger family humour; Guildford Grammar School's archivist Rosemary Waller for help with research; Barry and Liz Garner and to many others for sharing their insights and allowing me to use their words.

To Gemma Jones, a fellow reporter on the *Daily Telegraph*, and my News Limited colleagues in New York and Los Angeles, Stefanie Balogh and Peta Hellard, go my admiration and special thanks. You are good!

The encouragement of my agent Margaret Gee, my editor Tricia Dearborn and my commissioning editor Colette Vella has been inspirational.

Other material has been sourced from court records in Perth and New York, documents in the State Library of Western Australia and interviews given by Heath to journalists and newspapers, magazines and websites throughout the world including the *Daily Telegraph, Sunday Telegraph, Australian, West Australian, Sydney Morning Herald and Sun Herald*; the books *Heath Ledger*

Too Good to be True by Grace Catalano and *Say It Out Loud* by Adam Sutton and Neil McMahon; *Vanity Fair, Vogue Australia, LA Weekly, Empire, People, Who Weekly, Variety, Newsweek, New York Daily Post, Brazil* magazine, *New York Times, New York Daily News, Wall Street Journal, The Times, Guardian, Cinema Confidential, Los Angeles Times* and *New York Observer.* Thank you.

Janet Fife-Yeomans
Sydney, August 2008

INDEX

Chief Executive: Juliet Rogers
Publishing director: Kay Scarlett
Commissioning editor: Colette Vella
Editor: Tricia Dearborn
Concept and design: Reuben Crossman
Layout: Susanne Geppert
Production: Tiffany Johnson

Fall River Press
122 Fifth Avenue
New York, NY 10011

ISBN: 978-1-4351-1651-1

Printed and bound in the United States of America

10 9 8 7 6 5 4 3 2 1